MIND LOST MIND FOUND

The Story Of JoAnn DeJoria Smith

© 2011 By Stan and JoAnn DeJoria Smith

Mind Lost Mind Found

by Stan & JoAnn DeJoria Smith

Visit our website at www.MindLostMindFound.com

Printed in the United States of America
First Printing: May 2011

ISBN 978-0-9715405-3-8

Library of Congress Control Number: 2011903565

Dedication

by JoAnn DeJoria Smith

To my precious daughter, Heather Lynn, and her father, Bob DeJoria, who was too young to die.

I'll never know if all the things that I was told about your father were true. They certainly were the compasses that set our lives on a treacherous journey. I have learned that people have the capacity to be incredibly kind and incredibly cruel.

With all my love, Mom

To my husband Stan. This book could have never been completed without you. Some people never know what it is to love or to be loved unconditionally. I have been given that gift in you.

There are no words to thank you for all you have done for me, and how meaningful my life has been with you.

There is only one thing that reaches beyond the grave, and that is love.

Yours forever, JoAnn

Foreword

by John Paul DeJoria

They say if you remember the 60's or early 70's, you weren't there. I remember the 60's and 70's and I was there. JoAnn was definitely there too, way "out there".

We go back to Washington Irving Jr. High School. JoAnn lived less than a mile from our home. In fact, during our high school days I went out with her best friend and neighbor. One Halloween, JoAnn and I got a bit wild and took off in search of prime targets to throw eggs at. Our first "throw by" was through the Beverly Hills Hotel. I whipped the car around the valet parking and we egged a couple of black limos. We then headed up to Mulholland Drive, where lovers would park on the side of the road to "enjoy the view". I screeched the wheels around the turns and JoAnn threw eggs at their windshields and we had a great time.

We were young, wild, and thoughtless, like a lot of other teenagers then. I hope we didn't hit any of your cars. If so, we are sorry.

JoAnn was my good friend and a lot of fun to be with. We pulled a few other capers during our crazy teens while she was going steady with my brother Bob. She ended up marrying him and they had a great relationship.

JoAnn had many exciting jobs working in the entertainment industry over the years. She worked for Capital records and transcribed Timothy Leary's odyssey with the Grateful Dead, and then worked for Universal studios and a few more record companies before landing a job at a large talent agency, working for an agent.

My brother was an entrepreneur who started the first low-cost copying businesses in Beverly Hills. The first two towers in Century City had just been completed and we made the rounds to every business.

She had been a housewife, though Bob had spoiled her with a full-time live-in maid so they could both have days off just riding his Harley or going to the beach.

When my brother died, JoAnn's life took a turn. If someone wanted to write a story, they couldn't come up with the kind of real life adventures she had. My sister-in-law packed more life into a week than most people do in a year. In those days, that meant a lot of adventures.

She was like a ship that had lost its anchor and she was out of control. Her avant-garde lifestyle became more and more outrageous. To top it off, she was confused and beautiful, and she had money. I never knew what she would do next.

JoAnn would move in and out of our home without giving me any notice unless she was calling me to rescue her from one of her insane boyfriends. She would take over the spare bedroom and sometimes the house. She was so out of control that she would yell at me if I made too much noise in my own home and woke her up.

I had to work, and she would often stay out very late or not come back until the sun was coming up.

One time JoAnn showed up unannounced, and I had a roommate renting the spare room. JoAnn took all of my roommate's clothes and put them on the street, so she could have what she considered her room back! When the girl came home in a confused state, JoAnn kicked her out of the house and locked the door behind her. Somehow it ended up causing trouble with my friends who lived next door.

Before long, JoAnn loaded her Porsche up one night and drove to Marin County so she could move back in with her artistic boyfriend who made incredible leather clothing. He ended up with a clothing shop on Rodeo drive and sold clothes to famous movie stars.

Now you might be skeptical reading this story because her life was so outrageous. But I assure you: it's all non-fiction.

At this point we can all laugh, but she really is fortunate to still be alive. Her daughter Heather has grown up to be a lovely young woman, who is now the vice president of a major corporation.

This book is a detailed account of JoAnn's outrageous and unbelievable life. You may have to remind yourself at times – this book really is a true story. I know; I was there for a lot of it, and I never knew what would happen next.

Author's Note

by Stan Smith

As John Paul noted in the Foreword, he knows this is a true story because he lived through much of it himself.

I didn't live through any of it myself, but JoAnn kept a diary. I double-checked all the facts I could, met some of the people, visited several of the places, and interviewed JoAnn many times. I've tried to make this book as factual as possible.

Of course, we can't claim that every conversation happened exactly as it did in this book. JoAnn didn't transcribe conversations in her diary thirty years ago, nor can she recall them perfectly now. But we did our best.

Further, we changed the names of most of the people in this book. But if you read the name of someone you've heard of, that name is probably accurate. In each case, the remarks made by JoAnn and her friends dovetailed with the public perception of the people involved.

With all the names we had to change, it seems likely that someone will find his or her name in the book. All such occurrences are entirely coincidental and unintended.

Contents

One

The Mock Funeral

"Bob always told me he'd get killed on that horrible Harley." I yanked a blue dress off a hanger from my bedroom closet and pulled it on. My best friend Rebecca was sitting on the bed. "I don't want to go through with this charade."

"Are you kidding? You don't have a choice." She was right; I had already seen people gathering outside, and I needed to be out there greeting them.

"But I can't think straight," I protested. I saw her red hair tumbling gracefully over her shoulders as she bent down to rummage for something in her bag. "This counterfeit funeral is crazy."

"No it isn't. Having a phony service for the family and their friends is brilliant. It'll satisfy them, and tomorrow we can have the real funeral Bob wanted, with the people he really wanted to be there."

"I'm not saying the idea is bad; I'm just saying I can't do it. You're the actress, Rebecca. You pretend for a living. I'm not sure I can pull this off."

"Of course you can do it. Everybody wears masks, my dear. The only difference between you and me is that I get paid for it." She lit a joint and took a long drag, then handed it to me. "This will help you."

Automatically I lit a stick of incense and I took a long drag on the joint before I snuffed it out. Her eyes widened with surprise. "Bad timing," I explained. "My family is here."

"Calm down," she teased. "We should get a few of them stoned."

I didn't get to answer. The bedroom door flew open and my great aunt Hazel barged in without knocking; wherever she went, she always assumed she was in charge. I had gotten rid of the joint just in time. "Blue!" said Aunt Hazel indignantly. "You can't wear blue to the funeral!"

"But this was Bob's favorite dress," I protested feebly. Out of the corner of my eye I saw Rebecca slipping out.

Aunt Hazel flung open my closet and started pawing through my wardrobe. "Haven't you listened to a thing I've taught you? I'll find something more suitable for you to put on." The toe of her sensible black pump was tapping impatiently. "And what's that smell in here? It smells like something burning."

"Incense," I said weakly. I always used it to cover the smell whenever someone lit a joint; for once, the habit was paying off.

"I can't imagine why you feel the need to burn incense," she mused, still riffling through my closet. Then she jerked a skimpy lace blouse from its hanger and whirled around. "What is this, JoAnn? It looks like a streetwalker's trappings."

"Bob bought it for me." I collapsed onto my vanity bench and it creaked beneath me. The old brocade rose fabric was starting to fray at one seam. I picked at it nervously.

Aunt Hazel smacked my hand. "Stop that!"

I felt like a chastised toddler. It was all too much: Bob's death, the counterfeit funeral, and now Aunt Hazel. I had to focus on something. I looked at my reflection in the mirror of my ornate Victorian dresser and noticed tears running down my face.

Aunt Hazel noticed too, and she turned and pointed her arthritic finger in my face. "It won't do you a bit of good to cry. You have to get over this and go on with your life. I won't stand for any tears." She squared her shoulders and pushed her thick brown-rimmed glasses over her beak-like nose. "Young lady, I've buried two husbands and never shed a tear. I expect the same from you."

She thrust a handkerchief into my trembling hand. I drew a deep breath and tried to obey my great aunt as I had done from childhood. All right then, I wouldn't cry. It was a simple decision, really, and I felt my grief falling down into a dark unreachable place in my heart, as though a ring had slipped off my finger and fallen into the sea. Numbly I dried my tears.

Somebody else knocked. "Come in," I said absently.

My mother peeked in. She was tall and shapely; the first hint of grey was just starting to creep into her long brown hair. She took one look at Aunt Hazel and tried to escape with the hurried announcement, "The guests are arriving."

But Aunt Hazel was too quick for her. "Georgette, come here. Look at what your daughter is wearing – stand up, JoAnn! – and get those sandals off your feet! Do you think you're going to the beach?" Actually, I had just come back from the beach. I had been there to try to collect my thoughts and write something to read aloud at today's ceremony.

My mother shrugged and turned to go. "That is what's wrong with your children, Georgette," Aunt Hazel said reprovingly. "You don't tell them what to do, and they run wild." But Mom was out the door. Aunt Hazel handed me a black wool suit and a tailored beige silk blouse; I had meant to take them to Goodwill and now I was sorry I had put it off. "This will do," she proclaimed.

"It's August, and she thinks this is appropriate?" I muttered as I slipped into the scratchy wool suit and stepped outside into the hot summer day. Why did I let my aunt control me?

It felt surreal as I joined the guests on the neatly manicured front lawn.

It had all begun just a few days ago on a peaceful afternoon when I was taking a nap. Bob was out, and our live-in maid Marta was looking after our two-year old, Heather. I must have fallen into a deep sleep. I dreamed that two policemen came to my door to tell me my husband Bob had been killed in a motorcycle accident. Then a phone rang, and it took me a moment to realize it wasn't just the dream; it was real. I answered groggily.

"Mrs. DeJoria?" a woman asked. "I'm calling from St. Johns Hospital. Your husband has been in a motorcycle accident. You need to come right away, but don't drive – find someone else to drive you."

Frantically I phoned Megan, who lived about ten minutes away. I was terrified; the dream was happening. While I waited for her to arrive I phoned Bob's younger brother Johnny and asked him to meet me at the hospital, then I called a couple of friends with the news.

Megan took me to the hospital and Johnny was waiting at the door. "I've been inside to check; our first stop is the admitting office," he said.

The lady at the desk had me fill out a form, then in the same flat tone of voice she might have used if we had asked where to look for the Coke machine she said: "Your husband is brain dead. There's no hope; he won't make it. You'll have to make the decision when you want to take him off life support."

What? I had dreamed about the death, but not about this. Sobbing, I turned to Johnny. "How could I ever do such a horrible thing to Bob? I just can't."

He looked at me intently, and along with the grief and compassion I saw in his eyes, I was surprised to see determination. "Don't worry,

JoAnn. I promise you won't have to make that decision. I will tell Bob to leave his body." We made our way to Bob's room in intensive care.

Bob was lying in the hospital bed and I rushed over to touch him. He was cold. I felt the pad he was lying on; it was filled with ice. Johnny and I stood silently and looked at Bob for a few moments. Bob and Johnny looked alike: ruggedly handsome features, piercing blue-green eyes, thick black hair. Johnny was a year and a half younger than Bob, and he was the more spiritual of the two; he had become an avid student of Scientology. He seemed to be waiting for me, and as soon as I glanced at him he began repeating in a monotone: "It's okay to go now, Bob; I will take care of JoAnn and Heather; it's okay to go now." He would keep this up for several hours.

I suddenly realized I had left Megan at the door. I went to the waiting room to check, and found it filled with our friends. "How's Bob?" they asked.

"He's in intensive care," I said. I couldn't bring myself to tell them Bob was brain dead. Instead, I chattered nervously about my dream, about the two policemen, about my certainty that Bob would die. My story angered Bob's best friend Duff; he stormed out of the waiting room.

Everything was unbearable. I didn't feel up to chitchat in the waiting room, and I couldn't really talk about what was happening. Was Bob alive or dead? It was the worst of both. I realized I needed to be with him while I could. "I should go back," I said, and I returned to intensive care.

Eventually a nurse noticed Bob was nearing death, and she pointed at the thin red lines zigzagging on his life support system. Its peaks and valleys were weakening. In a moment it flattened out. She shrugged and said, "That's it."

A spasm of rage shot through me. "That's it? It! How can you be so cruel? That's my husband!" I screamed and cursed.

Johnny put his arm around me. "Let's go," he said in a soothing voice. Others would see only that he was staying under control; I knew him well enough to hear a crack of raw emotion in his voice. But he knew me well enough to know I could be volatile.

I broke away from him to lean down and hug Bob. He was stiff and I knew he was gone. I rose, and Johnny put his arm around me again to walk me outside. I overheard one orderly telling another, "Looks like we're going to have a lot of bodies for the morgue tonight."

"Unfeeling beasts," I muttered. Johnny was doing his best to keep me calm as he led me out of the hospital. Surely this was only a dream and I would wake up and it would disappear. "It can't be true!" I cried out on the hospital steps, twisting myself free from Johnny's arm. I turned around and our eyes met and in a tiny voice I begged, "Can't I go back? I need to be with Bob."

Johnny shook his head and turned me back around. I gave in, and he walked me out to his old Mercedes convertible. I crumbled into the backseat.

"I've got to go back inside and get Cyndi," Johnny said softly. "Are you going to be alright out here by yourself?"

"Yes," I mumbled, because it was what he needed to hear so he could go back for her. But as soon as I was alone, I sobbed the real answer to myself: "No. How am I ever going to be alright?"

A moment later, Cyndi climbed into the front seat and reached out for my trembling hand. "JoAnn, I'm so sorry. I can't believe Bob is gone." We drove along the Pacific Coast Highway and it seemed odd to me that the rest of the world carried on as usual. When we reached my house, Duff's Harley sat in my dark driveway, and Rebecca and Allison pulled in behind us. It was about 3 a.m. I made coffee.

Bob -- always so strong and so full of life -- how could he be gone?

"The crazy thing about it all is that it almost seemed like Bob knew he was about to die," I suggested. I was too numb to cry right now, but occasionally I discovered that a tear had run down my face.

"Why would you think that?" said Rebecca.

"Just the other night we had company for dinner. In fact it was last night – it feels like a hundred years ago – and suddenly Bob asked everybody what happens after we die. It's not like him to ask something like that. We never think about religion."

"He's been asking that a lot lately," Johnny commented.

"You're kidding!" I gasped. "Not around me, he hasn't."

"I've heard him ask several people," he went on. "He must have known something was about to happen."

"I've heard him too," Duff admitted. "He's asked a lot of people. But I don't know if I buy all this business about him knowing all this stuff ahead of time."

"Well," I retorted, "there's more. While our friends were talking about reincarnation and going on to a higher plane, Bob started describing the funeral he wanted. It was weird. He said it had to be something cool – nothing like the funerals they do in church." I gave them the detailed description he had given us all at dinner. "Then he leaned forward and pointed his finger at me, like he was giving me a warning, and remarked, 'I'll never leave you a rich widow.' I couldn't imagine what made him say something like that. Why would I want to be a rich widow? But I couldn't get a word in edgewise. He went on to say that if I remarried, he didn't want someone marrying me for my money. 'He'd better be man enough to take care of you.'"

"He must have known," Johnny repeated.

Duff tugged on his mustache. "It's really far out. But one thing's for sure: he's told you what kind of funeral he wants and you're gonna have to do it."

"But how?" Allison objected. "What'll your family think?"

"Don't worry about that," Rebecca said. "If anyone can find a way to make the family happy and to honor Bob's last request, JoAnn will find it."

We talked through the night and into the morning. At about 10 a.m. the doorbell rang. I opened the door and saw the two uniformed police officers that had been in my dream.

"Are you JoAnn DeJoria?" the tallest officer asked softly.

"Yes."

He took a deep breath. "Your husband, Bob, was involved in a motor-cycle accident yesterday in Topanga Canyon." The officer cleared his throat and hung his head. "He passed away early this morning at St. John's hospital in Santa Monica.

"I know."

"Usually the families are already aware in these situations," the shorter officer explained as he took off his hat and mopped his brow, "but it's our policy to inform them in person. We're very sorry."

I nodded and closed the door. Everyone in the room stared at me in disbelief. I shrugged and said, "I told you they'd be here."

Rebecca was right; I can always find a creative way to deal with impossible situations. It hadn't taken long to figure out that the only way to make the family happy and to give Bob the funeral he requested was to have two funerals, one phony and one real. So I told my family when we'd have their funeral – I didn't mention the second one – and Mom came to stay with me in the guest room.

The night before the funeral I tucked Heather into bed and told Mom goodnight. It was hard to get to sleep; Bob's absence was everywhere. Suddenly at midnight, Heather began screaming and Mom and I almost collided in the hallway as we rushed to her room.

Heather thrashed about in her brass crib. "Hot!" she cried. Her flushed face was contorted in pain. Her blond hair lay matted in damp curls on her head. "Hot," she wailed again and again.

I reached for my daughter, but she struggled out of my arms.

"Hot!" Heather clenched her tiny fists. The crib shook violently as she threw herself from end to end, all the time screeching, "Hot!"

I grabbed my mother by the arm and pulled her away from the crib. "Let's leave her alone for a minute," I said uneasily.

"What do you think is wrong?" my mother whispered.

A terrible thought flashed through my mind. I whispered hoarsely to my mother, "Johnny told me Bob could enter into another person after he died."

"Hot!" Heather screamed hysterically as she reeled against the side of the crib. "No! Hot!"

I had to do something. What if Johnny was right and Bob was here? I was terrified, but I spoke out. "Bob, please leave her alone."

Heather shook her head. "Hot!"

"Bob, this isn't right for Heather! She's got to have her own life!" I insisted. "We love you, but there has to be another way. I know you'll find it. Please leave her alone, now!"

Suddenly, Heather relaxed and dropped to the mattress. I reached for my daughter and pulled her close. She snuggled against me.

"Mommy, please – outside." Now her voice was tiny, broken, delicate.

I carried her through the dark house and out the front door into the night. My mother followed closely. Heather raised her tiny arm toward the sky. "I love you, Daddy."

My mother and I exchanged frightened looks.

The next morning, I called the crematorium. "This is Mrs. DeJoria. Can you tell me when my husband, Bob, was cremated?"

"Hold on, I'll have to check the records," a woman replied. Soon she returned with the answer I feared.

"Last night at midnight."

The time came for the counterfeit funeral. I made my way across the back lawn, carrying a letter I would read aloud to the guests. After that, I wasn't sure what I would do. The suit was horribly uncomfortable and I grumbled to myself: why couldn't I find a way to outmaneuver Aunt Hazel and wear something else?

I looked at the crowd as I made my way across the lawn. There was Ma, my grandmother. She was younger than Aunt Hazel but the deep wrinkles in her face made her look as old as time itself. She had always been kind to me, sweet and gentle. But my mind went back to the cards.

Ma's Uncle Henry would sneak down to the river and hang around with the gypsies when he was a small boy in Russia. They taught him to tell fortunes. Because Uncle Henry favored her, she was the only one of the five sisters he revealed the fortune-telling secrets to. He ended up dying with the death card in his hand. He left his cards to her – Aunt Hazel was insanely jealous – and Ma used them only once. They predicted my grandfather's death, and he died in a fire later that day. She freaked out, put the cards away, and refused to get them out again. Decades passed, and the cards lay untouched.

But I got her to read them for Bob and me. At first she resisted, but I kept begging until she gave in. With a sigh she fanned out the cards. I picked one, and she looked at it and announced, "Change." Change? This sounded like fun.

Then Bob took one and handed it to her, and the look of fear that spread over her face frightened me. "What is it? What is it?" I asked, but she shook her head as she quickly gathered the cards. "Trouble," she admitted as she took the cards and withdrew into her bedroom. I could never get her to say any more about it.

I saw her today and told myself for the hundredth time, it was the death card, wasn't it? And I suddenly realized the change she saw for me would not be the fun I had expected.

I got to the cliff at the edge of my yard and turned to face everyone; behind me was a stunning view of the Pacific. They saw me standing and waiting with a piece of paper in my hand, and they became respectfully silent. I read them the letter I had written on the beach a few hours earlier, pouring out my heart to Bob. Then I turned and looked out over the ocean. I didn't quite know what to do, but I glanced around as though I did. And there it was, off to the left: a plane heading out over the water. I pointed to it and pretended to sniffle, as though Bob's ashes were being scattered. It worked. I heard a symphony of mourners weeping and blowing their noses into handkerchiefs. In her heavy French accent Bob's mother Yvonne cried out with anguish, "My son! My Robert!"

The ceremony ended when the plane disappeared from view. Now the friends and family came to share their condolences one by one. Though the ceremony was a fake, the grief was real. "I'm so sorry," said one. "I can't believe he's gone," said another.

When my grandmother hugged me I asked, "Ma, was it the death card he drew?"

"Yes," she sighed. "But how could I tell you? At least he had a few more months." Her body drooped with resignation and she looked into my eyes with the deepest sadness I had ever seen. Then her eyes left mine and she walked away.

Yvonne came slowly towards me, her eyes swollen as she reached out to embrace me. "My Robert, my son, my Robert is gone! Why did this terrible thing have to happen?" I had no answers.

A few people said, "It's as though Bob were right here, watching over us." I probably should have been able to take it in stride, but after Heather's experience the night before it gave me the creeps.

Finally the people started leaving and Rebecca sidled up to me, sympathy shimmering in her large hazel eyes. "I'll be back tomorrow for Bob's version of a funeral," she whispered. She smoothed her short grey skirt over her shapely hips. We both saw Aunt Hazel raise her eyebrows indignantly. "We'll have a great time."

Then she looked both ways to make sure nobody was listening. "Incidentally, that plane you pointed to – the one that supposedly scattered Bob's ashes out to sea – was a commercial airliner taking off from LAX." She winked. "I may be the actress, JoAnn, but you pulled it off. Now you can give Bob the funeral he described."

"I hope so," I sighed.

Rebecca hugged me, but suddenly I felt her pulling away. "Oh no," she whispered. "Here comes old Witch Hazel. I'm out of here." She released me and rushed through the front gate.

Aunt Hazel walked up, her eyes following Rebecca out the gate. "Who is that tramp?" she snapped.

"A friend, someone from work," I stammered.

"Is that where you get your wardrobe ideas from? That was the shortest skirt I've ever seen! And be sure you don't ever cake on your make-up like that girl. I certainly hope you get her out of your life immediately. She can't possibly be a good influence on you." With that, Aunt Hazel turned and left.

What a day! I was glad when it was over, but the mock funeral had presented one final challenge. Mom was planning to take Heather home with her for a few days. I had to get her out of the house before the guests arrived for the real funeral the next day. I didn't want to have to try to explain the funeral Bob had said he wanted: "Get my friends together, bring out a big basket full of our homegrown pot, and have a party!"

Two

Contact From Beyond The Grave?

The good news was that Mom didn't suspect a thing. The bad news was that she was showing no signs of getting on the road, and the clock was ticking. We'd already had a leisurely breakfast; Mom was relaxing in an armchair and I was sprawled on a sofa while Heather played with her blocks by the picture window.

"What time do you have to be at the airport?" I asked. "Traffic can be brutal on the 405. Of course it isn't rush hour, but all it takes is someone with a flat tire and it'll cause a bottleneck when the gawkers slow down to look."

"Oh, I'm not worried," she said. "They always want you to be at the airport so early, and what for? You hurry up and wait, just to sit in the lobby." Mom was so easygoing and so practical that it was creating a problem for me. The crazy thing about it was that if I could just tell her I was expecting guests, she would have done everything she could to help. I felt guilty that she was so sweet, and here I was hiding some-thing from her. She probably would have understood, but I couldn't bring myself to risk it.

Just then the phone and the doorbell rang at the same time. Heather toddled to the screen door as Mom went to the kitchen to answer the phone. I sat up to try to see who was at the door and heard Rebecca say-ing, "Hi Heather; is your Mommy home?"

"Come on in," I called as I jumped up.

She had a large cast-iron pot in one hand and loaves of French bread in the other. "I brought some food for..." she said, but then cut it short because she spotted Mom in the other room. She elbowed the screen open, and in a conspiratorial voice mouthed the words, "You know – for later."

There was no friend I'd rather see than Rebecca, but sometimes her timing could be incredibly bad. Mom's back was turned, so I hurriedly motioned for Rebecca to get the food out of sight. She scurried around to the side door by the garage and I returned my attention to my moth-er's phone conversation.

"Yes, Sister Theresa, Bob was in a motorcycle accident. He passed away on Tuesday." Mom paused and waved for me to come to the phone. "She's right here, Sister; I'll get her for you."

I shook my head vigorously. "No, Mom, tell her I left," I whispered.

Rebecca padded back in the room and listened. "Who in the world is Sister Theresa?" she asked.

"My father's aunt. She's a Catholic nun, and I'm definitely not in the mood to talk to her."

"You've got a weird family: Jews and Catholics."

I shrugged. What did it matter that my mother's family was Jewish and my father's was Italian Catholic? Other than Sister Theresa, none of us really believed one way or the other.

"JoAnn, Sister Theresa is waiting to talk to you," my mother insisted, holding her hand over the receiver. The call would be uncomfortable, but why put it off? "You may as well get it over with," she cajoled, and she was probably right, even if I didn't want to admit it now. I reluctantly accepted the phone and sat at the kitchen table.

"Hello, Sister Theresa." Heather was playing with her blocks again and Mom and Rebecca had nothing else to do but to listen in on my conversation. Sister Theresa was full of questions. Had I had called for a priest? "Well, not really, Sister. You know Bob wasn't Catholic." Where had I had the funeral? "His ashes were scattered over the ocean in the front of our home yesterday."

This brought a gasp. "Your father, God rest his soul, raised you a Catholic! If he was alive, he would be very upset that you gave your husband a pagan funeral."

"It's what Bob wanted."

Sister Theresa decided it was time to deliver a mini-sermon, but I was watching the clock and trying not to sound as impatient as I felt. Did I even believe in God? I couldn't imagine how this could matter, especially right now. "Truthfully, Sister Theresa, I don't know what I believe anymore."

She let out an indignant snort. "I will have Mass said for Bob, and you will certainly be in my prayers. Goodbye."

"Oh, Mommy, I wish you hadn't let her know I was home," I moaned. "It was dreadful."

Mom shrugged. "How could I lie to a nun?" She scooped Heather into her arms. "We'd better get you some lunch before we leave,

Sweetheart."

Rebecca stood in the driveway and waved goodbye as I pulled away to drive Mom and Heather to the airport.

I rushed back to Malibu and found Rebecca sleeping on the sofa. She sat up and rubbed the sleep from her eyes. "You got back quick."

"Or maybe you've been snoozing awhile." It wasn't fair; I was the one who needed a nap. I stretched my head over my arms and yawned. "Wow, it's a good thing my Mom didn't see all the bread and that huge cast-iron pot. Where did you hide it?"

"I stuffed the French bread in the washing machine and threw some laundry on top of it," Rebecca answered. "Then I hid the cheese fondue in the garage."

"You airhead! The dog is in there." We ran to the garage and found my German shepherd licking up a puddle of cheese by the overturned pot. He looked up at us; cheese was all over his face and his fur. "I wish I could throw him in the washing machine. What a mess!"

"Then he could eat the bread," Rebecca giggled. "You know, I really wasn't thinking. It's kinda gross that I piled the dirty clothes on top of it. Don't worry; I'll run down to the store to get more." She lit a joint and handed it to me. "But smoke this first. Take a minute to relax. Everybody will be here before we know it."

We walked back into the house and sat together on the overstuffed sofa. It was good to have a friend to talk to; this was my first chance to unwind since the mock funeral. The words tumbled out. "I sure hope today is better than yesterday. It was horrible. I felt like a zombie standing on the lawn. Aunt Hazel told me not to cry, and now I can't. I wanted to cry last night after everyone left, and I couldn't. It's like my tears were locked up."

Rebecca tapped me on the shoulder. "You're letting the joint burn out. Give it to me."

Handing her the joint, I continued. "Anyway, I overheard someone yesterday commenting that I must not have cared much for my husband because I was so composed. I don't get it. Ever since I was a kid, I've heard people gossip how the widow grieves, as if there is some sort of rule written about it. I hate it. Nobody can know what this feels like. I'm numb. I feel like I'm losing my mind. A voice inside keeps screaming at me that I'm not doing anything right, that I should throw a fit or faint. How do I know what's right? I haven't watched anybody my age lose her husband. And what good would that do, anyway? Nobody can feel someone else's feelings and then imitate them. I don't want to imitate anything. I'm so messed up. Am I doing it right, Rebecca?"

"You're doing everything just fine," Rebecca said, still puffing on the joint. "Don't worry about what people think. We'll get so stoned we'll be oblivious and won't have to use our brains." She handed the joint back to me.

Rebecca was wonderful. She always knew just what to say; with just a few words, she could snap me out of my darkest moods. "Yeah, you're right; who cares what people think? We'll just absorb the atmosphere," I said.

"Atmosphere? What atmosphere?" She sounded puzzled, but my friends were always telling me I tended to come up with things out of left field.

I explained without a word. I took another deep drag and blew the smoke in her face.

People began arriving, and I was acting like a robot, not a hostess. Faces blurred, and I didn't acknowledge anyone. But who cared what anybody thinks? I could get away with it. Today's crowd would be Bob's close friends, and none of them were hung up on the expectations and demands I had faced the day before.

When it seemed everyone had arrived, I walked to the same spot I had used at the counterfeit funeral, where I could stand with the ocean behind me. Sometimes sunlight sparkled on the ocean as though a thousand diamonds were floating on its surface, and today it put on its best display. I stood between two fragrant and majestic acacia trees on the edge of the cliff. Megan and Sean had brought a beautiful floral wreath with a ribbon that said "In Memory" and hung it on one.

Bob and I had picked out the house together. It had taken us a year; my realtor had shown us dozens of houses before we had seen this one. It hadn't bothered her if we showed up at a house on Bob's Harley instead of in the Jaguar; she wasn't put off by our hippie attire or his long hair. I knew she called the sellers to tell them we might seem eccentric, but we were qualified buyers. Was it that she enjoyed jolting the stodgy owners of these expensive homes? Somehow she had treated the whole process like a joyful adventure, and we had become friends.

"JoAnn, remember the street in Malibu with all the trees?"

"Of course. Cool Oak Way. I've always said that's where I want to live."

"Well, I listed a house on that street this morning. Better bring your checkbook."

She'd never said bring the checkbook before and I knew she must have found something good – she wouldn't pressure us with sales gimmicks. Bob was at work, so I went alone to meet her in Malibu.

As we walked through the little wooden gate leading to the yard, a blanket of peace wrapped itself around me and I knew I was home. Everything was immaculate; the landscaping was lush and well planned; the house had the perfect layout for our needs.

The view of the Pacific was extraordinary. The house sat on a point of land, with no other homes visible from any part of the property. The living room windows showed the northern coastline curving beyond the Malibu pier, and the southern coastline down past Santa Monica with the planes taking off from LAX, and then all the way down to Palos Verdes. I could see the skyscrapers and much of Los Angeles. It was breathtaking.

I called Bob and he came immediately to meet me. Tears filled my eyes. I was overcome with the beauty of the place, with the sweet smell of earth mingled with the ocean breeze. I followed Bob to the edge of the cliff where he stood and scanned the panorama. "I want this place."

"But, Honey, you never even looked at the house!"

"I don't care about the house. I love this place. We're done looking."

I had expected a lifetime in this beautiful and secluded spot; instead, we had had about a year and a half.

Now as I walked to the cliff and turned to face the people, I heard the airplane overhead. The pilot would circle the house three times to identify himself, then fly out to sea, scattering my husband's ashes. In the briefest of moments, I watched my childhood sweetheart disappear in a fleeting smear of grey.

All eyes were on me, as though I could know what to do next. I turned to face them and reread the letter I'd written to him at the beach. Then it was time to honor his last request: to throw a big party.

People shuffled in and out for the rest of the day. The house was filled with a thick fog of marijuana and tobacco smoke.

But before long I'd had all I could take. I spotted my friend Allison, a friend it was easy to relax with. "It's too crazy out here," I confided. "I'm not really in a party mood anyway. Let's go back to the bedroom and talk. I need to get away from the crowd."

We plopped down on the bed and I lit a joint. "You could get a contact high just by sitting in the living room," I remarked. I took a shallow drag and handed the joint to Allison. All my friends smoked pot, but she was the sanest of them: sweet, clean cut in a girl-next-door sort of way, and utterly devoted to her children.

"It's sure weird that Bob told you about all this the night before he died."

"Well, I hope he's happy with it." A couple of things had already happened that I wasn't sure were what he had had in mind. One man had walked in, glanced around the house, and offered to buy it; he said he was sure I wouldn't need it now that Bob was gone. Another friend gave me a gift-wrapped box; I opened it and found a sex toy. Peals of laughter followed as she told me this would help me get by without Bob. Was this really what he had wanted?

But Allison had missed all of that. "JoAnn, you gave him exactly what he asked for. You should be proud. I'm sure he's looking down from heaven enjoying every minute of it." That was Allison, always finding something encouraging to say.

Allison's four-year-old came in the bedroom. "Where's Daddy?" he asked.

"I don't know. Look first, and if you don't find him, we'll go help you." Allison laid down the joint and snuggled her head in the pillow.

"I already did, Mommy. I can't find him anywhere."

Reluctantly, Allison and I followed her little boy around the house looking for her husband, Duff. Unable to locate him, we went outside and continued the search. We found him in a secluded spot beside the house making love to Rebecca.

Allison plucked her son off the ground and turned away screaming for her daughter. I watched her run down the gravel path with her son in her arms and her daughter close behind. Then her tires screeched as she sped away.

I turned to Rebecca and Duff; by now they were sitting side-by-side on a swing. "Have you lost your minds?"

Duff just shrugged his muscular shoulders. He tried to look noncha- lant, dropping his head on Rebecca's shoulder and looking at me disinterestedly through half-closed eyes.

But Rebecca's face was mischief itself. "If it feels good, do it. Whatever it takes to get through the day or night, my dear. Besides, I know exactly what you need, and I've already called him."

Duff got up and swaggered away. "I'll catch you later," he said over his shoulder.

Whenever I saw Rebecca giving her half smile – there was only a slight upturn at one side of her mouth, but her eyes were dancing – I knew she was up to something. "Who'd you call, Rebecca? What are you talking about?"

"Warren. He's promised me. Look at it like this: he's a special present from me to you. You've been sheltered all your life, and I know from experience he will treat you right. I want you to start with the best." She smacked her lips and blew me a kiss. "A gauge to judge the others by."

What next? I buried my face in my hands and shook my head. "I don't believe this. I don't want to be with another man."

"Listen to me. I'm very serious about this, JoAnn. You have to go on with your life. What are you waiting for? Who made up the rule that a certain amount of time has to go by? Who cares what people think? Eventually you'll be fooling around, so go for it now. Bob's gone and he's not coming back. Are you supposed to sit around mourning for a year doing some sort of self-imposed penance? This is the Age of Aquarius. We're enlightened. Why waste time? Life is short." Rebecca lit a joint and handed it to me. "Stay stoned, have fun."

"This is crazy." I took a deep drag. "You're in a hurry for me to get over this. You don't understand. Give me a chance to –"

"No," Rebecca interrupted, pointing at me just as Aunt Hazel had done the day before. "You're the one who doesn't understand. I'm your best friend, and I know what's good for you. Warren will be good for you. I guarantee it. You're trying to follow a set of rules that 'they' made up – whoever 'they' are. Look at the mess 'they've' got the world into: Vietnam, bombs, chemical weapons. Someday we'll take over, and it'll be different."

"Look, it doesn't make any difference anyway." I passed the joint back to Rebecca. "Warren would never look twice at someone like me."

Now her eyes began to twinkle. "You don't give yourself enough credit. You don't realize you're really a looker. He'll like you. Men love tall, shapely blondes." She stood and ran a hand over the curve of her hip. "Short red-head actresses don't do so bad either. Talk to him. He's absolutely irresistible." She turned and went into the house.

I followed, deciding it was time to try once again to mingle with my guests. I saw Nate leaving and walked him to his new Mercedes convertible. I had been his personal secretary at a large talent agency in Beverly Hills before Heather was born, and we had remained friends. I had always found Nate dazzling. He was the first man I ever knew who had a college education and wore suits to work; he looked like a male fashion model; he lived in an exclusive neighborhood in Beverly Hills, and when Bob and I had gone to a party at his home we saw original paintings by Matisse, Picasso, Dali, and Van Gogh.

I had always had a crush on him, just as a first-grader might have a crush on a teacher, and it seemed harmless because he was out of reach. He was as unlikely to look at me twice as Warren was. Why should he even notice me? Starlets often came to the office, and many of them would climb into his lap and flirt. He always resisted their advances. And whenever anyone in the office made a pass at me, Nate always protected me. "She's shy," he would say, "and very married."

His office was on the twenty-fourth floor, and one day we had been waiting for an elevator. We were talking and he was behind me, so I had turned to face him and wasn't looking at the elevator door. The chime rang and I heard the door open, and I went to step in. But he grabbed me by the waist and stopped me – the door had opened but the elevator wasn't there. I would have dropped to my death in the empty shaft. Nate had saved my life. I didn't think; I threw myself into his arms and pressed my lips to his. He did not respond and I broke the embrace. Our eyes met, and wordlessly we both knew it would never happen again and we would both act as if it hadn't happened.

That had been a few years ago, but now we got to Nate's car and, without warning, he put his muscular arms around me and kissed my lips softly. Then he released me, but our eyes were locked for the next few seconds and I was breathless. A breeze ruffled his thick sandy-colored hair and I didn't know how to read his brown eyes. It was as though we were back at the elevator.

Then he broke the spell as he got in his car and drove away. Why had he kissed me? I was confused. I had always considered him off-limits because I was married, and I suspected that his respect for Bob and me had made him consider me untouchable too. But what I had thought was a harmless crush had proven to be a fire that could blaze out of control. I was angry with myself for enjoying the kiss – Bob hadn't been gone even for a week yet – and for wanting the comfort of his embrace. What did it all mean? And was this the party Bob had wanted?

I wasn't doing well, trying to connect with people. I gave up and went back to my room for a couple of hours. I locked the door behind me.

I heard a knock at the door, and it was Rebecca. "We're going out dancing at the Topanga Corral. Come with us – let's get wild!"

"Get wild? What do you think you've been doing all day? You go! I don't want to." It was our favorite hangout; while Malibu had a Hollywood flavor, the Topanga Corral was like a piece of Woodstock that had somehow been transplanted to California. But to get there, we would have to drive down the stretch of road where Bob had been killed.

"Don't be a drag," Rebecca said. "Let's go. We need to get out of here and dance. Get out of bed; I can't leave you here by yourself."

Reluctantly I unlocked the door, and then eight of us squeezed into a car and off we went. Everyone else was chattering, but I wasn't in the mood. I couldn't believe I'd agreed to go out dancing. As we went around the curve where Bob had lost control of his chopper, I thought to myself, if Bob were here, he'd be so mad at the way our friends are acting, he'd kill us all.

Suddenly, the screech of brakes sent terror streaming through me. I smelled burning rubber and felt the impact as another vehicle slammed into us. We'd been hit at the sharp curve where Bob had had his accident. Fortunately, nobody was hurt and our car wasn't badly damaged. After the police arrived and took a report, I groaned, "I just want to go home."

We returned to my house and everyone went to their cars and left, but Rebecca tore herself away from Duff and said, "I want to talk to JoAnn a minute." She grabbed my hand and pulled me aside. "I called Warren, and he's going to be in Malibu tonight." Then she slipped some pills in my hand. "And whenever you want to go to sleep, take one of these."

Then she jumped in the car and sped away, leaving me standing alone in the dark driveway.

My heart pounded with fear as I ran toward the swinging gate and entered the yard. Moonlight was scattered over the ocean. Eerie shadows and shapes stood where trees and bushes ought to be. I hurried toward the front door and was fumbling for my keys when I heard movement nearby and screamed. My panic only made it more difficult to find the key, but in a moment I did and I opened the front door. The neighbor's cat scurried out of the bushes. Only a cat, I assured myself as I slipped inside.

The empty house was uninviting. I tried to relax by drinking more wine, and then I lay down on my bed and smoked a joint. I turned off the light and heard the floor creak. What was that? I wondered. Trembling, I fumbled for the light switch and heard the floor squeak again. I turned on the light; then for good measure I got up and turned on all the lights in the house. When I went back to bed, I took one of the sleeping pills Rebecca had given me.

The phone woke me up at about two a.m. I was really groggy, and the caller hung up. Was it Warren? It couldn't be…or could it? I wasn't sure if I wanted him to call or not. It seemed foolish to think he even would. When I had seen him in a movie, I had thought Warren was the most handsome actor I'd ever seen. I had fantasized about him many times, but these weren't the kind of fantasies that become real.

And then, of all things, he'd become romantically involved with Rebecca. Rebecca had a thing for powerful men; lately she'd said she was trying to find a way to conquer Castro.

I loved Rebecca. She was always wonderful, always outrageous, always full of surprises. Now she wanted to straighten me out in her own unique way. I realized it would happen if I said yes. But one thing puzzled me: how did my single friends carelessly pass their lovers around like a bag of potato chips, as though it was only polite to share?

Rebecca, what will you come up with next? I wondered as I drifted back to sleep.

Three

Minus A Quarter Of A Million

The phone rang again and woke me out of a sound sleep. Groggily, I knocked the receiver off the hook and watched it dangle in the bright morning light. I rubbed the sleep out of my eyes and retrieved the phone. "Hello?" I groaned.

"It's Allison. You need to tell me what's going on with Duff and Rebecca."

I felt defensive right away. Why did she sound mad at me? I hadn't had anything to do with any of it. "I don't know," I protested.

"You must know something," she said curtly. "She's your best friend."

"Look, I'm not even awake yct, but this whole thing is as much of a surprise to me as it is to you. I don't know anything about it, and I refuse to get in the middle of it. It isn't fair."

"It isn't fair? How do you think I feel?" said Allison, and then she hung up.

What a thing to wake up to! I stumbled out of bed and made coffee. I had just filled my cup when the phone rang again.

"Tell me about Allison and Duff's marriage," Rebecca purred. I couldn't believe it: first Allison, now Rebecca. And Rebecca was maddeningly smug; it was hard to keep my temper.

"First, it's all messed up now that you have entered the picture. Second, I'm not even awake yet, and Allison just hung up on me for not telling her what you and Duff are up to. So, third, I'm going to hang up now before I explode; but I'll tell you the same thing I told Allison: I refuse to be put in the middle of this mess."

"Oh, it doesn't matter anyway," Rebecca said in a singsong voice. "I can't be serious about Duff. After all, he's just a flunky; he carries cement to bricklayers all day. Why would I get involved with him when I've got Elvis Presley and Henry Kissinger? It must be temporary insanity. I guess Bob's death is affecting us all."

Leave it to Rebecca to get me laughing when I was so mad I was about to hang up on her. But it was true: she had a thing about powerful men. Bob and I had had a surprise visit when Elvis had sent one of his boys all the way from Texas in his private jet to pick some of our homegrown pot because Rebecca had bragged about it. "Somehow it's hard enough to connect Elvis and Kissinger, without throwing Duff in the mix; and what about Warren?" I laughed. "Does this mean it's over between you and Duff?"

"Of course! You won't hear another word about it from me. He really isn't my type – did I tell you I'm working on Castro? And I was getting to Warren – that's my next question. Did you hear from him?"

"I don't know."

"JoAnn, how can you not know?" She sounded dumbfounded. "How stoned were you?"

"I was out of it. I took one of those sleeping pills you gave me and washed it down with a glass of wine. The phone rang in the middle of the night, and the caller hung up on me."

"He must have realized he woke you up." She sounded thoughtful; I could tell wheels were turning. "I'll have to make arrangements when he gets back from location."

"Arrangements! I don't need you to make arrangements! How about if I let you know when I want to meet him? It just doesn't seem right. It's too soon after Bob's death. It's like I'm being unfaithful to Bob's memory." I took a sip of coffee and looked out the window. I saw deer eating the tops off my roses.

"Don't be silly. It's not like Bob was Mr. Faithful."

I didn't know what to believe. Bob was handsome, and women often had seemed to throw themselves at him. Which was better: to put up with it, or to nag? "Look, Rebecca, I just can't get into it right now. Besides, I've got to run – I just saw deer eating the flowers."

But she wouldn't let it go. "Warren is what you need. You can't hang on to the past – catch you later."

I raced outside, waving my arms at the deer and shouting, "Shoo! Get out of here!" and they gave me a startled look and scampered down the hillside. Sometimes they'd try to come back, so I stood with my hands on my hips and glared after them as they ran away. But the phone rang again and I had to rush back inside. I wasn't ready for another call.

It was Megan. "JoAnn, you won't believe what happened last night after my husband and I left your house. It was really far out."

"Right now I can believe almost anything."

"Well, Sean and I took Bob's wreath down to the Malibu Pier, like you asked us to. Sean threw it out to sea as far as he could. Then we went into Alice's Restaurant and belted down a few whiskey sours. We were in Alice's about an hour before we went home." Megan paused and took a deep breath.

"When we got home, the wreath was on our front porch! I almost stumbled over it when we came up the steps. It must have washed up at high tide." Neither of us spoke for a few moments. Then she offered, "It was like Bob was reaching out to us to say goodbye."

After I hung up, I pictured the wreath floating and bobbing on the waves after Sean tossed it. How could it have traveled the three miles from the pier to Sean and Megan's place in one hour? True, their home sat right on the beach in Malibu, but how could the wreath direct itself to their front porch? What guided it there? Or was it just a coincidence? I tried to grasp its meaning. Was Bob really trying to communicate with us? Could he?

Another phone call interrupted my thoughts. A man demanded, "Is Mr. DeJoria there?"

"No, he's..." I couldn't bring myself to say the words.

"He's where?" asked the caller sharply.

"He's not here. That is, he's no longer living. He's dead."

"Dead? Who is this?"

Despite the man's offensively abrupt tone, I answered, "His wife."

"Well then, Mrs. DeJoria, you owe Xerox $100,000!"

Shocked, I said nothing.

The emotionless voice continued, "We need to arrange a meeting to settle this matter at once."

I hung up and stared out the picture window. It was the same window I had looked out every morning for the past year, yet everything looked different. $100,000? This couldn't be right; Bob had never said any-thing about it.

Suddenly I longed for my daughter. I quickly dialed my mother's number. "Mom, how is Heather doing?" I asked as soon as she picked up the phone.

"She's been fussy, Honey. She wants to come home and keeps asking for you."

"I wish she was here right now so I could hold her," I said miserably. "But I have to get down to my store right away." I didn't mention the disturbing phone call. "I let my maid go till the end of the week. Could you please keep Heather till Marta gets back?"

Mom sighed. "I'll do the best I can."

"Can I talk to Heather?"

"Okay, just a minute."

The next thing I heard was Heather breathing softly through the line.

"I miss you, little goose," I said as cheerfully as I could.

"Mommy, I wanna come home."

"Soon, Baby," I assured her. "Hold up all your fingers – just the fingers on one hand. That's how many days before you come home."

"Okay, Mommy; I see," Heather said sweetly.

I had her give the phone back to my mother. "I've got to run. Give my baby a big hug and kiss from me."

I threw on some old clothes, and as I drove into Beverly Hills I thought about how we had started our businesses. While working for United Parcel Service, Bob had gotten to know the manager of a four-cent copy business that operated in a coin-laundry near U.C.L.A. After listening to her, Bob decided to talk to a Xerox salesman. The salesman was more than helpful, telling Bob how to cheat Xerox and make a huge profit. "I can show you how to turn off the meter and you'll never get caught," he assured him. "Even the largest printing establishments in the area turn in false meter cards each month."

I didn't like the idea. We would need to begin with a $2000 investment. I had the money – I had saved it before Bob and I had gotten married – but it seemed risky. "It took me a long time to save that money," I protested. "And this is crazy. How do you know Xerox won't find out? I don't even understand what you're trying to do."

But Bob was convinced. "Honey, I know this will work; I just know it."

If we had had the conversation just once, we never would have gone into business. But he thought about it every day while driving his UPS truck, and then he would come home excited. "This is our chance. We've got to do it." Eventually his enthusiasm wore me down, and we opened in Long Beach. I was pregnant with Heather, but we worked hard to promote our venture by passing out flyers at the state college and local businesses.

We opened our second store in Beverly Hills. They had just started building high-rises in Century City. Again we did a lot of promotion, personally visiting the offices in every high-rise in our area. We ran ads in the *Hollywood Reporter* and *Variety*; that brought in a lot of screenwriters and people involved in the motion picture industry.

The Beverly Hills store was an immediate success. Suddenly, we had a beautiful home in Malibu, a live-in maid, and all the perks. Bob was only 28 and I was 26. We had worked hard; we were on our way. Shortly before he died, Bob opened a third store on Fairfax in the Borsch belt; it was holding its own but hadn't become as profitable as either of the other two.

Now that I had just inherited a staggering debt, I had to wonder: how did Xerox know? Was there a hidden counter in the meter? Had the salesman deceived Bob?

I arrived at Beverly Hills and went into the store. As always, it was filled with customers wanting copies, rubber stamps, stationery, and other office supplies. The copy machines hummed in the background. This was our most successful copy business, the one that had lifted Bob and me from the working class to the upper middle class almost overnight

"Looks like it's going to be a long day," I muttered to one of the counter girls.

"Yeah, work's really piling up. And machine #2 is down. I called the repair shop yesterday, but they still haven't shown up. "

Kim, the manager, yelled to me across the room. "Gino is on the phone."

Gino owned the shoe-repair shop in Long Beach where we had placed our first photocopy machine. The shop was near the state college and made a lot of money, even though it consisted of only one copy machine and a few employees working in shifts.

"JoAnn, Diana and I are very sorry to hear about Bob," Gino said in his thick Greek accent. Then without any warning or hesitation he continued, "We've made a decision. We're installing our own machine." He was trying to sound businesslike but I could tell he was nervous, as though his wife were standing over him as he made the call. "So you've got to get yours out of our store right away."

I couldn't believe what I was hearing. We had a good relationship with Gino; he and Diana had asked us to be their son's godparents only a few weeks before Bob's accident. "But we have an agreement," I protested. "You shook Bob's hand and told him we could have the space for as long as we wanted it."

"But there's nothing in writing, is there?" he replied coldly. It was like a kick in the stomach. Without a lease, I realized I was helpless to prevent Gino from putting me out and stealing my customers.

"I thought we were friends," I stammered. Our machine had brought a lot of customers into his store; our business had helped him succeed.

"Business is business," he said curtly. "Now get your machine out of here right away or you'll find it sitting on the curb. I've already ordered my own." Gino hung up.

At first I felt numb. I phoned my manager in Long Beach, and she had already heard. "I can't believe they're doing this to you. When I heard about it, I got so mad I decided to picket the store and let everyone know how they've kicked you when you're down." She was more concerned about me than about her lost job. The more we talked the madder I got, but I kept my rage in check.

As soon as I hung up I started screaming. "Do you know what they did to me? He's stealing the whole Long Beach store! I wish I could stomp that miserable creep and kick him where it hurts!" I forgot that nothing but a flimsy partition separated me from the customers. Sensing their embarrassment, an employee rushed in to calm me down. My voice had carried through the whole store.

Oops – why unnerve good customers? This wasn't solving anything. I simmered down and called Xerox to have them pull the machine as soon as I could move my business somewhere else. I wasn't going to let this creep continue to make money off us! I had equipment, employees, loyal customers, and a good name – all I needed was a new location.

Then something went right for a change: I saw Johnny driving up in his vintage Mercedes. I ran out to meet him. "You won't believe what Gino did," I called to him. "He kicked me out of his store."

"He can't do that," Johnny said confidently.

"Yes he can," I replied. "I don't have a lease. There is nothing I can do to keep him from throwing me out and stealing my customers."

Johnny's green eyes flashed with anger. "That jerk! Look, I came over here to take you down to Milt's to find out about my brother's life insurance policy. So let's do that first, and then I'll drive you down to Long Beach." He led me out the door and down the block to the insurance agency. I knew he was fulfilling his promise to Bob that he would look after Heather and me. "We'll find another location. Do you have a reliable employee working there?"

"Yes," I said, breathing hard as I tried to keep up with him. "The manager is great. I was talking to her just before you drove up. She is so furious that she is going to picket the shoe-repair shop and tell everyone what Diana and Gino are up to."

"Far out. I like her style! All we'll have to do is find another location, and you'll be up and running in no time at all, and that jerk won't steal your customers."

We entered the insurance agency and stale cigarette smoke greeted us in the dingy reception area. "This little dump doesn't fit in with Beverly Hills," I muttered to Johnny. "I feel like I'm in Tijuana."

Soon Milt called us back to his crowded little office. I had already called to tell him about Bob's death. "I'm so sorry about what happened to Bob," he offered awkwardly. He was pale and his hands shook as he lit a cigarette. "I need to make one more call about your policy," he apologized, "and there's no room in here for you to sit. Can I ask you to wait outside?"

So we sat on a long wooden bench in the hall; through the closed door we could her him arguing on the phone. About ten minutes later he came out and shook his head. "I don't believe it," he sighed.

"What's wrong?" Johnny asked as Milt sat down beside him.

Milt looked miserable. "Bob let the policy lapse twelve days before he died. It was a double indemnity policy, so you would have collected $250,000. But he didn't send in the $32.00 premium," Milt said as he stood up. "I'm sorry. There's nothing I can do."

Johnny looked stunned. "Are you sure?" he asked.

"Nothing," said Milt, shaking his head again. "I've already checked every way I can."

"Well, thank you for trying," Johnny said as he shook Milt's hand. "We'd better be going."

Milt looked at me through watery eyes. "I wish I could do more for you and Heather."

"Thanks for all your help, Milt," I said. "To tell the truth, it doesn't seem right to get paid for Bob's dying, anyway."

Johnny and I walked out into the warm sunshine. "Remember when I told you that Bob said he wouldn't leave me a rich widow?" I said as we started back to my shop. "This must be what he meant."

"Yeah, I remember." He shook his head. "But it's hard to believe that this has happened for thirty-two bucks."

I stepped into the shop to tell them I'd be out for a few hours, and then Johnny drove me to Long Beach. We spent several hours looking for another location, but nothing was available. Finally around six in the evening, I turned to Johnny in frustration. "Let's forget this. I still have the store on Fairfax and the one in Beverly Hills. This place is so far away it could turn into a big hassle if the manager should leave."

"Are you sure? I'll help you look again tomorrow," Johnny offered.

I shook my head. "That's okay. I think it's the right thing to do. Look at the distance between the three stores. And what if a key employee gets sick, or quits? It was hard enough to keep up with the workload when Bob was alive; I'm not sure I can do it all alone."

He didn't try to talk me out of it.

The hazy sun dipped behind the tall buildings, casting long shadows on the tree-lined streets as we approached the Beverly Hills store. Traffic was light and the sidewalks were nearly deserted. I envied the office workers who were already home with their families, snug and safe in their homes. I had nothing but an avalanche of work waiting for me.

We arrived at the store and the tires screeched as Johnny made a hasty u-turn to let me off near the door. "I've gotta pick up Cyndi," he said, letting the engine idle as he waited for me to get out of the car. The "Closed" sign hung in the window; everyone was gone. I spotted Duff sitting on his chopper in front of the store.

I had never felt comfortable around Duff and I didn't really want to be left alone with him. I turned to Johnny. "Can't you come in with me for a minute?"

"Sorry, Sis; can't hang around." I got out of the car reluctantly as Johnny waved to Duff and sped away.

Duff was handsome in a rugged sort of way, half surfer and half biker. He had chiseled features, and his well-defined muscles bulged out of a tight black t-shirt. With a sinister grin he announced, "There's something you need to know."

"What?" I tried not to sound too impatient but I wanted to get this over with. Every time he revved his Harley, the sound made me jump. I wasn't in the mood to stand out here talking to Duff in a cloud of exhaust fumes. I think my eyes told him I wanted him to get to the point.

He shut down the engine, swung his leg over the seat of his chopper and stood up, towering over me. "Bob had a hundred thousand bucks stashed in a safety deposit box. He showed it to me a couple of months ago." His blue eyes flashed as he ran his fingers through his blond hair.

"Where'd he get all that money?"

Duff shrugged. "He didn't say, but he was using it – look, it wouldn't be right if I didn't tell you this – he had extra cash stashed and was using some of it to pay his girlfriend's rent. She lived somewhere in the valley." He got back on his Harley.

Girlfriend in the valley? If so, why was Duff telling me about her? Sometimes there had been evidence that Bob was seeing other women, but I didn't trust anything Duff had to say.

I looked at him long and hard, and his eyes betrayed that he enjoyed hurting me with his "information". Maybe I could check up on it.

"Which bank?" I called out over the noise of the engine.

"Can't remember. I was pretty stoned that day." Duff revved the engine and took off.

Four

Revenge

I let myself into the store and found piles of work waiting for me. Bob and I had always finished the day's work after all the employees went home, but tonight I would be alone with my thoughts.

My hands did the work automatically as my mind went back over the day. It had begun with the mysterious call from Xerox, saying I was $100,000 in debt. Why hadn't Bob told me about this? Then it had been the phone call from Gino, and in moments one of our three businesses was gone. None of this would have mattered if Bob had kept up the insurance policy, but instead he'd decided, "I'll never leave you a rich widow." Could I hang onto what we had?

My hands kept working, and so did my mind. It was more than the businesses, the house, the Jaguar, the maid. My father had been an invalid and we had lived in the wrong part of town. I had always been snubbed by the "in-crowd" – I particularly remembered how it had stung when I was turned down for membership in a social club, the Gammas. But self-pity has never been my style. I had decided then that I would have money when I got out of school. Hard work had gotten us this far, and somehow I would find a way to hold things together.

And what about the $100,000 Duff said Bob was keeping in a safe deposit box? Was it really there? It would be great if it was; it would pay the debt to Xerox. But I couldn't reconcile Duff's words with a recent argument between Bob and me. It had seemed unfair that, in addition to his Harley, he always drove the nice car – first the '63 Corvette, then the Ferrari, and lately the new Jaguar – and I was stuck with the aging Firebird. I had said I wanted a new car; he had said we couldn't afford it, but I had persisted. So one day he had proudly given me a bankbook in which he had written, "For JoAnn's new car." He had opened the savings account with $50.00. And now Duff was telling me Bob had been using a hidden stash of $100,000 to pay another woman's rent?

Paying another woman's rent! This was the last straw. Years of suppressed anger welled up. I grabbed the phone and called Rebecca. I would get even with Bob. I'd been afraid to retaliate when he was alive, but now he couldn't hurt me.

"Rebecca," I blurted out when she answered the phone. "I've made up my mind. I want to spend that evening with Warren." I didn't need to tell her I was fuming inside.

She responded immediately. "Good. That'll cheer you up. I'll give him a call and then let you know where to meet him." She laughed playfully. "You won't be sorry – I guarantee it!"

I hung up the phone and boiled over like an old pot that had been left on the back burner to simmer. Revenge! What would it feel like? I looked towards the ceiling and screamed, as though Bob could hear me. "I hope you know this is happening! Now you check this out, Dude! You've had your secret days and nights, and now I'm gonna have mine! But it's not gonna be a secret to you…"

Suddenly I realized I was staring at the ceiling and shaking with anger – but I still couldn't go home until the work was done. I went back to work, and around 2 a.m. I closed up shop and drove home.

At eight a.m., the housekeeper knocked. "Coffee?" she asked. If a shadow could talk, that was Marta.

"Yes, Marta." I fought away the sleep I so badly needed, and the single cup of coffee on the nightstand was a picture of desolation. My anger from the previous night was gone; all I knew was that I missed Bob. I wanted to pull the shades and hide. Instead, I had to gulp down the coffee, get dressed, and rush to the airport to pick up Heather before I went to work.

My mother had sent her on the morning flight, and the stewardess escorted Heather off the plane. My heart leaped when I saw her. Her delicate features reminded me of a blond porcelain doll I had once seen in an antique store. Her soft green eyes sparkled with delight as she held a red lollipop up for me to see. It was still wrapped; she was treasuring it. "Mommy, I got this because I was a good girl."

I gathered Heather in my arms and as she snuggled against my chest I buried my nose in her hair, savoring its smell. This was the first normal moment I had had in days. It struck me that she was too young to realize how deeply her life had changed; she was simply glad to be home, and I was glad to be holding her. "You are my littlest angel," I sighed, and we held each other even more tightly.

Then we rushed back to Malibu, weaving in and out of the morning traffic, and I left her with Marta so I could get back to work.

Warren's apartment was the whole tenth floor of the Beverly Wilshire Hotel. The elevator went only to the eighth floor, and then I had to climb two flights of stairs to reach his door. I knocked timidly; I knew it wasn't just the stairs that had caused my heart to pound so hard. I looked back at the stairway, a possible escape route.

Warren was on the phone, and with a boyish grin he motioned for me to come in. I entered the plush hotel apartment. My throat felt dry and I could barely catch my breath. What am I doing here? I wondered as I hid my fear behind an artificial smile.

He covered the mouthpiece and motioned for me to sit in an over-stuffed chair. "I won't be long," he whispered. Whoever he was speaking with must have asked who had come into his apartment because he said, "A friend."

Then they began to quarrel.

I squirmed in my seat as I realized he was talking to his girlfriend, Julie. Warren wandered out onto an enormous rooftop garden to finish his phone call. He was about 40 feet away; I had seen hotel suites, but nothing as large and plush as this. It seemed as if I were visiting a private screening of a silent film. He leaned against the railing and continued his animated argument. He was even more handsome in person than on screen.

His conversation ended abruptly and he walked back into the living room, where I sat with nervous fingers drumming on the silk damask chair. Warren's eyes reflected tenderness and he quickly made me feel that we were old friends. "Sorry I was on the phone so long. How are you doing?" We fell into an easy conversation and I relaxed.

The evening was more than an escape from Bob's infidelity, from the bills I was stuck with, and from my anger. He was everything Rebecca had described. For one wonderful night and morning, I was in a fairy tale world and I didn't think of Bob.

But I had to get back to reality the next day. The store was filled with customers wanting their orders filled immediately. Around noon I was daydreaming and trying to pay bills. A lady in a nasty mood picked on one of the counter girls. I shot out from behind my desk and ordered the woman out of my store. She snapped at me and I lashed back at her like a lunatic. I saw shock on her face, and her rudeness drained out. A flood of my loud curses followed her out, and then an uneasy silence filled the store.

"She deserved it," I said with a chuckle as I returned to my desk. I would never have gotten away with such an outburst if Bob had been around, but he wasn't. It was delicious not to have to be nice to rude people.

Over the weekend Marta went home, so Heather and I were alone. I was nervous about being so isolated. The weekend dragged by, and I couldn't wait to pick Marta up on Sunday afternoon.

Heather and I waited in the Jaguar at the bus stop Sunday as the passengers got off. The last person stepped down and the doors closed. Marta was nowhere in sight. I knew the score. That was the way most of the maids quit: they simply never came back. I'd been through this before with a few other girls.

This meant I had to find someone to look after Heather. First I put her in a nursery school, north of our home in Malibu and about an hour from work. I would drop her off in the morning, drive to Beverly Hills, and pick her up at 5:00 when the school closed. Then I would have to drive back to the store because there was so much work to do.

Heather always wanted my attention and I couldn't get much done. What could a two-year-old find to do in a print shop? I would put her in her playpen, but she would always manage to escape. It was frustrating when she spilled files or overturned piles of paper; worse still, the running machines fascinated her, and I had to make sure she didn't get hurt.

I would try to put her to bed around 8:00 p.m. each night, but she couldn't get to sleep and she would climb out of her crib or cry. Eventually she would fall asleep; then at midnight when I was ready to go home, no matter how gently I gathered her out of her playpen, it always woke her up. This went on for several days, and it wasn't working for either of us. We were both exhausted.

I kept looking for a housekeeper. A neighbor said I should take Heather to her daughter-in-law because she took in children.

"She's so far away!" I protested. Maria lived in Simi Valley, an hour and a half away. I would have to leave Heather with her for days at a time, bringing her home on weekends.

"Go visit Maria," she suggested. "Talk to her, and then decide."

I didn't like the idea, but what could I do? Nothing else was working,

and like it or not, I had to do something. Marta wasn't coming back.
And with Bob gone and with the $100,000 debt to Xerox, I had to put
more time than ever into the business. Life had spun wildly out of
control. Unless something else turned up, I realized I would have to visit Maria and see if she could provide a temporary solution.

Heather playing
with Bob's headphones.

We drove into the neat little neighborhood. Children were everywhere. Heather's eyes brightened as she looked out the window. "Mommy, Mommy, can I play with the children?"

I was glad to see her so excited. Bob and I had always made a point of finding things Heather liked to do. Sometimes there were other children to play with when we took trips to the park or walks on the beach, and at home we made sure she had plenty of fun – she especially enjoyed her paints and her easel. But I suddenly realized that our home was so isolated that she had never been in a neighborhood full of children.

"Yes, Honey, you can play," I said. As soon as I took her out of her car seat, she tried to run off. "Wait," I pleaded. This was happening too fast.

Two meticulously dressed little girls with hair in neat braids ran up to the car. "Are you Mrs. DeJoria?" one asked politely.

"Yes."

"I am Sharon. I am 6 years old, and this is my little sister, Janet. We are Maria's children and have been waiting for you."

"Can Heather come and play with us?" Janet asked shyly.

"Can I, Mommy, please? Please? Can I?" Heather asked eagerly.

"Yes, Honey," I said reluctantly. As soon as the words came out of my mouth the children ran off, holding hands and giggling happily.

One glance showed the home was centered on children. There were play areas inside and outside the house, and small tables with crafts in a corner of the family room. Maria, who spoke with a rich German accent, was obviously a good mother. It was amazing that she could be so tender while remaining firmly in control. It was hard to get Heather to leave, but we promised to visit again soon.

But I kept hoping I was wrong about Marta. I drove to the bus stop for the next three Sundays in case she might come back. Each time the last passenger disembarked my heart sank. Reluctantly I took Heather and visited Maria again, but I still couldn't decide. Back in Malibu, I tentatively asked Heather if she would like to stay at Maria's. "You mean I can sleep at the house with all the children?" she asked.

"Yes, Honey … if you want to."

"Can we go now, Mommy?" she asked simply.

"I'll see if we can go tomorrow," I said. I suddenly realized I'd unconsciously allowed Heather to make the decision. I wondered if I was too easily led, too unwilling to make decisions myself.

The next day I packed her little suitcase and we drove to Maria's. Heather wanted to run off and play as soon as we arrived. I explained that I was going to be leaving and she simply said, "Bye bye, Mommy – can I go play now?"

Heather was excited as I set her suitcase in the bedroom. The children showed her where she would sleep on the lower bunk and they giggled, probably looking forward to secret conversations after the lights went out at bedtime.

I held her tight. I didn't want to seem upset. "Bye bye," I said.

"Can I go play now Mommy?" she asked nonchalantly. This was the reaction I wanted, yet somehow it wasn't.

I drove away, choking back tears. I hoped I was doing the right thing. Would Heather even miss me?

If I had misgivings, my friends didn't. They had already assured me it was the best thing I could do. They said I was expecting too much of myself if I thought I could run the businesses and look after Heather without any help. It was easy for them to say; none of them had children. To them, it was just a baby-sitting service. To me, it was as if I had torn my heart out by the roots and left it at Maria's.

I longed for Heather to have a normal family life. Bob and I had loved her so much we would sometimes come home and wake her up at 2:00 a.m., just to see her and hold her. But what could I offer her now?

Nights in the store while I ran copies and she had nothing to do? Bob and I had given her joy, but Bob was gone and I was desolate. Was this an emotion to share with a child?

My friends also had urged me to move. "Too many memories – build a new life – start over and give yourself a chance." Meanwhile, Rebecca's ex-husband Everett had relentlessly tried to buy my house. I wasn't ready to sell, but I was considering a lease. Of course, this would mean finding another place to live.

Now that I had left Heather with Maria, the house was emptier than ever. I lay down to rest.

Bob had died just a few weeks ago, but it seemed like a decade. His memory would seem to fade, but then another vivid recollection would well up from nowhere and pierce my heart again. I wished I could cry until it didn't hurt anymore. What was wrong with me? Was it normal to have all these feelings, and not be able to get them out? Oh God! – my thoughts reached towards a God I wasn't sure I could believe in – will it ever stop hurting? It was anguish one moment, numbness the next.

Restless, I walked outside. I smelled a fresh ocean breeze blowing across the lawn. I ran my hand over a tree trunk where Bob had carved a heart just a few weeks before. My fingers caressed each letter, "Bob Loves JoAnn." We had been childlike that day, full of life. My heart screamed in protest. How could he be gone? Why? I decided that if there really is a God, he must be insane and cruel to allow us to suffer such pain.

I went back inside and lay down again. Everything reminded me of Bob. I saw the vase where the flowers should have been; he was always bringing me flowers, even if it meant he had climbed a hillside to pick them himself. My closet was full of beautiful clothes and my dresser covered with jewelry he had bought me – every item an expression of love that was gone and would never come back.

The phone rang. I grabbed a joint as I answered.

"JoAnn, I want to take you to meet one of my friends." It was Rebecca, and she was excited. "I talked to her about all the things that happened when Bob died, and she can explain them."

Rebecca's friend had been a star on the "Mod Squad", a popular television series, and had given up her acting career to marry a multi-talented musician and producer. They lived in a cute place on the beach in Malibu. She was warm and friendly and seemed confident that she had the answers to life. Like Johnny, she had studied Scientology. As we went over the story, she explained that Johnny had assured Bob that everything would be okay so he would be free to leave his body. She said Bob had tried to enter Heather's body the night she was screaming she was hot, and he was trying to reach out to us when we got in the accident.

The words were strangely comforting, but hard to believe. Rebecca and I left. "JoAnn, you should move into my apartment while I go to Spain," she said as she dropped me off at home. "You can come anytime you want."

"Thanks," I said as I got out of the car. It was nice of her to make the offer, but I wasn't sure I was ready for such a step.

Rebecca drove off and I was alone again. The sun was setting, and my sense of dread began to grow with the lengthening shadows. I had always loved horror movies as a child, but now whenever I was home alone at night it felt as if I were living in one. Some nights were so terrifying that I slept with all the lights on.

It had been fine to sit in a living room with Rebecca and her friend and say Bob was trying to contact me after his death. But do the dead return? Do ghosts exist? Demons? This didn't feel like Bob. He hadn't given me the creeps when he was alive; why would he be terrifying me now?

Meanwhile, Everett was waiting to lease my house. Heather was with Maria. Everyone said I needed a new start. Rebecca's offer wasn't a permanent solution, but I wouldn't have to endure another night of terror. Maybe at Rebecca's I could at least sleep.

Rushing into my room and grabbing a few things, I left as quickly as I could. I got out before dark, and headed for the safety of Rebecca's apartment in Beverly Hills.

Five

Magic Mushrooms In Suffrage City

I got in the habit of spending the night at Rebecca's, but by day my hub was either at home in Malibu or at work. Allison called me at work one afternoon and wanted to go to a nightclub that night. She was upset about Duff and Rebecca, and she wanted to talk. It would be awkward to tell her I was spending my nights at Rebecca's, but I got around it by volunteering to drive to her house to pick her up.

I looked forward to an evening with Allison, especially since she was upset with Duff. I had never understood the attraction between them. True, they appeared well matched: she looked sweet and innocent with her ready smile and pixie-cut black hair; Duff was tall and rugged, handsome with intense blue eyes. But if she was wholesome, he was reckless. I had taken one look at him and foreseen trouble, an impression he repeatedly proved correct.

Bob and I had been content to smoke pot until Duff led us to try something more powerful: elephant tranquilizers, brown powder in a hand-wrapped package. It was bad enough that we were so stoned we sped to a party in Bob's Ferrari and didn't realize a tire had gone flat – we arrived and found that we had finished the drive on the rim. But the worst of it was Allison's frantic call the next morning. "Amber swallowed the elephant tranquilizer, and now she's in intensive care." This was their three-year-old; Duff had left the powder in the living room and she had gotten into it. Allison was sobbing. "Oh dear God, JoAnn, the doctors don't know if she'll live. They sent Duff home to get the tranquilizer so they can have a lab analyze it to see if there is any antidote." It was touch and go for several days but Amber pulled through.

Then it was Duff who talked Bob into buying the Harley, in spite of my protests. So one beautiful Sunday afternoon, Duff and Bob raced down the freeway, with Allison and me clinging to them. Our speed topped 100 mph, and suddenly Duff invented a game: he would jerk his bike across several lanes of traffic, get off at the exit ramp, and cross the intersection to get back on the freeway. Bob raced after him. I was screaming in terror, but Bob wouldn't slow down. At a red light I found a chance to jump off; I cursed at Bob but he ignored me, gunning his engine and drowning out my cries. The light turned green and again he took off after Duff. I stood there trembling and wondered if they would return. I waited; they didn't. I spotted a hitchhiker with long matted hair. I didn't care that he looked and smelled as if he hadn't bathed since 1950. "Can I come with you?" I asked. "Sure," he said. He stuck out his thumb and I did the same. Someone picked us up and left us at his house. He drove me the rest of the way home. When I walked up our driveway, Bob was tinkering with his Harley. He glanced at me and wordlessly turned back to his new love, his motorcycle.

Allison was upset with Duff? I could sympathize. For years I hadn't had the luxury of venting my frustrations about Bob and about men in general, but now I could.

I stopped to pick Allison up, and she didn't look like herself. She was wearing more eye makeup than usual, her lipstick was a bolder shade of red, and her jeans looked tighter – was this the effect of her high-heeled boots, or had she bought new clothes? She saw me eyeing her but before I could comment she said, "Let's go." And with a toss of her shaggy hair she and a cloud of perfume she headed for the car.

We went to a local hangout near Redondo Beach and were downing one tequila sunrise after another. Suddenly she said, "JoAnn, I think we should meet somebody." I should have guessed she was thinking something like this, but still it was out of character. Knowing Allison, it must have taken a struggle for her to put these thoughts into words.

"Who?" I asked, looking around the bar as I twirled the paper umbrella stuck in a chunk of pineapple in my drink. I noticed she wasn't looking at anyone in particular.

"Someone to talk to, someone to dance with," she slurred. I had never seen Allison drunk. "What are you waiting for? Bob's gone, and letting a bunch of time pass isn't going to change a thing."

She was right. Haunted by Bob's infidelity, I felt a fresh surge of anger. I looked around the room, determined to meet someone. "Yeah Allison, but who? There isn't one guy in this place that I want to talk to, let alone dance with. Most of them look like they just fell off their surfboards and did a belly roll in the sand."

Now Allison looked around too. "You're right. Maybe we should go somewhere else."

Just then, the next band started their set. The lead singer was the best looking man in the place, and knew I had to find a way to meet him. "Not yet," I said. "I want to listen to this band. And I'm going to find a way to meet that singer." I pointed him out, and while we listened, I schemed.

The set ended and we went out to my car. "It's simple," I explained. "The Jaguar will be the hook, I'll be the worm, and he'll be the fish." How was this happening? I, who had no experience, was teaching Allison how to pick up a man. I drove down the street and turned around so I could watch the door. Eventually he came out, carrying his guitar. I slowly drove by.

Redondo Beach was Volkswagen territory, and the black Jaguar stood out. He noticed it immediately. "Hey are you some sort of rich liberated women?" he called out. It was working. I stopped the car and he came up to the window.

Drink had made me bold. "Yeah. Want to come home with me?"

"Why not?" he said. He hurriedly waved his band away as Allison climbed in the backseat. "My name is Drew," he said as I drove Allison home and turned towards Malibu; I knew it wouldn't be scary because I would not be alone. He told me about his home in Michigan, and as I expected, he stared with astonishment as I showed him the view from my yard. I told him I had been widowed recently. "Your husband was one lucky man," he sighed.

We became friends, and for the next few weeks we would have an on-again off-again relationship. I had never considered my friends in California complex or pretentious – really, they weren't – but in a way I had never seen before, Drew was straightforward and uncomplicated.

I called the shop the next morning and my manager said everything was under control, so I decided not to come in until the end of the day when I would take care of any unfinished work. I drove Drew home later in the morning and then had time to think as I drove back to Malibu. How had last night happened? I wasn't trying to meet someone; Allison was. And what had happened to my morals? Did morals even matter anymore? Who made those rules anyway? Hippies were happier. Maybe I should be a hippie like them.

I got home and wandered around the house. Family pictures took me back to the love Bob and I had shared, even in the difficult times. I sat under a tree to smoke a cigarette, and then a joint. I was drifting. I went inside and fell asleep on the sofa.

I woke up and felt overwhelmed. Here I was, unable to look after my two-year-old because I was working around the clock to pay off a debt I hadn't even known about, and living in a house I was afraid to be in after dark. Before long, Rebecca would return from Spain; then it would be time to move back to Malibu or to find another place to live.

I realized I was exhausted. I was working too hard. I almost never got a chance to kick back like this or even to think. And the day was slipping away quickly; before I knew it, it would be time to get back to work.

What if I found a new manager for my business – not just someone who managed the other employees during the day, but someone who could run the whole thing? He could give me a check every week or month and I could live on the income, but the responsibility for the business would be his, not mine. It would be a great opportunity for him and I could get a break. It wouldn't even matter if he made most of the money, as long as I had enough to live on. What more did I need? And as for a place to live, a few weeks at Rebecca's had made me realize I really did need to move.

Then something in my mind argued, Ha! Where are you going to find a manager for your business? How are you going to find a place to live? You've never lived alone; you've never had to make decisions. It was true: I had lived with my parents, then my grandparents, then Bob. Now that I was alone, I realized I didn't have the confidence to find my own way. This is why I had followed Allison's suggestion to look for a man; this is why I had let Heather talk me into having her stay with Maria; this is why I had accepted Rebecca's gift of Warren and then her invitation to stay in her apartment while she was in Spain.

I got my things together and started the drive to work; I didn't want to be late or I'd have to fight rush hour traffic. But I kept thinking as I drove, and it occurred to me I wasn't doing so badly after all. Drew had been nice and I knew I'd see him again. Heather was happy at Maria's. The night with Warren had been a fantasy fulfilled, and my stay at Rebecca's had helped me realize I needed to move. True, other people were causing me to make choices I might not make on my own – I couldn't imagine Aunt Hazel being steered into any of these choices, but did I really want to be like Aunt Hazel? Maybe I'd found the key: my friends could give me better advice than Aunt Hazel could, and things would work out fine.

So I went back to work and back to Rebecca's, but whenever I was out with friends I told them I was thinking about finding a manager for my businesses, and I needed to find another place to live. And sure enough, within a few days I struck oil. It turned out to be simple after all.

One of Rebecca's neighbors knew a couple of men who were going to be released from jail that week, Vinnie and Ray. "Don't let the 'jail' business scare you off," she said. "They're really nice guys and they've made a mistake, but now they've paid their debt to society and they need jobs. I'm sure they'd be glad to manage your business. Don't say no until you've met them."

So I met them a few days later and she was right: they were both very nice, and I could see they would be perfect for the job. Ray was the outgoing one, very agreeable. "It's your business, Mrs. DeJoria," he assured, "and you're the boss." Vinnie was less talkative, but there was no overlooking his strength. I wished he'd been around to handle Gino in Long Beach.

An attorney drew up the papers. "I always include a six-month probation period," he said, "so you can terminate the agreement easily if things don't work out."

"How often do people need to use that clause?" I laughed nervously. I didn't mind having the safety net; after all, I really didn't know these guys.

"Almost never," he replied, "but it doesn't hurt anything to put it in."

And it was reassuring when Vinnie added, "That's good. You'll want to have guarantees. It's just good business." And I felt better and better about the deal as I spent the next few days training them to run the businesses. Ray was going to work with customers, Vinnie would take care of the back office, and I would be free.

Meanwhile I also found a place to live. Someone said to call Wayne, whose house was on a turnoff from Topanga. This would be just a few miles from my house in Malibu, which meant I'd still be close to the beach, but Topanga was another world. A lot of hippies had begun to settle there. "They don't get uptight about things like codes and building permits there. You can live in a teepee or a geodesic dome there. But don't worry; Wayne's place is nice – it's really peaceful – you can't even see it from the road. Take your hiking shoes; you'll have to climb a steep hill to find it."

So as soon as my business was rented, I drove out to Topanga to take a look.

I followed directions to the house and, sure enough, I couldn't see it from the road. Only after I trudged up the steep hill did the large two-story cabin come into view. I knocked timidly; Wayne answered the door. He might have looked intimidating, six feet five inches tall and dressed in patched blue jeans. But he had a boyish face with a welcoming smile and friendly blue eyes, and his long blond hair looked as if it had been cut with a bowl. He looked as innocent as a child.

"You must be JoAnn," he said. "I heard you'd be coming. There's plenty of room." He spread his arms with the expansive gesture of the lord of the manor. "The owners built the place themselves. They're American Indians – they don't even live here – they're out with a group in Arizona, protesting for their rights." They had also built a couple of outbuildings, and Wayne had rented those out too. I wondered if they knew how many people were living on their property.

We stepped into the living room, and I could see they hadn't hired a decorator to furnish the house; probably someone on a budget had shopped at Goodwill. The three sofas were frayed and I suspected the coffee table doubled as a footrest. They were arranged to face an enormous stone fireplace, which filled the house with the cheery scent of a wood fire. Indian blankets, baskets, and fetishes covered the walls. Funky but comfortable, I told myself.

"I'm sure you want to see your room," said Wayne, leading the way down the stairs. "It's in the basement, where you'll get some privacy and have your own entrance and a view out the slider."

It was cold, damp, and filthy. No bed or even box springs; just a stained mattress on the bare cement floor. No carpet; just dirt and trash. An orange crate served as a table, decorated with a small green ashtray overflowing with butts. But it was a walk-in basement with a large sliding glass door, and it did have a view of sorts, if you liked to look out into the woods.

I didn't care about the dirt. I was still numb from Bob's death, and I was a little worn out from all the business details I had handled in the last few days. I could put up with the mess for a few days until I felt up to cleaning and decorating. For now I simply needed to move; a friend had led me to Wayne; the place was available. I agreed to rent it and moved in.

My first night, I wondered why so many people were going in and out. I crept upstairs to the main level of the house and saw Wayne measuring out white powder on a scale and placing it in bags. I interrupted him between visitors.

"What is that white stuff that you're measuring out? Is it cocaine?" I'd seen coke once before. My sister's boyfriend had brought it to our house, and I'd kicked him out.

Wayne laughed. "You don't know for sure, huh? Well, come sit right down here, little lady, and I'll give you a real treat." He began to dance around me and took an Indian rattle off the wall and shook it over my head.

"What are you doing?" I asked.

"An Indian fertility dance." He laughed as he laid the rattle down on the coffee table and took off a necklace. It was the tooth of a large animal I couldn't identify, hung on a braided leather cord. He poured the white powder onto a mirror and carefully chopped it with a razor.

Did everyone who rented rooms from Wayne have radar? As if they had gotten a signal, they began to appear and quietly take their places around the big stone fireplace. The only sound was the crackling fire as he ceremoniously rolled up a hundred dollar bill and sniffed up a couple of lines.

He passed me the mirror and I carefully mimicked Wayne.

I didn't know what to expect. All I felt was my eyes watering and my nose starting to run. I tasted cocaine. Sniffling, I watched the plate go around the coffee table until I it was my turn again. I sniffed a little more. This time my mind perked up a bit and I felt more awake.

The plate went around and around until the sun came up. A David Bowie album was playing over and over in the background, stuck on one song. I finally went downstairs to lie down. The floor with its dirt and debris looked cleaner than the mattress, so I lay on the cement, too stoned to feel a thing.

Loneliness crept in and I searched through my suitcases to find my diary, hoping I'd be comforted if I wrote Bob a letter.

"Dear Bob:

I pray that you will come and visit me in my dream. Please, Honey, let me know if there is really another life. I want to die if it means

I can be with you. I feel dead anyway. I hope you have found happiness. You've been gone three months and haven't come to see me in one dream. The only thing that keeps me here is that I'm not sure that there is life after death, and what about our Heather? I gotta go. I don't want to think anymore – it hurts too bad."

I dropped the pen and lay down again on the cold floor. The room was spinning and I thought I was about to pass out. I fell into a deep sleep and woke up disoriented. It was either sunrise or sunset; I wasn't sure which. It felt as if my head had been fastened in a vise. I tiptoed upstairs to find out what was going on. It turned out it was sunset, and like bats we had slept all day and waited for dusk before we had stirred. Everyone left with the final rays of sunlight, except Wayne and me.

About 9 p.m. there was a knock on the door.

Wayne opened it and his face lit up with joy. "Stash! Come on in – I haven't seen you in ages." Stash nodded and they shook hands. He looked like a rock star who had made it: neatly styled black hair that was long and shaggy, craggy face, prominent cheekbones, a shirt in a bold pattern with bright colors, a wide belt with a huge silver buckle, pants stuffed into the tops of his high-heeled patent leather boots. He was very good-looking, but not my type at all. I would later learn he managed a few major groups.

"I've got something I've been saving for a special occasion and the right people to share it with," Wayne said, his bright blue eyes sparking with excitement.

"What have you got?"

"Mushrooms!" He looked as pleased as a little child telling a precious secret.

"You mean the real thing?" Stash inquired hopefully.

"Yeah, I picked them myself in the desert and I sold all the coke last night so nobody will bug us," Wayne said.

"Oh yeah! Let's do it, man!"

Wayne pulled a jar from the refrigerator. Its contents looked detestable. He removed the lid and handed some to both of us.

I couldn't imagine putting it in my mouth. It was deformed and slimy. I sniffed it suspiciously, wrinkling my nose. I recalled stories of people who died after eating mushrooms they'd found in their yards or while hiking in the woods.

Stash and Wayne didn't hesitate, so I figured I'd better get it over with quickly. I popped the gunky thing in my mouth and swallowed it fast.

Within minutes I felt wonderful and saw delicate rainbows everywhere. Stash spent the next few hours in a chair and stared at a Salvador Dali book. The David Bowie album was playing again, stuck at top volume on the same song, "Suffragette City."

The mood changed a few hours later when Wayne started rummaging around in the kitchen cupboards. He found a big cooking pot and put it on his head, untroubled by the crust of burnt food stuck on the bottom. He sat on the kitchen floor and put another pot on his knee, and then grabbed a pastry cutter and beat out a rhythm.

Stash went out and came back in, wearing a pirate's hat. "Where'd ya get the hat?" Wayne asked. His eyes were at half-mast.

"Found it on the wall in your room," Stash said. He twirled about, grabbing a kitchen knife and slicing it though the air as if it were a huge saber.

We laughed until we ached, with tears running down our faces. We ended up on the floor, all of us playing music on the dirty pots and pans.

The David Bowie song was still playing when the sun came up. We ate a little more mushroom before Stash left. The house was still and the fire crackled in the cool morning. Wayne carried me into his room.

A few weeks later I went for a walk on the beach and ran into Megan and Sean. "I can't believe what has happened to you!" Megan said with a laugh. "A few months ago you were a normal looking Malibu housewife – a bit square, actually – and now here you are, looking like a full blown flower child!"

I realized she was right. I had given up my trips to the Beverly Hills for overpriced hair styling, manicures, and facials; now my hair hung straight down, haphazardly parted in the middle. I was barefoot and wearing one of Wayne's embroidered shirts and a pair of faded, torn jeans. Did it really matter whether I wore my own clothes or Wayne's?

My old lifestyle was too much work. Life with Wayne was much easier. Heather was thriving with the family in the Valley; I had rented my business and was receiving a monthly check; I slept through much of the day and was up all night, when Wayne made all his deals. Most were outside the house. We'd even get calls at 3:00 a.m. and go make deliveries.

Wayne's never-ending supply of drugs kept me numb to the past and the future. When I'd wake up late in the afternoon in Wayne's huge waterbed and roll over, I'd always find a straw and a few lines of coke to get me going. A little more coke or even a joint would pick me up later if I started thinking of Bob or missing Heather. Nothing mattered but feeling good for the moment. Some would call it a delusion, but so what? It felt good to feel good. Only a few weeks ago I had envied Megan's well-ordered life and her sense of style; now I didn't. I knew better.

Life was ticking along smoothly until I got a call from Drew. He wanted to see me because he was having problems with his girlfriend. It only seemed right to meet him; he'd been there for me when I had needed a shoulder to cry on, and now he needed me. But what would Wayne think? I told Drew I'd call back.

Wayne was throwing another log on the fire.

"Do you mind if I take off with my friend Drew for the weekend?" I asked. "He wants me to go to Santa Barbara. He's a guy I was seeing for a while before we met."

"Of course not," Wayne said.

It didn't seem to bother him at all, so I called Drew and told him I'd be right over. I threw some things in an overnight case and Wayne walked me to my car. He kissed me goodbye as if I were going off to see my Mom.

"See ya when you get back," he said, smiling broadly and looking like an overgrown six-year-old.

When I got back, things were never the same between us.

Wayne never said anything, but I could tell my weekend with Drew did bother him. He liked to think of himself as liberated, but deep down inside he was more old-fashioned than he realized. Our relationship became a convenience rather than a romance.

One morning we learned that a neighbor, another coke dealer, had been blown away with a shotgun along with everyone else in the house. I wasn't sure if I wanted to live, but I knew that wasn't how I wanted to die. I grabbed my things and drove down the hill to rent the first vacancy I could find on the beach.

Six

Rolling Stones In Hawaii

There were always places for rent along Pacific Coast Highway, so I turned right off Topanga and headed towards Malibu. A strip of homes and apartments separated the highway from the sea; some were upscale and some were run down. I saw a "For Rent" sign and hit the brakes when I saw a parking place.

A red Corvette had been riding my back bumper, and his brakes squealed before he shot around me, yelling and giving me the finger. This road is a racetrack, I muttered to myself. I had to parallel park quickly before another cluster of motorists rounded the bend, and I almost hit the car ahead.

It was no better on foot. I dodged traffic and ran across the four-lane highway. One couple actually yelled at me as they sped by, as though I were trespassing on their personal property.

I could see that the complex was aging, but maybe I'd get a good deal. I didn't need much – I still had my house. I saw the word "Manager" on one of the doors and knocked. A short woman with matted hair and rumpled clothes answered, opening the door with one hand as the other hand dragged a cigarette from her face. A TV was blaring in the background and smoke seeped out of her mouth as she rasped, "Yeah?"

"I'd like to see what you have to rent," I said.

"Oh you would?" she snorted skeptically, looking me up and down. I could tell my appearance looked less promising to her than hers did to me. "It's $1,000 cash up front," she warned. "No credit. You pay in advance each month or you're out." She gave me a self-satisfied look.

"No problem," I said, looking her straight in the eyes. I could afford it.

Her eyes narrowed and she took a long drag on her cigarette. "Then let's go," she said as she took a large key ring from a hook and grabbed a dirty hat to pull down over her ears. "Follow me; it's upstairs. I'm Margo, by the way," she said as she headed toward the stairs.

She opened the door to #5 and the pungent odor almost knocked me over. Didn't anybody even clean around here? Margo was tiny and she pressed herself against the wall, motioning me past her. "Have a look but make it quick. I ain't got all day."

The L-shaped miniature apartment was barely large enough for one person. A huge slider looked out on the Pacific and the first thing I did was to walk across the tiny living room and open it. A fresh Pacific breeze swept in. I took a deep breath and savored the comforting crash of waves below the balcony.

"As you can see, it comes furnished," Margo said, "so you'll have everything you need. Utilities are included in the rent, all but the phone. If you want a phone, you'll have to get your own."

The sun had bleached the pattern out of the frayed couch and thread-bare carpet. The coffee table and end table were a set, with peeling finish and frayed rattan. Nothing else matched. A lamp with a dingy shade sat haphazardly on its tacky orange base. I reached up to straighten the picture on the wall, a tiger painted on black velvet. Vendors would buy these hand-painted works in Mexico, to sell for next to nothing in America on the side of the road.

While I was inspecting the apartment Margo was inspecting me. "Most single women can't afford a place like this," she said suspiciously. "You sure you got the dough for this place?"

"I'm sure," I said as I walked past a small counter with two decrepit bar stools and into the tiny kitchen. There was a two-burner stove and an old refrigerator with rounded corners and its white finish worn through in places.

"Well, I've learned the hard way," she continued. "You can't count on alimony. It doesn't matter what the judge says; men always find a way to get around it. So if you're expecting to live here on alimony…"

"I'm widowed," I snapped. It came out sharply, but I didn't care. I didn't want her telling my personal business to everyone else in the apartment complex.

For the first time, her eyes softened. "Viet Nam?"

This really wasn't any of her business. "Motorcycle," I said defiantly.

Her face hardened again with disapproval, and I could tell I had just failed a test. "Well, I'm just saying I've had people think they could afford it and then find out they couldn't. But if you're sure…"

I wanted to get this over with and I stepped into the bedroom for a quick look. It was no worse than the rest: a queen size bed by a large picture window, a curtain where the closet door should have been, a small desk in one corner, and the in the other corner a door to a cramped bathroom with deteriorating fixtures. It was a dump, but the view from the slider was incredible.

"I'll take it," I said quickly. I was ready for Margo to leave and the chatter to end. I wrote the check and handed it to her as she took my keys off the ring.

She inspected the check carefully, then shook her head and walked out, saying, "I'll be calling the bank as soon as I get to my phone, girly. So if this check ain't any good, don't bother getting comfortable."

At last she was gone. The first thing I did was to open all the windows and turn the heat up to 72 degrees; after all, utilities were included. Then I went to the car and brought in my things. I had a few candles and sticks of incense, and I lit them all to get rid of any lingering odors.

By now the sun was setting and it was high tide. Was it my imagination, or could I feel the motion of the waves? I went back out on the balcony and looked down. My whole apartment was built on stilts, and it was weaving and creaking as the waves crashed. I couldn't believe my good luck. I went back to the bedroom and lay down, covered myself with a coat, and fell fast asleep as my bed gently danced with the sea.

Days melted into weeks, and now that I was living alone and didn't have to go to work, there was nothing to do. I began each day by stumbling out of bed and lurching to the refrigerator, where I chose between Southern Comfort and champagne for breakfast. I listened to a lot of Janis Joplin tapes. Reality was so painful that I kept myself numb with a pill or a joint or another glass of booze.

Life was a giant sewer. Once in a while I'd take a hard look at myself and realize I was going downhill, but it didn't jolt me enough to make me want to change. I got the idea I was becoming the kind of person I should protect Heather from. She's happy at Maria's, I would tell myself. Why mess things up by going to visit?

But I loved her. December rolled around, and I bought a mountain of toys, had everything gift-wrapped, and drove to Maria's to sneak it into the house and spend time with Heather.

Then a few more days slipped by and I was staring at the ocean one afternoon while sipping champagne on my balcony, and suddenly I realized tomorrow was Christmas. Why ruin it for Heather? I called Maria. I concocted my story as she picked up the phone. "Hello?" she said in her thick German accent.

"Maria," I said, faking a raspy voice and a cough. "I'm very sick and can't come over tomorrow. Do you think Heather will be alright?"

"Of course she will." Her voice was soothing. "She's very excited about Santa. You sound terrible, JoAnn. Be sure and get a lot of rest today. I will tell Heather. Call her tomorrow when you wake up."

I hung up and sank further into despair. I opened another bottle of champagne and lay down. The high tide roared under my bed as the sun set.

I woke up drunk around 3 a.m. and tried to get back to sleep. I thought about calling Heather but realized it was the middle of the night. Waves pounded and I fought back tears as I remembered all the wonderful Christmases with Bob. I dozed for the rest of the night, in and out of sleep, with restless thoughts and dreams.

Morning arrived eventually, and at 9 a.m. I put on a cheerful voice and called.

"Hi, Honey, Merry Christmas!"

"Mommy, Mommy! I got new toys! Santa brought them!" she exclaimed. This was the first year she was big enough to get excited about Christmas.

"What did you get, Honey?" I asked.

"I got a dolly and a stroller like Jenny's and I got teddy bears – and Mommy, I wanna go play now, OK?" I had never heard of Jenny, but she turned out to be one of Heather's friends.

"Yes, Honey; go play." I was relieved that she was having so much fun.

"Are you going to come and see the toys that Santa brought me pretty soon? I got some more too," she said.

"Yes, in a few days," I said, "when I feel better." We said goodbye and hung up.

What a relief! She at least was having a good day. I had done the right thing; my dark mood wouldn't spoil her Christmas.

I went to the refrigerator and popped another cork. I walked out on my deck, plopped down in the old blue and white striped canvas lounger, and raised my morning glass of champagne towards the pounding surf to offer a toast: "Merry Christmas, Christmas." I put the glass to my lips and drained it in a single gulp.

I smoked joints and drank all morning. By the time the sun broke through the fog around noon, I'd forgotten I could pour the champagne into a glass and was drinking straight from the bottle. In another couple of hours, I couldn't quite get it into my mouth; a lot of the champagne dribbled down my chin. I left an unfinished bottle on the deck and found it later. It had gotten warm in the sun and I threw it out to sea.

I wish the phone would ring, even if it were just a wrong number. At least I could say "Merry Christmas" to somebody, I thought.

I smoked another joint. "Where is my home?" I screamed. "How can I find it? Do you hear me? I don't want to be what anybody wants me to be. Looking in the mirror I only want to see a reflection of me."

I went back onto the deck and saluted the sunset. Christmas was over at last! Then I drank myself to sleep.

I woke up with a blinding headache and still dressed in yesterday's clothes, feeling shipwrecked in my own bed. I needed to get out for fresh air; at least I was already dressed. I downed a glass of Southern Comfort and fumbled for a Marlboro. I stepped out into bright sunshine, locked up, and went down the stairs onto the beach. It was low tide and I could walk in front of my apartment. I would have to get back before the tide came in; otherwise, I would have to walk on the Pacific Coast Highway.

I sat down on a big rock and needed another cigarette. It was tricky to light up in the wind, but I'd invented a new method: I would cup one hand and light four or more matches at once with the other. It always worked. Today it took only three tries.

"Do you live on this beach?" a guy said as he crouched next to me and lit a joint.

What a typical line. "Yeah," I said, turning my attention towards some rocks and watching as waves splashed against them and created foamy mysterious patterns.

He handed me the joint, and now I looked at him as I took a hit. He was good-looking and the pot was great.

He chatted about nothing and then said, "Wouldja like some coke? I've got a stash at my place down the beach."

Coke? Magic word. Now that I wasn't living with Wayne, it cost $50.00 to $100.00 a day to keep up the lifestyle he'd gotten me used to. Guys were always using coke as their bait to try to pick up girls. I looked him over and decided to go along with it, resolving that it wouldn't go any further than I wanted it to.

Six surfer-type guys were crammed into his little living room, and I was relieved to see other people there. They greeted me enthusiastically and someone shouted, "Party time!" They were smoking joints and drinking wine.

We smoked more pot and then they passed the plate of coke. It wasn't as good as Wayne's; it had been cut a few times. But Wayne had always gotten his from someone who brought it straight from Colombia. He had taught me the key: the best quality coke is always closest to the source. Though all dealers would claim their coke was pure, every middleman would cut it with one thing or another for better profit margins. Wayne had spoiled me.

But why complain about a free lunch? I leaned back in my chair. We smoked a little more pot and laughed about things that had happened that summer. The room began to get blurry and I slumped down in my seat. The guy next to me put his hand on my leg and I jumped up like a bolt of lightning. This had already gone too far. The others were leering at us, waiting to see what would happen next.

"Hey baby, what's the matter with you?" the guy asked, apparently surprised at my reaction. "Most women would love to have the attention of so many men! Come on now, don't be a drag!"

I flew out the door and heard them all laughing as I ran down the stairs and took off running down the beach as fast as I could. I got home, ran up the stairs, and locked the door behind me. "How can they be so cruel?" I screamed, catching my breath.

Some guys were just creeps. I thought of a night about a week after Bob's death, when I was trying to talk with my friend Sarah in a crowded restaurant on the Sunset Strip. The tables were so crammed together that the two guys next to us kept trying to start a conversation. We weren't interested in them, but they wouldn't take a hint and kept bugging us. Finally, Sarah politely asked them to leave us alone because I'd just lost my husband and we wanted to talk. The one sitting next to me said sarcastically, "Well big deal!"

That pushed me over the edge. I took my glass of milk and threw it in his face. For a delicious moment I watched the milk drip all over him, but then he jumped up, made a fist, and was about to hit me. Thank goodness the waiters stepped in; they grabbed him and wrestled him to the floor as he hurled a string of curses at me. A couple of big guys got up from their tables and helped the waiters escort the milkman and his friend out.

Bob had always protected me. I had no idea the world could be so cruel. Was this how life would be? Depression began setting in, and I needed a diversion. I called Wayne and he came down to visit me. He brought coke, the good stuff. It was good to spend the day with him and to feel safe.

After Wayne left the next morning, the phone rang. I answered reluctantly, hoping it was someone I wanted to talk to.

"Hi, JoAnn. It's Amelia – do you remember me?"

"Amelia! Of course I remember. What's up?" I had met Amelia when Rebecca was in Spain and I was staying at her apartment. An Englishman had called to ask Rebecca to go out with him and I told him she was out of the country. "Well this is a bit awkward," he said, "but the fact is, I've been invited to a dinner party at Scandia's and I need a date. We don't know each other, of course; but I wonder if you'd be so kind as to go with me." I had never known a man who was so polite, and I went. Amelia had been one of the people at the table, and we had hit it off at once.

"I'm trying to get tickets to the Rolling Stones concert," she continued, "but it sold out right away. Then I remembered that you used to work in that crazy business, and I guess at this point you'd need connections to get in…"

Amelia wasn't a bum trying to get a free ticket; she was a model, tall and blonde and beautiful; she was living with an older man in Bel Air, a wealthy architect. "Gosh," I paused, running through a mental Rolodex. "Let me call a few agents and see if I can get us some comps. You'll want good seats, and the comps are always in the first twelve rows or so."

"Can you get eight seats? That would include you and your date."

"I'll get back to you when I find out."

I hung up and called around to see if I could get some VIP tickets. One of the agents said, "Sure, I can give you the tickets, but I don't have anything local. You'll have to fly over to Hawaii in three days for the concert."

Everyone loved the idea. Amelia booked our flight and hotel reservations. The architect stayed home, but he and Amelia had an open relationship and her date for the trip was Michael.

The day of the concert, I sat down on the beach with Amelia and Michael. He unwrapped a wad of tissue paper and brought out three tiny black specks. They each took one and they offered the last to me.

"What is it?" I asked, leaning closer for a better look.

"It's acid," said Michael. "Amelia and I talked it over and decided you'd be an okay person to drop with."

"Yeah," Amelia added reassuringly. "I don't do LSD with very many people. It can get too weird."

I stuck the black speck on my tongue and continued sun bathing. I'd never dropped acid before, but Amelia was level headed and I trusted her judgment.

"Let's go get a drink," Michael said as he stood up and stretched.

Stairs led down to a bar, dark and smoke-filled. We went in and ordered Mai Tais. I looked around and realized we were in the bottom of a swimming pool; our end was dry, but behind the bartender was a wall with a large glass window, and people were swimming on the other side. Soon I was coughing. "Let's get out of here. The smoke is getting to me." I led the way, taking two stairs at a time and trying to adjust my eyes to the bright sunlight.

"WOW!" was the only word I could say, and it echoed and floated away and formed bubbles. One by one they burst, each echoing its own "wow" until the last faded into a whisper. Everything was alive and moving like the surf: rainbows ringed the hotels that towered over Waikiki Beach; people of all sizes and shapes thronged the beach; all were surging back and forth with the liquid motion of the waves. A fresh ocean breeze rippled through my hair.

We plopped down and I ran my hand across the warm sand. "What a trip! The sand is alive." I caressed a handful and sifted it through my fingers. Each grain throbbed like a tiny pearl. I filled both hands with animated sand and dropped it on my head. Amelia looked at me questioningly. "I'm making a Head And Shoulders commercial," I explained with a laugh.

Within seconds we all were dumping sand on our heads, concocting our imaginary commercial. We laughed and got so carried away we lost track of time.

Suddenly we noticed the beach was empty and Michael looked at his watch. "Oh no, we're running late."

"I'm sure our friends will wait for us," I reassured him. "I have the tickets." But we still had to go to our rooms to shower and get dressed.

Within minutes we met again in the lobby, found a taxi, and arrived after most of the people had already gone in. Michael looked at the bright side. "Oh well, we missed the crowd."

The concert was sold out and scalpers were everywhere. I had forgotten to look for a date, so now we had an extra ticket.

"We've got to give this ticket to someone," I said. Michael and Amelia quickly agreed. We decided to choose the lucky person together.

"I'm sure we'll all agree on the same person since we're on the same wavelength," Amelia chirped.

She was right. We all saw the same kid at the same time. We nodded at each other and went over to him.

"Wanna go to the concert?" Michael asked.

"I can't afford a ticket, man; I'm broke," he said, turning away.

"Well, do you want to go?" I asked.

"Sure I wanna go. I flew here from Kansas because I heard the concert was going to be free. I spent all I had just to get to Hawaii. Now I'm busted and can't buy a ticket."

"Well then, you can go for free!" we all chimed in together as I handed him the ticket.

He looked at it in disbelief. "What do I got to do for this?" he asked.

"Just enjoy the concert," I said as we walked towards the entrance.

Suddenly he realized we weren't jiving him and he began jumping up and down with excitement and ran in ahead of us.

We had great seats in a balcony that almost hung over the stage. We were in the very first row above the Stones. Which was better, the concert or the kid from Kansas in the seat next to me? Once in a while he would glance at us suspiciously, unsure if his good luck would hold out. But after the concert he realized we'd simply given him a ticket with no strings attached. We all hugged and said goodbye, and the next day it was time to fly home.

As soon as I got back to California, I drove out to Simi Valley to see Heather. I stopped the car and saw her playing with neighbor kids. She was having as good a time playing a silly game with them as I had had with Amelia and Michael on the beach.

She didn't notice me until I got out of the car and shut the door with a bang. She looked up and saw me, and then she left her game and ran to me, reaching for my open arms. "Mommy!" she squealed. "You surprised me, huh?" We hugged one another for a long time.

"Let's go to the park," I said. And as I spun the merry-go-round for her and pushed her on the swings, I wondered if I was giving her what she really needed. My friends all said leaving her with Maria was the right thing, but how could they know? None of them had ever had children. Still, Heather always seemed to be happy, and she always seemed glad to hear from me when I called and excited to see me when I visited.

We had a wonderful day together and I stayed until her bedtime so I could tuck her in and read her a story.

"Mommy, will you be here in the morning?" she asked.

"No, Honey," I said with a pang.

"Why, Mommy?"

"Because I don't live here."

"Can you live here, Mommy?" The question broke my heart, but what could I do? I felt helpless.

"No, Honey, I can't live here. But I hope that someday soon we'll live together again. Okay?" I said.

"Okay, Mommy. Will you read me Cinderella?"

"Yes, Honey," I said, picking up the book.

Seven

Outrageous Bank Deposit

I had rented out my business because I didn't want the responsibility of running it, but responsibilities kept seeking me out. For one thing, Xerox still said I owed them $100,000. By now I had learned Bob had been planning to buy the machine in question; this would have eliminated the problem with the false meter cards. Bob had died with the check made out to Xerox in his wallet.

But there was another wrinkle in the story. Bob had applied for a loan to buy the machine, and the Bank Of America had required him to take out a life insurance policy for $35,000 to secure it. Bank Of America was the first beneficiary; I was the second. Now that Bob had died, our insurance man Milt wasn't sure if he could get me that money because Bob had paid only a $25 deposit on the machine and hadn't gotten the rest of the payment to Xerox before he died.

Meanwhile, I had a bad feeling about the guy who was running my business and knew I'd better check things out. At first I had found it amusing that Vinnie carried himself like someone in the Mafia, but I was starting to hear rumors that he really was connected. But was there any real evidence? Maybe people were just jumping to conclusions because he had the classy but intimidating looks and the surly east-coast accent we always saw on Mafia shows on TV.

I went down to the store and Ray was busy with customers at the counter. He was in work clothes and was good with people, always eager to please. I said hi to Ray and walked through the door to the back office. Vinnie was in a dark suit and working at one of the desks.

He saw me and jumped up with a smile. "Well, well, what a surprise! How are you?" His words were warm but his eyes were wary.

"I'm okay," I said, walking past him towards my desk, but he saw what I was doing and managed to get there ahead of me and slide into my chair. He was smooth; it almost made me wonder if I had walked in just as he was about to move from one desk to the other.

"What's up?" he asked, looking up at me; his voice now showed the first hints of a hard edge.

"I'm here to see the books," I said.

"No dice."

"What do you mean, 'no dice'?"

"I mean no," he said. "When you rented me this store, the books went with it. You gave up your right to look at the books."

It went back and forth but he wouldn't back down. Finally I said, "This is going nowhere. I guess I'll have to go see the lawyer who drew up the rental agreement. You'll be hearing from him!" I rose to leave.

"I'll look forward to his call," he said defiantly as I walked out.

The attorney called Vinnie, and then got back to me. "He's clearly in the wrong, but I've done a bit of checking and this guy is bad news. I couldn't get anywhere with him – I told him we could settle it in court, and he ended up threatening us – and here you are, a woman living alone – I really couldn't advise you to fight him. Even if you won you wouldn't gain much, and you've got too much to lose. Everybody tells me the same thing: this guy's just plain scary."

I couldn't believe it! The lawyer backed down! So I called my brother-in-law.

He said he'd talk to Vinnie, and then called back the next day. "It went better than I expected. There's always a way to break a stalemate."

"You're wonderful!" I exclaimed. "I don't know if it was your optimism or your negotiating skill, or maybe just that you're Italian and male and in my family." Johnny really was a good negotiator. He always chose to believe the best about people, and it worked like magic. And it didn't hurt that Johnny too could look menacing if the need arose.

"I can't take all the credit," he said. "When you told me the lawyer said Vinnie was in the wrong, I got John Rocca to go with me. You know how he is – always polite, always smiling. He's such a nice guy that nobody ever realizes that he's a genius at catching the subtle nuances of fine print."

I laughed as I pictured it. "I can't believe it. The lawyer got scared and backed down, and you guys had him purring like a kitten. I should have called you first."

"But JoAnn, we haven't gotten to the good part yet," he went on. I had seen him in this mood before; he was so excited about the deal that he couldn't be bothered to stop and receive accolades. "John has a friend who works for Xerox, and it turns out it would make sense to get another machine. There's a way to do it where everyone would make more money."

"What? Another machine? But we haven't finished working out the $100,000 debt! How can we afford another machine?"

"We need to talk about that, and John and I want to bring his friend to your apartment so we can go over it all together. He'll explain it, and I think you're going to see it makes a lot of sense."

So that night the three of them came to my apartment: Johnny, John, and their friend David. David explained printing equipment to us and I knew I needed to focus on business, but somehow I was distracted by his kindness, his gentleness, his beautiful dark eyes. Was he married? I nodded my head occasionally, as if I were really following what he had to say. Johnny and John were listening more intently, and we all said goodnight and agreed to meet in the store the next evening. I fell asleep thinking about David.

The next morning I woke up early and searched through the refrigerator for a bottle of champagne. There wasn't an open bottle and I didn't want to hassle with popping a cork, so I drank Southern Comfort instead. I took a few hits off a joint and went for a walk on the beach.

The mail brought a letter from my insurance company. I opened it slowly, wondering if it would be the money Milt thought he might be able to get me, or a letter saying I would get nothing.

I stared at the check. "Pay To The Order of JoAnn DeJoria the sum of Seventy Thousand Dollars." It was a double indemnity policy in case of an accident. I could use the money, but it felt strange to get paid for Bob's death. I stuck it in a drawer.

The day passed and I got ready to go to the store. This wasn't business as usual; I needed to make sure David would notice me. He was so conservative! He had even worn a tie to my house.

I washed my hair and put on a little eye makeup. I had gotten away with jeans and t-shirt last night, normal attire for people who live on the beach, but now I dug through my closet for something that wouldn't look hippie. For once I was glad Aunt Hazel had imposed her taste on me. I chose a pair of black pants but none of my tops looked right until I opened a storage box and found a plain sweater in a blue that would set off my eyes. I put it on and looked in the mirror.

My rings! I had gotten in the habit of wearing a ring on every finger, but this wouldn't be the right look for David. I took them off and put on a simple pearl necklace instead. I studied my reflection in the mirror and laughed. I could still look conservative.

Vinnie and Ray had already gone home when I pulled up to the shop, but Johnny, David and John were already there. I let them in and they looked through the books and talked a lot about numbers. I tried to care and tried to listen, but all I could think about was how great David looked. Clean-shaven, he was wearing a nice blue suit with a crisp white shirt. Most of all, there was no ring on his left hand.

"Would that be all right with you, JoAnn?" David asked.

What on earth were they talking about? I hadn't been listening. "Oh, sounds fine," I said. I hoped Johnny and John would speak up if I were making a mistake. They all seemed to think that the papers I was signing that night would take care of the $100,000 debt to Xerox. I never understood how it could work. For now, all I could see was David.

"Great. Then why don't you have dinner with me tonight?" he said confidently. He opened the car door for me and I climbed into his new Cadillac. I was used to hippies in jeans, driving a Porsche, Jaguar, or Mercedes. But the spacious Cadillac, driven by a handsome man in a suit, seemed exotic and foreign to me. He pulled up to valet parking at a plush restaurant in Beverly Hills and escorted me inside. I had never felt so elegant

It was dark and romantic, with candles burning on every table. He ordered a bottle of champagne. As we began talking, the chatter at other tables and the live-band's music all faded into the background. His dark eyes made me feel as if were floating and drowning at the same time. The evening was incredible. He walked me to my car after the long dinner and kissed me on the cheek.

The next morning I didn't want a drink or a joint. It felt wonderful to be alive. I was in love, and I had something to do: I had invited David for dinner. So I had to go out and buy some respectable clothes and a couple of nice steaks.

We had a beautiful romance and David always treated me like a princess. He took me to all kinds of ritzy places: nice restaurants, the country club, dancing. He tried to interest me in golf and horseback riding. I would take him for walks on the beach, but he never quite looked relaxed, carefully keeping his golf shoes from getting ruined in the surf and the sand. For weeks I did my best to be conservative, but after a while I needed to be myself. He was so straight he didn't even smoke pot.

So I brought some with me, determined to turn him on. It was my birthday, and he was taking me to Palm Springs. He was reluctant but I convinced him it was harmless.

He choked as he took his first hit and coughed out all the smoke. David didn't even smoke cigarettes; he was always trying to get me to quit.

"Come on, Honey, hold it in" – I grabbed the joint from him – "like this." I took a deep hit. He tried again and started laughing, so he didn't get any in his lungs that time either. For a moment I wondered if it would be easier to turn him onto coke. After all, he had the money to buy it. No, I decided; bad idea; better not press my luck. I coached him until he got in a few good hits and we went out dancing.

A slow song was playing and David stopped in the center of the floor and looked at me.

"JoAnn, I want you to marry me," he said. "I want to give you and Heather a home."

I was stunned. It was more of a statement than a question and I was relieved that, for a moment at least, I didn't have to say anything.

"I'll take good care of both of you," he said, waiting for me to answer.

"Well, I'll think about it," I said. My mind was racing. "We haven't known one another very long, and marriage is very serious to me."

I began looking at our relationship differently. It had always brought relief from the pain of Bob's death, but what kind of future would it bring? For the past few months, I really hadn't had to think about the future very much. Now I would have to make a decision.

What would it be like to build a family together? The longer I was with him, the more uncertain I became. He was goal oriented and determined to be a multi-millionaire. He was well on his way and most of his life revolved around work and business deals.

I watched Heather to see if she was bonding with David. She didn't seem to avoid him, but I noticed that when the three of us were together, she always stayed very close to me.

David took me to meet his parents. There was a twinkle in his father's eye whenever he looked at me and I could tell he approved, but his mother clearly didn't. She was polite, but I could tell she was making an effort just to tolerate me. Her manner towards me did soften when she found out my mother's mother was Jewish, but even then I had been brought up Catholic. I knew I would never quite measure up in her eyes.

"It's my decision, not hers," David said defensively when we were alone. "And besides, she'll come around. No woman on earth could possibly be good enough for her sons – you'd have thought the world was coming to an end when my brother got married. And of course she wants me to marry 'a nice Jewish girl' because she doesn't want Gentile blood in the grandchildren. But she'll come around. My father likes you, and he'll work on her. She came around after my brother got married, and it'll be the same for you."

That was David's family. But my grandmother thought David was the best thing that had ever happened to me – she was the one I talked to because she lived in L.A. "Well, you're going to marry him, aren't you?"

"I don't know, Ma."

"What's the matter with you? A nice Jewish boy? He would take care of you and Heather. You have to marry him!"

"But Ma, I don't know if I love him…"

"Love, schmove! He'll give you security, stability for you and Heather. He's a nice Jewish boy; he's got ambition. Already he has a Cadillac and his own home! What's the matter with you?"

"But…"

"But?! There's no but about it!"

"But Grampa isn't Jewish…"

"Yeah, and he doesn't have a Cadillac either, does he? He has a Chevy! Look at this ring" – she stuck her hand in front of my face – "Can you even see the stones in it? Now I bet David would get you quite a rock…"

"But Ma, David's mother doesn't want goy blood in her grandchildren…"

"She'll get over it! She'll get over it as soon as they're born."

In the end, I couldn't worry about David's mother and I couldn't marry him just to make my grandmother happy. Was I in love with David, or was I in love with being in love? I had been living with him much of the time but had kept my apartment in Malibu. One morning after David left for work I decided to go home. I needed to get away from everyone else's influence so I could sort things out.

I had left my apartment vacant for a couple of weeks and now the smell of cold and damp greeted me. I opened all the windows and a fresh ocean breeze rushed in. It was high tide and I lay down on my bed, listening to the surf crashing under me. I lit a joint and began to plan.

What if I took a long trip? That would help me find out if I was really in love. I had a friend in South America; there I would be far enough away that David couldn't come visit me for a few days, and he was much too busy to go on an extended trip.

I opened the drawer next to my bed to look for some matches and noticed the $70,000 check from the insurance company. It had been there for weeks because I just hadn't felt right about getting paid for Bob's death.

I spoke to Bob as if he were in the room. "Well, Honey, I guess you'd tell me to cash it if you were here. But you'd want me to have some fun and blow someone's mind, wouldn't you?"

Why hadn't I thought of this before? It had seemed cold and commercial to cash in after Bob's death, but if I made it into an outrageous adventure it would be a sort of memorial to Bob. I smoked another joint and wheels turned. I would find a very elegant bank in Beverly Hills, dress like the wildest hippie they had ever seen, and make my deposit there.

So I put on some funky clothes, left my hair a mess, and walked barefoot down the Pacific Coast Highway until I reached a spot where I could walk on the beach at high tide. A couple of joints had lifted my spirits, and now it felt good to walk along the surf, getting the bottom of my pants wet, and then to sit down in the damp sand. This would be the foundation of my outfit.

I hopped in my Jaguar and headed for Beverly Hills. The car looked too respectable, so I parked out of sight and walked in. I stood in bare feet, dirty and tattered blue jeans with patches, a thick leather belt, a skimpy crop top, three Indian necklaces, several bracelets and rings, and a funky leather hat with feathers hanging down the back. As people noticed me, I saw raised eyebrows. Whoever I looked at would quickly turn away.

A woman got up from behind her desk and walked over to me. "May I help you, young lady?" she asked, peering down at me through glasses propped halfway down her nose. It could have been a young version of Aunt Hazel: the beak, the glasses, the disapproving stare.

"I would like to deposit this," I said nonchalantly, as though I made $70,000 deposits every day.

I handed her the check and her disapproval vanished instantly, replaced with gracious professional courtesy. "Yes, I see," she said, adjusting her glasses. "Let me escort you to Mr. Meriwether, our president." She walked me to his desk. "Mr. Meriwether, this is Mrs. DeJoria and she would like to open an account with us."

The Meriwether eyes bulged and his face reddened as he glared at his employee, looked me up and down, and quickly surveyed the customers to see who was looking at him. He cleared his throat. Poor man; his image is shattered, I thought, trying to keep from laughing. Bob, you would have loved this one.

The lady handed him the check and he saw the amount.

"Oh, please have a seat," he said, clearing his throat again as a wide smile transformed his face. "I make it my rule to meet new customers with substantial deposits, just in case you might require any special assistance. Would you like some coffee or tea?"

"No thanks." I smiled back at him. It took only a few minutes to process the new account, and as I glanced around I noticed the sandy prints of bare feet on the small oriental carpet in front of the Meriwether desk. I looked down and saw that my jeans were drying and I couldn't move my legs without a fine trickle of sand falling. It hadn't occurred to me I would make such a mess, but that would have to be a bonus. I wondered if he would call a staff meeting to change his policy of always meeting new customers with substantial deposits. They handed me my white passbook with embossed gold lettering, and now Mr. Meriwether and the receptionist dismissed me with smiles, handshakes, and the assurance that "It's been such a pleasure." Everyone's eyes seemed to follow me as I left, trailing more sand to the door.

With this errand done, I drove to a travel agency and bought tickets for Sao Paulo, Brazil. Only as I was driving home did I remember that Amelia had told me she wanted to go to Acapulco. Why didn't I think of this sooner? So as soon as I got home I called her and the words came tumbling out.

"Amelia, it's JoAnn. I need to get away for a while and I just bought tickets to Sao Paulo, but after I left the travel agent I remembered that you had said something about wanting to go to Acapulco. I don't know if you're free, but I could always call the travel agent and change my ticket…"

"I don't know," she replied. "Let me look at my calendar." She was silent for a moment, and then she spoke again. "I'm free now, but I have to be back next week for a photo shoot. Could you leave right away? It would have to be tomorrow."

She didn't allow herself to get excited about the trip until I got back to her with the news that the travel agent could get us on the plane the next morning. She would come back in time for her shoot and I would go on to Sao Paolo. Then she gushed, "I'm so glad you called! I've been wanting to go back to Acapulco for the longest time, and it just hasn't come together – and now you've made it happen! And we had such a good time together in Hawaii…"

I needed to see Heather before I left, and I called my grandmother to see if she wanted to go with me. On the way, I told her I needed to make the trip to Brazil to decide whether to marry David.

"JoAnn, be sensible," she said. "David is a nice Jewish boy. He's very successful and will take good care of you and Heather. You don't need to waste your money on a trip."

"Ma, I just don't know if I love him," I said, trying to calm her down. "I really need to get away to try and sort things out."

"But what about Heather? How can you just go off to South America and leave her?"

"Heather is fine," I countered. "She's happy, and I'll be gone just for three weeks." We took Heather to the park and she played on the swings while Ma kept working on me about David.

After a while it was time to take Heather back to Maria's. "Mommy is going to go bye-bye for a while," I said as I was leaving.

"Okay Mommy – you be back in this many days?" she asked, holding up four fingers.

"No, Honey, more days than you have fingers," I said. She opened and closed her hands several times. "This many days?" she asked, laughing as she made a game out of it. I began to wonder if I was really doing the right thing.

But Maria reassured me that Heather was doing fine. "She's adjusted well to our family life. There's no reason you couldn't be gone for a month if you wanted to."

I gave Heather one more hug and drove my grandmother home.

David called me that evening just as I was beginning to pack. "I got home from work and you weren't home – I wondered what's up. You're at your apartment? What are you doing there, Honey?" he asked.

"I'm on my way to Acapulco with Amelia," I answered, "then I'm going on to Brazil. I had to come here to pack."

"You're kidding, of course. Quit teasing me."

"No, I'm serious." I spent the next several hours trying to convince him this was the right thing for both of us. Not wanting any tearful goodbyes, I said I'd see him when I got back.

I finished packing and dropped into bed, but sleep didn't come easily. Was I crazy? Could I afford this trip? Sure, I had the $70,000 check. Vinnie and Ray were running the business. But did I still owe Xerox $100,000? I wasn't sure. Maybe David had come up with a way to clear the debt, but if so, I really didn't understand it. Meanwhile, David wanted to marry me. Why did things have to be so complicated?

Yes, I needed the trip. I was going to have to get away from it all for a few days so I could make my decisions. With that settled, I fell asleep.

Eight

Love Spell In Brazil

We left early the next morning, and Amelia was good company. I was excited about the trip and was chattering about everything and nothing, but Amelia was easygoing, purposeful, confident. I never knew what she was thinking and she didn't talk about her feelings, but she knew how to have fun. And though I didn't know her well, I trusted her. She always knew where she was going, and on the trip to Hawaii I had noticed something about her: whenever I was having a rough time, she always seemed to care.

We touched down in Acapulco around 10 a.m. I stepped off the plane and savored the warm tropical wind. Amelia flagged down a taxi and spoke to the driver in Spanish.

"What did you say, Amelia?" I asked.

"I told him to take us directly to the Via Vera – no rides around the block," she said. "These guys will drive you all over town rather than taking a direct route."

"What for?"

"To run up the cab fare," Amelia said as she lit a cigarette. "I can see I've got some things to teach you about traveling in foreign countries." She had been all over the world and knew the ropes.

"What if you don't know where you're going?" I asked.

"Just act like you do. Always have confidence and look them in the eye." We drove along the coast, past the many high-rise hotels overlooking the ocean. "But this time, I really do know where we're going. I've been here before."

Amelia had said we needed to stay at the Via Vera because it was the "in" place to stay, out of the way and not filled with tourists. So I wasn't surprised when the taxi turned away from the coastline and headed up a winding road. Our destination was a collection of sparkling white bungalows surrounding a beautiful pool with a bar in the middle. From the hilltop we had a panoramic view of Acapulco Bay.

This was the escape I needed. The days drifted by. We were as lazy as the palm trees swaying gently in the breeze. Always stoned, we lay around the pool and worked on our tans like everyone else. I had expected the scent of tropical flowers, but instead it was cocoa butter, the suntan lotion of choice. Our only exercise was the swim to the bar in the middle of the pool where we drank strawberry daiquiris. Everyone was relaxed and friendly, and it felt like a family gathering as we played backgammon, ran into one another at the pool by day and at the local "in" spots by night, and sometimes danced till dawn. We quickly found boyfriends.

Suddenly the week was over. Amelia and I went to the airport and she caught her plane back to California as I boarded my plane for Sao Paolo. I would miss her. She was savvy and reliable, and I looked up to her as though she were the big sister I had never had. I hoped I could carry myself with her elegant sense of authority when I arrived in Sao Paolo.

I landed sixteen hours later and found a cab, doing my best to be confident and to look the driver in the eye. I would be staying with my friend Sandra, and I gave him the address she had sent me. He raced through the dirty city, taking wild risks to pass other cars, weaving in and out of lanes, accelerating madly to gain a momentary advantage and then having to stomp on the brakes to avoid a crash. I was terrified. It was a relief to arrive at Sandra's apartment, though I suddenly realized I might not have exchanged enough currency at the airport to pay my fare. It was even more of a relief when Sandra opened the door and helped me settle up with the driver.

Sandra and her mother welcomed me into their little apartment and tried to make me feel at home. Her mother, a tiny woman with grey hair and dark sad eyes, didn't speak any English but communicated with a radiant smile.

Within a day, I knew I was trapped. Sandra went to work every day, leaving me with her mother. I couldn't go out; there was the language barrier, and they lived in a scary neighborhood. Mosquitoes thought I was an all-you-can-eat buffet. The apartment was confining. Just off the kitchen was a creepy little room that housed a shrine of some sort with statues and candles; though nothing was said, somehow I knew to stay out. Sometimes out of boredom I wandered around in the apartment, and her mother and I would pass each other and do an embarrassed charade of nods and smiles, as though we were somehow communicating with each other. Sandra took me to parties at night, but still I didn't connect. There were no cute guys; almost nobody spoke English, and I certainly didn't speak Portuguese.

I decided to go to Rio. Why Rio? Why not? At least I'd heard of it. There was bound to be more going on there than at Sandra's.

Nobody tried to talk me out of it. "I wish I could go too," said Sandra, "but I can't afford to miss work." She called the airline for me and arranged my flight – "Even if you find someone who speaks English, how good would their English be? It'll go faster if I just do it all in Portuguese."

Then Sandra said there was one more thing we had to do before I left: her mother was a white witch and wanted to put a spell on me so I would find a lover in Rio. "What does she want me to do?" I asked. Sandra turned to her mother and said something in Portuguese.

Her mother disappeared into the little room and came back out, and then things happened so fast I couldn't quite keep up with it all. She was holding something in a fist and I saw a bottle in the other hand, and she motioned for me to stand in the middle of the room. She began shrieking at the top of her lungs, dancing all around me and sprinkling me first with something wet and then with powder, back and forth between the two. I felt an electric atmosphere swirling around me. I stood as if paralyzed until she completed the ritual.

This was my sendoff. I went to the airport by myself the next morning because Sandra had to go to work.

Nobody at the airport spoke English so we communicated with sign language. I tried to carry myself with Amelia's confidence as I waited for my plane to depart. Suddenly a man in an airline uniform grabbed my hand and pointed to a small plane that had started to taxi. He tugged me and soon we were chasing it down the runway. I was running too hard to laugh, but it felt like a scene in a Laurel and Hardy movie. I couldn't believe this was happening!

My heart sank as the plane got away. My luggage was on it. I managed to catch another flight an hour later and arrived in Rio. Once again, nobody spoke English. I searched all over the airport and eventually found my bags.

I flagged down a taxi and the driver could manage a bit of broken English. I tried to tell him I wanted a hotel. He drove along the coast and stopped in front of a large place that looked like an apartment building. The currency resembled play money to me. I handed him some and he smiled so brightly I wondered if I had given him too much, but there was no time to find out. He drove off.

In the lobby I found a young man who spoke English, and he translated for me at the desk. They gave me a room but I had to drag my own luggage up the stairs. I couldn't put my finger on why my room gave me the creeps, but it was dark, dingy, and dirty. I lugged my suitcases back to the front desk and waited for the young man who spoke English.

"What's the best place to stay in Rio?" I asked.

"The Copa Cabana Palace," he said. "Then that's where I'm going," I said as I headed out the door.

At this point the cost was no object. I was exhausted and ready to be pampered. I felt right at home when my cab pulled up to the plush hotel and uniformed bellmen waved me in. The desk clerk spoke English. Someone carried my bags, and my room was clean, bright, and airy.

I changed into my swimsuit and sat by the pool, listening for someone I could strike up a conversation with. Everyone was chattering happily in Portuguese – or for all I know it was Spanish, Italian or Swahili. This was no better than Sandra's.

I strolled into town. I window-shopped. I looked for places to eat. I took in the sights. An old woman looked up at me and said something in Portuguese. "I'm sorry; only English," I said, thinking this would force her to leave me alone.

"You're beautiful," she said with a thick accent, "very beautiful." And she gave me a smile and a nod as Sandra's mother had done in the apartment. Poor thing; she must be crazy, I told myself as I kept walking. I knew I wasn't beautiful: once as a little girl I had studied myself in a mirror and I asked my Aunt Hazel, "Am I pretty?" And she had answered with a no-nonsense voice, "Of course not; you're ugly." I'd never had any reason not to believe her.

One lonely day passed, and then another. There was nobody to talk to – just a few words with clerks and bellboys, a few more when I placed an order in a restaurant, and the crazy old lady on the street who never failed to say "very beautiful" whenever I walked by. She never said any more; it may have been all the English she knew. Sandra's mother had put a spell on me so I would find a lover, and I couldn't even find someone to talk to.

I was sitting by the pool again and wondering if it was time to pack my bags and go home when I noticed a girl talking to a group of people. She looked like a hippie: long denim skirt, a lot of jewelry, no shoes. I walked around the pool and sat nearby to eavesdrop. She spoke with a British accent, and English had never sounded so beautiful. I waited for an opportunity, and introduced myself.

Her name was Daphne, and she told me she had just flown in from Barbados; her boyfriend was still there but would arrive in a few days. Then she added that she was waiting for money to arrive from England. Was this a scam? Maybe, but at this point I was so glad to meet someone who spoke English that I didn't care.

"If money's a problem, you could stay with me in my room until it arrives," I told her. "I'd enjoy the company."

"It's so kind of you to offer, dear," she replied with a slight laugh, "but it's hardly necessary. I'm quite certain the money will arrive soon." And she began introducing me to her friends.

They proved to be a group of famous French fashion designers and their models staying at the hotel. Daphne invited me to join them for dinner every night and then to visit the fashion show they were putting on in a large auditorium in downtown Rio.

I didn't know many of the people in the group, and they usually spoke in French. Most of the men were gay and some of the models were lovers. But among the entourage that followed the designers around I began to notice Jean Pierre. I couldn't figure him out: he was always with a woman about 15 years older than he was, yet he spent most of his time flirting with me in covert ways. One night a waiter handed me a note as I went to the restroom.

"Meet me in the lobby after the show. Love, Jean Pierre."

"Love?" He didn't even know me, but I was intrigued and went to meet him. "I've been waiting for a chance to talk to you without Fifi," he said. "There's a beautiful walkway along the beach – shall we go?"

We walked a long way, and suddenly he tried to kiss me. I pushed him away. "What's going on?" I demanded. "I thought you were going with Fifi."

He stepped back with a grin. "You're really naive, aren't you?" He waited for me to react and then burst out laughing. "You honestly don't get it, do you?"

"Don't get it? What are you talking about? The only thing I know is that she clings to you like you're going to run away. It's obvious you're not in love with her."

"My darling, she is my job," Jean Pierre explained. "She pays for the apartment I live in. She buys my food, my clothing, my car. She takes care of all my expenses."

"What job? What kind of job is that?"

"I'm at her disposal, and she pays for everything."

This was puzzling. "That sounds like the kind of thing a gigolo would do," I said, thinking aloud; and then I got it. "You're not a gigolo, are you?"

He laughed again, and soon I was laughing with him.

So I became Jean Pierre's girlfriend for a few nights, whenever he could get away from Fifi. Then Daphne's boyfriend arrived, and his brother Antoine came to the hotel with him. We spent the day by the pool and then had to dress to go to a Samba that night. We all met at Daphne's room. "I'm going to steal the lovely JoAnn away from you," Antoine said to Jean-Pierre with a wicked grin. "You can't hang onto her; you'll be too busy with your delightful Fifi."

I didn't take it seriously; men seemed to like to say that kind of thing to each other. But at the discotheque Antoine asked for a dance, and then while we were dancing he said, "Let's get out of here." Why not? We did, and he was right: he had stolen me away from Jean-Pierre.

One night Daphne dressed me up in some of her beautiful designer clothes and carefully fixed my make-up and hair. When we arrived at the fashion show, a man carrying a handful of dresses rushed up to me, grabbed my arm, and jabbered frantically in French. "What is he saying?" I asked Daphne.

Daphne laughed. "He thinks you're one of the models and he's saying you've got to hurry backstage," Daphne said.

In French she told him I wasn't a model, and the man rushed off.

I had just been mistaken for one of the French models? They were the highest paid models in Europe, and they all were very beautiful. How could he think I was one of them?

Something was going on. Men had always showed an interest in me, and I had just assumed they weren't picky. But why had Antoine made such a point of letting Jean-Pierre know that he would steal me away from him?

Then my mind jumped back to the old woman who kept telling me I was beautiful. Was I? How could I be? But now I had just been mistaken for a fashion model. Ever since childhood I had thought myself ugly, but what if I was wrong?

After the fashion show everyone met at the hotel for drinks. While they chattered I slipped upstairs to my room, sat down at the vanity, and stared at myself. It was as if another person looked back at me, and she wasn't bad looking. I wasn't ready to think of myself as beautiful or even pretty, but that night I realized I wasn't ugly.

A coincidence happened the next morning as I walked through the lobby of the hotel. A man I had never met handed me a dozen yellow roses. "I bought these this morning and told myself I was going to give them to the first beautiful woman I saw," he said in a charming Brazilian accent. And with a bow, he was gone.

I got a vase at the desk and went upstairs. I ran into Antoine in the elevator. He was already becoming quite possessive.

"Who gave you those?" he demanded. "What did you do to get them?"

"A man in the lobby – and I didn't do anything. I don't know why he gave them to me."

"I don't blame him," Antoine said as he put his arm around me. "I stole you away from Jean Pierre and now I will have to watch out that someone doesn't steal you away from me."

Suddenly I was getting a lot of attention from men, and I loved it. Did this mean the spell was working? Maybe so; it wasn't any stranger than Ma's experiences with the cards. All I knew was that I definitely had more than my share of attractive men interested in me since I had arrived in Rio.

A few days later Daphne told me she was going to go back to England. "I can't imagine what the problem is and this certainly hasn't ever happened before, at least not to me. But for reasons unknown, my money still hasn't arrived."

By now I was pretty sure she wasn't scamming about the money, but new doubts flashed in my mind. I quickly overruled them. "Are you sure there isn't some way I can help?" I asked.

"Oh, no," she replied. "I'm so touched that you would offer, dear." She looked me in the eye and for a moment I saw a puzzled little girl beneath her sophistication. Then she reined herself in. "But the embarrassment really is making it quite impossible to enjoy the trip. I may as well go home."

"When are you leaving?" I asked, hoping it wasn't too soon.

"Tomorrow at 10 a.m."

I couldn't believe it. "Daphne, do you really have to go right away?"

"Yes, I really can't stand being broke. The trip has become entirely uncomfortable. If you're ever in London, ring me up." She scribbled her name and address on a piece of stationery. She went home the next day.

Home. I was finding it easy to stay away from home. For the first time since Bob's death, my mind was breaking free from my past. Heather tugged at my heart, and I'd kept in touch with her by phone and sent her cards almost every day. If Heather weren't in California, I might never go back.

I rarely thought about David.

Now that Daphne had left, Rio became boring again. The models and designers were busy or they didn't speak English. Antoine worked all day, selling jewelry; besides, he was charming but I wasn't in love with him and I knew he wasn't in love with me. Within days we began quarrelling and our relationship quickly broke down. What was keeping me in Brazil?

The models were leaving soon, and I decided to leave when they did. I packed my bags and Antoine took me to the airport. Our relationship may have ended, but Antoine wasn't one to just dump me at the door and leave. He took me to the airport's best restaurant as we waited for my flight to begin boarding. To our surprise, we saw all the French designers and models. They were returning to Paris.

Tan, a good friend of Daphne's, invited us to join them at his table. He was gay and was crazy about Antoine, but Antoine was straight. For days, Tan had been very friendly with me just so he could get close to Antoine. He was quite obvious about it and Antoine endured it. One day when we were alone I had asked why he put up with Tan's overtures. "What choice do I have? He's famous; he's well connected; he's successful. I have to put up with him if I want a future in this business."

So now we sat together at the table and drank champagne as we waited for our flights to depart. Mine would leave for Montreal at 9 p.m. and their chartered plane would leave for Paris at the same time.

"JoAnn, why don't you come to Paris with us?" Tan asked suddenly, looking around at the other models and designers at our table. "It would be just wonderful, darling. And we shall call Daphne and get together."

"Oh yes," everyone else gushed in broken English. "Come with us on our plane. You simply must see Paris in April."

"Well, it's 8:30 now," I said. "If you can get my bags on your plane, I'll go with you." I continued sipping champagne as someone rushed to find an agent. Would it work? I didn't know, but either way, it was exciting; if nothing else, I wasn't used to having such a glamorous crowd making a fuss over me. At 8:45 they began boarding the planes and I had no idea which flight I was on. At 8:50 p.m. I was notified my bags had been transferred to the charter flight. Everyone cheered when we got the news.

The flight was exhilarating, everyone else was happy to be returning home, and I was happy to continue my escape.

Nine

First Class: London, Paris, St. Tropez

Twelve hours later we landed in Paris, and Tan and I took a cab to his apartment. I could see the Eiffel Tower in the distance. I rented a room in a little hotel across the street and went to bed. It would be great to see Paris in April, but right now I needed sleep. Jet lag had messed up my schedule; I was used to being up most of the night, but now I fell asleep, as it was getting dark. The next morning, Tan called Daphne.

"Darling, guess who is here with me!" he said. "Yes, isn't it wonderful? Just at the last moment we squeezed her onto our plane." In a moment he handed me the phone.

"I'll be there tomorrow about noon to take you to a party in London," Daphne announced. So much for Paris, but so what? At last I'd be in a country where the people speak English. Besides, I'd always dreamed of visiting England.

Daphne and her boyfriend arrived the next day and visited Tan for a while. When we got to the airport I started to buy my ticket to London, but Daphne put her hand across the counter. "This trip is on me," she said. "You're not paying for anything."

We flew first class on Air France. The stewardess doted over us, never allowing our champagne glasses to run dry, and the food was wonderful. In no time at all, the captain announced we were landing in London. The words sounded like magic to me.

"Let me tell you about the party," said Daphne as we drove through London. I did my best to listen but my surroundings were a dream come true. From time to time she gave me a bit of history as we passed the buildings of brick or stone, many half-hidden behind walls with antique gates, and usually half buried in ivy. "This house dates back to the 16th century," she would say, and my mind would try to go back to America's beginnings, and then jump back even earlier. It was like being in a fairy tale; I imagined kings, queens, and nobles riding their coaches past the same buildings on the same streets centuries ago. I'm afraid I missed most of what she said about the party.

Suddenly we turned up a cobblestone lane and stopped. We were there. We stepped into a tastefully decorated flat and the host and hostess were greeting the visitors and directing them to a table where uniformed waiters were serving tea. Everyone else was formally dressed and calling one another Lord This and Lady That – everyone but a young man, Daphne, and me. We were in jeans.

It seemed like a movie set, not real life.

I had never felt so out of place: the manners, the clothing, even the polite snobbishness that somehow said "You're not really one of us, but we can't be rude enough to come right out and say so." First I told myself the only people here I could hope to relate to were the waiters, then it struck me that even they were far more sophisticated than I was – if I needed a job, I'd never manage to get hired to serve tea in a place like this.

It was crazy; it hadn't bothered me to dress like a hippie and make a scene at the Beverly Hills bank. No comparison. That was for Bob, and I was close to home and knew what to expect. Besides, the people at the bank were pretending to be rich and important; these people were the real deal. Ha! the scene at the bank may have been for Bob, but this wasn't for him and it sure wasn't for me. I wished I had dressed differently – even Aunt Hazel couldn't have gotten me ready for this party. I was so uncomfortable I wished I could disappear.

Daphne had left me on my own to mix with the guests. For a moment I wished she were introducing me to her friends, but they all seemed to be saying exactly what they were supposed to say. The crazy thought flashed through my mind that they weren't conversing at all, but were simply reciting lines they had memorized years ago; only if they followed a mysterious and complex set of rules could they know which line to say next. I knew I couldn't hope to get it right. I've never been good at small talk; my tongue felt like a giant blob of suet in my mouth. If only I'd filled up on champagne on the jet! A good buzz would help right now.

I took my chances and introduced myself to an elderly gentleman in a pinstripe suit and a grey bow tie. "Delighted to meet you. Let me guess," he said, glancing at my outfit. "I'm sure you're from America, but would it be California?" Soon we were chatting happily and he was introducing me to his friends, though they didn't all take to me as warmly as he did. "Have you met JoAnn? She's come all the way from California to be with us today as the guest of Lady Lunceford."

Lady Lunceford? I was too embarrassed to correct him, whoever Lady Lunceford was. But he seemed delighted to introduce me to people, even if it did make me feel like a new exhibit at the zoo. Everyone was unfailingly polite. The young man in jeans turned out to be Jack, one of Daphne's boyfriends. Someone told me Jack frequently had tea with the queen.

I was out of my league and kept hoping we'd leave soon. At last we said goodbye and walked out the door. "We'll go get a room now," Daphne announced.

The desk clerk at Claridge's smiled widely as we checked in. "We were hoping you'd be back again soon, Lady Lunceford," he said. So this was Lady Lunceford! I glanced at Daphne, who was signing the registry. She had looked like a hippie to me, but I decided to swallow my surprise. "We shall bring your trunk to your room," said the desk clerk, whose discreet nod sent the bellman out the door.   Daphne finished checking in and we headed for the elevator, where the bellman was waiting for us with a huge trunk on a trolley. I wondered if Daphne lived in hotels. She had left a trunk full of beautiful clothes at the Copa Cabana in Rio.

I'd thought Warren's place was elegant, but it was nothing like this. We had a sitting room and marble bathroom. Next to my bed was a button I could push, and a bellman would appear almost instantly to satisfy any whim.

"JoAnn, I want you to get whatever you want, whenever you want it," Daphne said. "Not many people have done anything for me in my life without expecting something in return, and I want to repay you for South America. You had no way of knowing I was really telling you the truth about my money not arriving. That's a scam a lot a people use when they're traveling."

"Oh Daphne, don't be silly," I said as I plopped down in an overstuffed chair. "You don't have to pay me back. I was being selfish. I was starving for companionship."

"No," she insisted. "You have no idea how rare real caring is." This led to hours of talk about Daphne's loneliness. She was buying her boyfriend Jack a Porsche to keep him happy; he was jealous because she'd told him she missed her boyfriend in South America and was sending him a ticket to Europe. I realized she had everything, yet she had nothing.

"Let's face it," she said. "The men I like wouldn't look at me twice unless I use my money to buy them off and give them the things they can't afford themselves." She wasn't unattractive, but I had noticed that her boyfriends were ten to fifteen years younger than she was. I felt sorry for her. Did she have any friends she could really talk to? Or was it always like the parties we had just attended, with formal but stilted conversation? We talked until sleep overtook us.

I woke up, pushed the buzzer for room service, and fell back to sleep for a few moments. Suddenly a young man was standing by my bed, ready to take my order. I mumbled something and he disappeared. I dozed again until I heard a tray being placed on the nightstand.

"I could get used to this," I murmured, savoring the smell of the coffee. We took our time getting dressed, and Daphne made phone calls. Suddenly I began giggling. This was the woman who said she was waiting for her money, and I had wondered if it was a scam?

"What's so funny?" Daphne asked absently as she dialed another number.

"Nothing," I said. I didn't feel like trying to explain what I was thinking.

"Well, I'm making just one more call," she said. "Jack won't be coming by today. He's a bit upset about Alex's arrival, so I've hired a car. It will be here in a quarter of an hour." Whoever she called must have picked up the phone; she disappeared into another conversation and I tried to hurry so I could be ready to go in fifteen minutes.

Daphne finished her call. "It's alright, JoAnn. You don't have to rush. We can take our time; they'll wait for us."

It took half an hour to get ready and go downstairs, and we were the center of attention as the hotel staff greeted us. "Good morning, Lady Lunceford...it's so good to see you...I trust you slept well, Lady Lunceford." She acknowledged each greeting with a crisp nod as we walked out to the street.

I couldn't believe my eyes. I was expecting a taxi; instead, a chauffeur was waiting for us, standing by the open door of a Rolls Royce. We climbed in and he closed the door behind us. "We're going to see the sights of London," Daphne announced as we headed into traffic.

It was hard not to feel important as people stared at us when we drove by, and I especially enjoyed getting in and out of the car with the chauffeur tending to our every need. As the sun began to set, Daphne told the driver to take us back to our hotel.

Back in our room, Daphne said, "We are invited to a very private club tonight." We took our time getting ready and left about 11 p.m. The chauffeur was still waiting for us where we'd left him hours earlier. The Rolls pulled up to the club, and I heard music blaring. A doorman let us out and we headed downstairs into a dark room.

It was a typical nightclub scene, though many of the people looked familiar. I wondered idly if they were people I had met at yesterday's party. Nobody looked interesting. I spotted two of the Rolling Stones at a table; one locked his eyes on mine and followed me wherever I went. It began to feel like a cat and mouse game. Was he expecting me to introduce myself to him? Maybe he was so used to women falling all over him that he'd forgotten how to make the first move. I wasn't sure and didn't care. He might be a star, but he wasn't my type.

Daphne was hanging on a man's arm all evening and announced that she was going to leave with him. She wanted me to take a cab; she would use the hired car. With that settled, they left.

I decided to go back to the hotel. I finished my drink, checked my coat out, and started up the stairs. One of the Stones said, "The blond is leaving," and then I heard footsteps behind me. I found the exit and ran across the street to catch a taxi. I looked up and down the street but couldn't find one. Instead, I heard squealing tires and the howl of a racing engine. Here he was in a red Ferrari. He slowed as he passed me and I pretended I hadn't noticed him, and then he took off with another roar.

I heard him circling the block, and again he slowed down as he drove by. This time he peered at me intently. For a moment I was tempted to respond. Instead, I saw a taxi and flagged it down.

Daphne didn't get back that night. I spent the next day in my room. I watched TV. I ordered a beef Wellington dinner and a few snacks from room service. Will she hit the ceiling when she sees the bill? I wondered. Nothing here is cheap. But she did say to order whatever I wanted. And besides, I can't go out because I have no idea when she'll show up.

Daphne returned at noon the next day. "Let's check out and go back to Paris," she said. In minutes, we were ready to leave. I listened in as she paid her bill for two nights, 1100 pounds. This was a little more than $2000, enough to buy a small car in California – nothing fancy, but at least it would have been brand new. Two nights! I would have gone over the bill line by line, but she barely glanced at it.

In Paris we checked into the shabby hotel across the street from Tan, taking separate rooms because they were so small. This hotel was as shabby as Claridge's had been elegant. Did Daphne sometimes like to go slumming? She seemed to adapt well, whatever the circumstances.

We spent our evenings in wonderful restaurants with the designers we had met in South America. After each long meal, we would go to nightclubs and dance for hours, sometimes till dawn.

One night I had slept for only a few hours when I heard a loud knock at my door. The sun wasn't even up yet. I buried my head in my pillow. "Go away," I moaned, hoping the knocking would stop. It didn't. Reluctantly, I opened the door. There stood Daphne with her suitcases.

"Let's get out of this flea bag hotel," she announced. "I've rented a yacht and we're off to Cannes."

I rubbed the sleep out of my eyes and gathered my belongings. Don't ask me when, but Daphne had bought a battered old Volkswagen. Soon we were driving out of Paris. We stopped to pick up Tan's brother Bang. He giggled in the back seat like a schoolgirl most of the time.

The sun rose, and I caught my first glimpse of the French countryside. The little cottages looked like something in a picture book, and I began to imag-

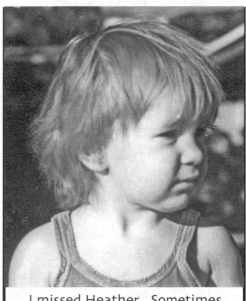

I missed Heather. Sometimes it was unbearable.

ine the families that lived there. Lights were on. I envisioned polite little children, sleepy and angelic, getting ready for school. I wondered what Heather was doing. Suddenly I missed California. I was floating on the edge of a whirlpool of depression, ready to spiral down. Maybe the radio would cheer me up. I turned it on and worked the dial, but all

I could get was static.

"Daphne, do you have a joint?" I asked.

"Certainly," she said, reaching into her large purse.

I lit the joint and took a deep drag, trying to get comfortable in the cramped little car. Soon the world looked bright again and excitement erased the gloom.

Crewmember and guests on the Northwind.

We arrived at the harbor a few hours later. We looked like three derelicts from the Sunset Strip. I wondered which yacht was ours.

We pulled up near the biggest yacht in the harbor; it must have cost millions. "This is it," Daphne said as she jumped out of the old car.

We approached the gangplank, where a captain stood at attention. "This yacht has been chartered by Lady Daphne Lunceford," he said dismissively.

"This is Lady Daphne Lunceford," I said, nodding towards Daphne.

He didn't flinch. He stepped aside to let us pass. How does he know we're telling the truth? I wondered as he escorted us around the magnificent vessel.

It was the second largest yacht in the Mediterranean – 180 feet long, with a crew of 11 men. The staterooms were lovely and the living room was of solid mahogany. The captain informed us that Jackie Kennedy, Winston Churchill, and the queen had all chartered it at times. He left us to choose our rooms.

Daphne's boyfriend arrived the next day from South America and Tan took the train from Paris. Now there were five of us, along with the crew of eleven. We left for Villa, France. We found the village charming and romantic, but there was no nightlife. Why stay? We headed out for an overnight trip to San Tropez.

We arrived at noon. Several yachts were berthed in the harbor, and a row of colorful umbrellas faced them. As we neared the shore I saw hundreds of people crowded into restaurants, watching everyone on the yachts.

"When we dock, don't fraternize with anyone except the people on the other yachts," Daphne instructed me.

"But how will I possibly know who's who?"

"Don't worry, my dear. We all will stick together, and we know who is socially acceptable. Many of those people sitting in the restaurants spend their days just trying to get a name so they can scheme their way on board."

We docked and went out for drinks. Wherever we went, everyone watched us. Daphne and her lover had eyes only for each other. I found Tan boring, and his brother whined incessantly about wanting a man. I drank glass after glass of champagne. We went back to the yacht for more of the same.

Soon I felt restless. "Can we go for a walk?" I asked.

"If you pay close attention to Tan and me, we may," Daphne said. She led our little group back down the gangplank.

As soon as our feet touched the gravel, people thronged us, smiling, jostling, and competing for our attention as everyone shouted a question. Daphne looked like a "hippie" but there was nothing common about the way she carried herself. She ignored the people around us and continued talking with Tan. The rest of us looked straight ahead and followed after them like dogs that had been to obedience school. The crowd got the signal and quickly dispersed.

We window-shopped and made our way to a little out-of-the-way cafe. Daphne and Tan seemed to know everyone in the place so I assumed these were the people we could socialize with. Everyone was chattering excitedly about either the Grand Prix or the Cannes Film Festival, two upcoming events. I was lonely and bored. I scanned the room for a good-looking man, but saw none. What a waste of time, I thought as I stirred my drink with the straw.

We returned to the *Northwind* and got ready for an evening at the local "in" spot. It wasn't any more exciting than our afternoon excursion to the little cafe. The same people were there.

Ten

Bored With Riches

I wasn't the only one who was bored at the nightclub, and we all went back to the *Northwind* early. Bang and I thought we were in for a dull evening – neither of us could find an interesting man – but suddenly he brightened and suggested that we spend the evening trying on my clothes. For the rest of the night, I helped him into one outfit after another. I couldn't stop laughing; it was like being a little girl again and playing with a doll, except now the doll was alive, laughing and giggling with every new outfit. I genuinely loved him by the end of the evening. He was like a kid sister.

The next morning I slipped out of bed before anyone else stirred. I wanted to get out; the yacht was starting to feel like an elite prison. As soon as I appeared on deck, someone poured me a cup of coffee and several crewmen stood at attention waiting for me to order.

The shore beckoned with a promise of freedom. I envied the people sitting and eating in the open-air restaurants. Already the restaurants were packed, and I noticed many of the diners were staring at me. It was funny; I wanted to be in their crowd, and I suddenly realized that they wanted to be in mine.

I couldn't do anything for them but I could do something for me. I abandoned my coffee and went for a walk. But it hadn't occurred to me that my stepping ashore would be like turning on a porch light on a dark night: instantly it attracted every bug within half a mile. They were waiting for me at the end of the gangplank, and a small crowd of jostling people followed me wherever I went, pelting me with questions: "Who does the yacht belong to?" – "Who are you?" – "Are you a millionaire?" – "Hey movie star, can you get me onboard?"

Couldn't I just take a stroll and have a leisurely breakfast and visit a few shops like a normal tourist? Apparently not. I had left the confinement of the yacht for the prison yard of the shore. I tried to act like Daphne; they kept pestering me. I ducked into shops; they were always waiting for me by the door. I ignored them but I couldn't get them to ignore me. Finally I gave up. I walked briskly back to the *Northwind* and waited for my shipmates to get up.

Everyone gathered at the table at 11 a.m.

"Why don't we go to Crete or somewhere exciting?" I asked.

"Oh my dear, none of us like the motion of the yacht," Tan laughed.

"You mean that's why we stay here day after day?" I asked in amazement.

"Well, we will be leaving for

Sitting still on the NorthWind.

Cannes in a few days for the film festival but we'll stay close to the shoreline," Daphne explained. "If we actually went out into the open sea it would be quite rough."

"Oh yes, and we wouldn't want to get seasick," Bang chimed in.

"It is rather funny, don't you think?" Daphne mused, sipping her morning tea. "Here we are on this beautiful vessel paying thousands of dollars a day just to sit here."

I was starting to wonder if these new friends were in competition to see how much they could spend every day. Though all our meals were provided on the yacht, we had gone out for dinner every night and the bill was never less than $500. New friends would fly in for a day just to sit on the yacht, and then another group would arrive the next day. Someone was always stationed at the gangplank to make sure nobody came on board without permission from Daphne or Tan.

One night a few designers arrived from Paris and we went to the little club to dance. More yachts had docked in the past few days, so I saw new faces. When the club closed, someone invited us to visit another yacht that was almost as big as ours. We all sat on board, chatting and drinking champagne. The owner of the yacht sat next to me and made some advances, which I ignored. I wasn't interested in him and he made me uncomfortable. I asked Daphne and Tan if we could go back to the *Northwind*.

"JoAnn, you are the reason we were invited on this yacht," Daphne said. "This gentleman is a very important person and we can't be rude. Just go along with it and let the rest of us enjoy ourselves, my dear. He's had his eye on you for days." She disappeared into the crowd on deck.

How did I get myself into this? I wondered. The yacht's owner was staring at me. Was I expected to go to bed with this creep so everyone else could have a nice time? I asked someone where the restroom was; I needed to get away for a moment. I felt like a prostitute.

I found an empty stateroom and sat down. Maybe he would become interested in someone else as the evening wore on. One of his friends suddenly barged in. I jumped up and headed for the door, but he blocked it.

"Playing a little hard to get!" he teased.

"I don't know what you're talking about," I said as firmly as I could, though I felt as if my knees were about to buckle. I sensed danger.

He tried to push me back into the stateroom and I struggled to get out. The owner walked in and I was glad to see him, even though I'd been hiding from him moments before.

"What's going on here?" he thundered.

I took the opportunity to slip out. I ran up to the deck and looked for anyone I knew.

The owner found me again and he wanted to make a deal. "I have a beautiful apartment that overlooks the bay, and that's where you can live. You will be free to come and go as you please and I will treat you like a queen. Tomorrow afternoon I will have a new Maserati delivered for you to use as long as you are here, and we will go to the Grand Prix together."

I shut out the rest of what he said. The dirty beast didn't even know my name, I thought. I knew the *Northwind* would leave tomorrow at 6 a.m. If I could just endure his advances for the next few hours, I'd get away safely. This was the worst prison yet; I had to spend all my time outwitting the predators. Somehow I got through it. We returned to the *Northwind* and I went to bed at 5:00 a.m. It was hard to get to sleep with the noises and jolts of the crew casting off. The yacht started to move, and sunlight spilled through my window. I was tired, but at least we were leaving San Tropez and its "very important gentleman."

It was too early to get up, but I still couldn't sleep. My mind went back to California. I wondered what Heather was doing and longed to hold her in my arms. I had mailed a card almost every day and had called as often as I could; she always sounded cheerful and told me what she was doing. Then I would feel torn, wondering if I should jump on the first flight home, or should I take advantage of the opportunity to see Europe? At home, I would face the enormous challenge to get my life and business in order. Somehow I kept choosing to postpone reality and continue my escape. Heather always took it in stride. She never cried or made me feel guilty.

We arrived at Cannes and left the *Northwind* so we could walk around the city. The streets were jammed with people who had come to the film festival. Banners and posters were everywhere; excitement was in the air.

We had been celebrities in San Tropez because we had been on a yacht, but here in Cannes the celebrities were actors, directors, and producers – anyone involved in filmmaking. It felt good to be a nobody again. I could go wherever I wanted. Perhaps I'll find a lover here, I thought.

But it wasn't happening; everyone seemed to be gay. I had often sat with other women and complained about the shortage of desirable men, but now I was having these same conversations with Tan, Bang, and their male friends. So much for the Brazilian love potion.

I felt numbed by the whole scene. Men and women were snuggled up together in dark corners or flirting at the bar. Suddenly a very handsome man kneeled down in front of me and was pleading with me in French.

"What is he saying?" I asked Tan.

"He wants you to dance with him. He's telling you he's going crazy because there don't seem to be any real women in all of France. He's a friend of ours, but he's straight – too bad for me!" Tan sighed.

After we danced a few slow songs he picked me up and carried me over to the table, again saying something to Tan in French.

"Ooh la la, you lucky girl!" Tan said, laughing coyly with his friends.

I struggled, trying to get this handsome Frenchman to put me down.

He held me tighter. "Tan, please tell him to put me down," I pleaded.

"Oh no, my dear," Tan said. "He's going to carry you off to Monte Carlo. He'll bring you back to us in a few days."

That was the beginning of a crazy romantic affair that filled a few lonely days. We had a lot of laughs and communicated with sign language. He returned me to the *Northwind* one sultry afternoon as the

Cannes Film Festival was coming to an end.

I found Daphne and Tan discussing where to have dinner; it had to be a place that would impress their friends. We met the friends at a restaurant and went through the ritual of introductions and ordering our food. Then as we began to eat, nobody noticed the food at all. They all were bragging about who had spent the most money at their dinner parties. It was like housewives competing to find the best bargains, except this group wanted to see who could spend the most.

I couldn't take any more of this. While they talked, I planned my escape. Should I go back home? Not yet, I needed to see a bit more of Europe. I'm part Italian; maybe I owed it to myself to see Italy.

I said my goodbyes after dinner and went back to the *Northwind* to pack. Tomorrow I would leave for Rome.

It was like being in South America again. The train station was crowded, I had to drag my luggage around, and I couldn't find anyone who spoke English. I saw trains stopping and people getting on and off, but I couldn't figure out which train I wanted.

Finally I found a lady who spoke English, and she directed me to the right platform. A man in a beautiful grey silk suit and perfectly polished shoes was sitting on his suitcase. He kept looking at me and smiling. Eventually he got up, moved his suitcase next to mine, and asked something in a language I didn't recognize.

I shook my head and shrugged, to let him know I didn't understand him. He motioned for me to hand him my ticket, which I did hesitantly. He glanced at it and gave it back. "No problem," he said in very broken English.

When the train arrived in the station he picked up my suitcase and carried it on board for me. I was grateful. He motioned for me to sit in a seat and left.

I knew this wasn't my seat. I had bought a ticket for a private sleeper and was anxious to stretch out for the long ride to Rome. In a moment he was back, gesturing for me to follow him. I was thankful for his help. How would I have found my compartment without him?

I stepped into my compartment and saw his luggage next to mine as he followed me in. I shoved him out and tried to find the conductor. The man in the silk suit followed me.

I found the conductor but he didn't speak English. I moved from car to car with the stranger at my heels, looking for another railroad employee. A waiter in the dining car spoke broken English; I asked him to talk to the conductor about the man's luggage in my compartment. The three men talked heatedly, waving their hands as they spoke. My Italian grandparents had often talked to one another in this same animated way.

"This man's things will be removed from your compartment at once," the young waiter finally said.

"Why were they put there in the first place?" I demanded.

The young man shook his head and looked down at the floor.

"I want a reason," I said impatiently.

"The gentlemen you boarded the train with told the conductor you are a prostitute and he had paid you to stay in your room tonight," the young waiter said shyly.

I stood there speechless, boiling with anger. The man in the grey suit had disappeared. I rushed back to my compartment to try to catch him. The conductor was removing his luggage but he was nowhere in sight.

I fell asleep that night to the clatter of the train racing through the countryside. Suddenly light flooded the room. It was the conductor, coming through the door. I jumped out of bed and pushed him out. I locked the door and tried to go back to sleep. Five minutes later, I heard the key turning in the lock and he barged in again. I pushed him out again, locking the door and this time latching it with a chain. He knocked again several times in the night but I ignored him and tried to sleep. It was a relief when I got off the train in Rome the next day.

There were no porters, so again I had to carry my luggage. It was a long trek from the platform to the terminal, and it was hard to maneuver through the masses of people rushing about. I made it to the street and found a cab.

It was a long drive from the terminal to the hotel. When we arrived I handed him $10.00 and he motioned for more. I gave him another dollar and he shook his head, gesturing that I owed him much more. I handed him another $10.00 and he let me go, not even bothering to help me with my baggage. In the hotel, I learned the train station was just around the corner. So this was what Amelia had warned me about in Mexico.

Italy was nothing like France. I had already tasted the difference on the train: I couldn't go anywhere without being pestered by men. Now

I felt like a prisoner in my hotel room. Making matters worse, I had chatted with some Americans on the train and they had warned me not to use drugs in Italy because the penalties were so severe.

After two days in the hotel, I decided to go for a walk to see the sights. The streets were filled with young soldiers who whistled and tried to grab me. This wasn't working.

I went back to my room, removed all my makeup, tied an old bandanna on my head, and put on an oversized shirt and a tattered pair of pants. I went out again and strode purposefully towards the Coliseum. This time I was not pestered as much.

I spotted a couple of college kids in Coca Cola t-shirts. They looked like Americans and I walked up to them.

"Hi," one said with a friendly smile.

"Hi, I'm JoAnn and I'm from California," I said. "Where are you from?"

"We're from Iowa. I'm Greg and this is Ralph."

"Would you guys mind if I walked around with you?" I asked. "I've been here a couple of days and can't go anywhere without being pestered by these men."

"You don't know Italian customs do you?" Greg asked with a laugh.

"What customs?"

"Well, any woman who is out in public alone is automatically considered a prostitute," Greg explained.

"You're kidding!" I gasped, but I knew they weren't. Suddenly I understood the man in the grey suit and the conductor. "That's the craziest thing I've ever heard in my life. You mean I can't even see this country without being pinched and poked and jeered at by these nutty Italians?"

Ralph reassured me. "Don't worry, we are fellow countrymen and we can stick together."

"We're on our way to the catacombs; want to come along?" Greg asked. "We've got a van parked a few blocks away."

I felt safe, as though I were walking with a couple of younger brothers. I locked my arms in theirs as we headed towards the van. And I noticed the women, young or old, always walking two by two, arm in arm.

That night Greg and Ralph took me for a sightseeing ride through Rome. "We're going to show you where the prostitutes hang out," Greg said as he turned a corner.

There they were, strutting provocatively in their skimpy clothing.

This is what every man in Italy would think I was if I was on the streets alone.

"Why don't you check out of your hotel and come with us to Florence?" Greg asked.

Why Florence? Why not? "Sounds like a great idea," I said. I packed quickly and soon was off on another adventure.

We picked up a couple of hitchhikers. They barely spoke English, but they managed to tell us they lived in Florence and if we wanted, we could stay with them in their family's home. We stopped at different points of interest along the way and arrived in Florence after dark. The hitchhikers guided us through the filthy streets. My heart sank when we pulled up to a pockmarked old building. It looked like it might fall down at any moment. The stairs shifted and creaked as we stepped on them, and the stairway smelled like spaghetti sauce.

But if the building was decrepit, the family was warm and friendly. There were twenty of us in the small apartment and somehow we all found places to sleep. Several of us ended up in sleeping bags on the living room floor. It was like being in summer camp. I had more fun here than I ever did on the yacht.

I soon forgot about their poverty as I was caught up in their warm and cheerful lifestyle. So what if we shared our one outdoor toilet with mice and roaches? For a few days I had a family. They all called me "California" and we made a game of communicating with their snippets of broken English. Soon my heart was longing for Heather and though I hated to give up my adventure, I knew it was time to go home.

I called David to tell him when I would arrive. He said he'd pick me up at the airport.

I boarded my flight and made my way to the back of the crowded plane. It would be a long trip to Montreal; I wasn't ready to think about the layover and the flight to L.A. I squeezed into my seat. Babies were crying, children were fussing, and the old man next to me was hacking as he smoked one cigarette after another. I longed for the serenity of first class. *Daphne, you've spoiled me,* I thought. *I wish I didn't know what it's like up there.*

But how could I get an upgrade? I called a stewardess and made up a story. "Excuse me; I'm not feeling well. I just lost my baby and I need some peace and quiet."

The stewardess gave me a sympathetic look.

"I wonder if I might be able to upgrade to first class? My nerves are just shattered." I hoped there was room, and better yet, I hoped my sob story would get me the upgrade.

"Let me check," she said kindly. She disappeared into the other end of the plane and returned a few moments later with a wide smile. "It's all fixed up," she said.

I followed her up to first class. Nobody was next to me, so I could stretch out and sleep if I wanted to. But I didn't feel like sleeping. I enjoyed being pampered and talking to other passengers. And sometimes I kept to myself to think about what I was going to tell David.

Maybe the trip really had helped me decide what to do. Whenever I became homesick, it was always Heather I missed.

Connecting with Daphne and her friends had shown me what so many people were looking for: they called it money and prestige, but it was really just a high-class prison. That's what Aunt Hazel had gone after, and when had I ever seen her truly happy? And David was always talking about his business plans, but what did he know about freedom? He couldn't even go for a walk on the beach without worrying about what the sand was doing to his expensive golf shoes.

The family in Florence had gotten it right. In terms of money they had nothing, but in terms of fun and family they had everything. Who needs money? Money can't buy what they had.

But as I turned it over and over in my mind, I couldn't see myself living like the family in Florence. I couldn't picture myself putting up with the smell in the stairway, living with a large family that shared one bathroom outdoors, going up and down a rickety stairway every time I went out or came home. Who needs poverty?

Okay, I could see having financial security; but at some point there had to be enough. There had to be room to kick back and enjoy. I could be content with enough to get by.

As we prepared for landing the stewardess said, "The captain wanted me to tell you that the upgrade is complimentary – a gift from the captain – and he hopes you feel better."

Eleven

THUGS AND THREATS

When I'd called David from Italy, he had asked, "Have you decided to marry me?"

"We'll talk when I get home," I had said. But I knew the answer already. He had faded quickly from my mind as soon as I had gotten to Mexico.

I think he knew what I was going to tell him; when he met me at the airport neither of us wanted to broach the subject. He chattered enthusiastically as we walked through the long terminal, pouring out facts and figures about his business and anticipating how soon he'd reach his three million dollar goal. "Your printing equipment will be arriving in the store in just a couple of days," he added as he threw my luggage into the trunk of his Cadillac. It was as though I had never left and our relationship was picking up where it had left off.

I didn't want to go home with him. His monolog about business continued and I mumbled an occasional "umm" or "oh". He didn't seem to notice I wasn't listening.

We arrived at David's, and finally I blurted it out. "David, I just can't sleep here."

"Why, Honey?" I had burst his bubble. His brown eyes looked at me with innocence, surprise, and hurt, as though he were a puppy I had shooed off the sofa. This wasn't going to be easy.

"Because I just don't love you," I said bluntly.

"Oh, you'll change your mind," he said, brightening as he patted me on the shoulder. It seemed easier for him than for me, probably because he was confident that he could sell me on the marriage. But I didn't feel up to a sales pitch right now and he was sensitive enough to wait for better timing.

"You just rest now and I'll sleep in the other room," he said, helpfully stowing my luggage in his room and tucking me in bed. He kissed me on the forehead like a little child and closed the door as he went out. I slept like a baby after the long flight and woke up late in the afternoon.

I found David's note on the kitchen table. "I'll be home at seven. Be ready to go to a special place for dinner. Love, David."

The sales campaign was underway, and I knew I had to get out of there before he came home. But how? My car was still at my apartment, miles away. I called Johnny. "Can you give me a ride home?" I asked. "I'm trapped here. David picked me up at the airport and brought me to his place, but he's at work and I don't have my car to get home. And I need my car – I haven't seen Heather in a long time."

Johnny came over right away and took me to see Heather. I wanted to make her feel like a queen for a day, and Johnny was a good sport. Whatever game she wanted to play, we played. She and I found every opportunity we could to snuggle. I hated to see the day end, but bedtime arrived and we kissed her goodnight, leaving her curled up with a new teddy bear.

Johnny drove me home. Now that I'd spent an afternoon with Heather, I realized what was really important to me. I started thinking aloud. "If this trip showed me anything," I said, "it proved that my business can run without me. I don't have to be there every day."

"That's great, JoAnn! So things have worked out well with the new guys?"

"It's running like clockwork – all I have to do is collect the checks. So what's to stop me from finding somewhere else to live, a place big enough for Heather and me both? Then the business can run itself, and Heather and I will be together again."

"You're right; all you have to do is find a bigger place. And you've got the income to cover it?"

"No problem there," I replied.

The next day I got up early and went down to the store. Ray was working with customers at the counter and I walked into the back room where Vinnie was busy at his desk. Two creepy looking men I'd never seen before were there with him, apparently just standing around. Vinnie looked startled as I walked in and picked up a stack of mail on my desk.

I thumbed through it and found unpaid bills; some were overdue. Before I could speak, he jumped up and grabbed the bills out of my hand. "What are you doing here?" he demanded. "You've got no business here!"

Something was very wrong. "Your lease is up," I reacted. I wasn't sure, but weren't we near the end of the six-month probationary period? It didn't matter. Something in my gut was telling me I had to get rid of this guy.

"What are you talking about?" he said smugly. "I got an extension – you can ask your attorney."

"Extension?" I exploded. "I never authorized an extension! What makes you think you have an extension?"

"I can prove it," he said, riffling through one of the many piles of paper on his desk. "I've got the paperwork right here; I'll show it to you."

His desktop was chaos. I waited, seething as he looked through one pile of papers after another. "Don't you ever use files?" I muttered, but he didn't answer; he just kept looking. "Never mind," I broke in. "I don't have time to stand here while you look for your papers. I'll get them from the lawyer." I strode out.

First I went to the bank to go over the records; I couldn't see them because Vinnie had taken my name off the account. Next I called the accountant I'd hired to check the books while I was gone; his secretary said he wasn't in. I went back to the store.

"I want to see the books," I insisted. "You agreed to keep accurate records and agreed I could see them anytime."

"So what?" he said, glancing significantly at the two thugs in the corner. They looked like goons in a mafia movie. I didn't like the way the fatter one glared at me.

"You know, lady, I love to drop people out of 10-story windows," he said with a thick Italian accent. The thugs grinned at each other, as though sharing an inside joke.

I should have been afraid, but uncontrollable fury rose inside of me and I was fearless. "I want to see the records – now!"

"Get out of this shop!" Vinnie yelled. He turned my chin towards the two thugs. "How do you think she'd look with acid thrown in this pretty little face?"

"Real bad, Vinnie," the fatter thug said, shaking his head sadly. "Real bad. It would be a shame for such a pretty lady to have such an accident."

That rattled me. I left the store, drove over to the attorney's, and stormed in. "I've got to see Mr. Gaston immediately," I demanded. I threw myself into a chair, drumming my fingers on her desk while the secretary buzzed Mr. Gaston.

She didn't let my agitation penetrate her cool facade. "Mr. Gaston can see you now," she said in a moment. I walked into his office. I took one look at his huge desk and suspected he had bought it to project an image of power, but it didn't work. It dwarfed him and he looked like a little boy playing dress-up in his father's suit.

"What in the hell is going on around here?" I stormed. "Who gave you the authority to extend Vinnie's lease? He's closed my account at the bank, hasn't paid a bill, and now he has the nerve to threaten me."

"Have a seat and I'll explain," said Mr. Gaston. His voice was soothing but I noticed a twitch in his left eye. He leaned back in his chair and made a tent with his hands, staring at them thoughtfully. "It seems there aren't a lot of attorneys in this town who want to fool with Vinnie. After you left the country he started to threaten me, and I checked up on him. He's out of prison on parole and everyone says he's not the sort of character anyone should mess around with."

"Why weren't the books checked?"

"Vinnie wouldn't let us in the store." Mr. Gaston leaned forward to line up his penholder, his appointment book, and his telephone.

"What do you mean, he wouldn't let you in the store?" I was getting madder and madder.

At last he looked me in the eye. "I'm sorry, Mrs. DeJoria," he said firmly. "If I've failed you, then you can fire me and I'll send you a closing statement."

"A closing statement!" I raged. "A closing statement for what? I hired you to go over to the store once a month with the accountant and check the books. You know what I found when I got home? A pile of unpaid bills, and half of them were overdue. You're a jerk, Mr. Gasbag, afraid of your own shadow!" I rose to leave. "I'm surprised you've got the gall to think I'm going to pay you!"

I slammed his office door and poured a stream of curses into his reception area on my way out.

I had been angry before, but never like this – it was like being drunk. I drove back to the store and Ray wasn't at the counter. "I'll be right with you," Vinnie called from the back office, thinking I was a customer. I put the closed sign up in the window and marched into the back room.

The two thugs were gone and Vinnie looked up at me with surprise. I began screaming. "I'm calling your parole officer and telling him what's going on! I'll tell him about your threats, your unpaid bills! You'd better get out of the store right now!" I charged over to the desk and saw the lease Vinnie and Gaston had signed. I tore it up, threw the scraps the floor, and began stamping them with my feet. "Give me the keys NOW!" I was out of control and I knew it, but I didn't care. He had scared everyone else, but I had him on the defensive and it felt good.

"Now let's just calm down, JoAnn," Vinnie said, spreading his hands in a gesture of conciliation. "Why don't I give you another $200 a month?"

"You'll give me the key and get out of here right now!" I roared as I picked up the phone and dialed 411. "Information? I need the number of the Los Angeles County Probation Department."

Vinnie quickly reached for the phone and broke the connection. His eyes were smoldering and they locked on mine; for a moment our eyes did the talking and I sensed how dangerous he could be, but I didn't flinch. Then he gave in. "Okay, have it your way. But you'd better forget about calling the probation department, or you'll be facing those two guys you met earlier. You don't want to mess with me!" He defiantly slammed the key on my desk and left.

For a few moments I enjoyed my triumph. Then it hit me: now I would have to run the business myself, and now I would have to postpone finding a way to have Heather live with me again. I was back to square one.

If I had any doubts about getting rid of Vinnie, they evaporated as I spent the rest of the day calling creditors and canceling accounts. Vinnie hadn't paid the bills; he had run up debts; he was threatening everybody who tried to check up on him. And somehow he had managed to sign a contract with Xerox for another machine. It was a mess, but I realized I could work through it. I congratulated myself for getting rid of him before things got too bad. Ha! Not even the lawyer had been able to stand up to him. And just because things hadn't worked out with Vinnie didn't mean I couldn't find someone else. How hard could it be?

I made a list of possibilities and thought of Andy. He was a friend, someone I could trust. He'd been doing various odd jobs on our block for years and once had worked part time for Bob; Jack Benny even trusted him enough to use him as a chauffeur from time to time. I got in touch with him and within a few days he took the job.

Meanwhile, I was in the shop daily from 8:00 a.m. to midnight, trying to figure out where I stood. By the end of the week, I realized I was $28,000 in debt.

Xerox was threatening to pull the machine Vinnie had leased, so I brought them the contract he had signed. The attorney had drawn it up, and it said Vinnie was responsible for all debts incurred while he leased the business. But the official at Xerox read my document and said, "I'm sorry, Mrs. DeJoria. This document means nothing to us. Our contract relates to a machine at your business address. Whatever in-house agreements you may have made, we'll have to remove the machine from your business address if we don't receive payment."

Unbelievable! Xerox was going to cut me off because of a deal they had made with someone else? I called IBM and said I needed to lease a machine. "I'm fed up with Xerox. I'm trying to run a business, and their service is deplorable."

The salesman was quick to agree. "Well, we don't like to say anything negative about our competitors, but IBM is committed to service. I'm sure we can provide what you need to keep your business running smoothly." I signed a lease and apparently he never checked up on anything. I had a new IBM machine within a few days and didn't lose any business.

Cash was coming in, but there were a lot of unpaid bills and the pressure was getting to me. Andy was great working at the counter and running machines, but I needed help with the accounting. More than once I tried to get a friend to straighten things out. "I'll give you half the store's profits if you can sort out the mess." Several took me up on it; none lasted more than a few days, and they all left shaking their heads and saying, "Impossible...worst mess I ever saw."

Creditors were calling every day and I couldn't get anything done. Maybe an attorney could get them off my back. I decided to interview two and then choose one.

The first, Shane, was really nice; he asked me out for a drink. The second was as repulsive as a lizard in a suit. "I'll take care of everything," he assured me, looking me up and down. I told him I'd think about it and drove back to Shane's.

Shane's secretary buzzed him and told him I was there. Shane came into the reception room and escorted me back to his plush office.

"Well, what did you decide?"

"I decided I'd like to have a drink with you. But that means I'll have to hire Brunson, because I don't believe in mixing business with pleasure."

"Great!" he said with a smile. "Go ahead and hire Brunson, and instead of a drink, let's make it dinner."

Dinner was wonderful and now he wanted to take me out for breakfast the next day.

I agreed, but didn't expect the doorbell to ring at 8:00 in the morning. I threw on my robe and made my way to the door to look through the peephole.

"What are you doing here?" I asked as I opened the door. He was in tight jeans and a red t-shirt with white lettering that should have said "Coca-Cola" but instead said "Cocaine".

"You did say you'd go to breakfast with me, didn't you? I've got to go by the jail first to see a client and I thought you could go with me."

"Breakfast at this hour?" I yawned. "I never have breakfast before noon on Saturday or Sunday. But come on in. I'd better make coffee while I get dressed."

I threw on my clothes, we had our coffee, and soon we were at the county jail. A line of visitors stretched along several blocks. They all looked numb, as if they had discovered that life was bearable only if you shut off your feelings. I almost felt like one of them. I turned to Shane and asked nervously, "How long is this going to take?" I didn't want a long wait. "The coffee on an empty stomach is making me hungry."

"Not long," he said. "Follow me." Shane marched ahead, carrying his large elegant briefcase. It would have gone with a suit, but it didn't match his jeans and cocaine t-shirt. We were in and out in minutes, and as we left I felt sorry for the people who were still waiting to get in. They would get no short cuts. Maybe I didn't have anything in common with them after all.

We drove back to Beverly Hills for breakfast.

"JoAnn, what a nice surprise!" said Rebecca on the phone. "It's been a while since I've heard from you."

"I've been putting in long hours at the shop," I replied, "but I came home early tonight. I'm dressed for bed and have my glass of champagne, and I thought I'd call. I'm trying to come up with a way to keep my business running and to move Heather back in with me, but I needed to talk to somebody who wouldn't want something from me."

"What do you mean?"

"Everybody wants something. Xerox says I have to pay off the contract Vinnie signed with them, even though the paperwork says I'm not responsible. I shouldn't complain; the weird thing about Xerox is that they seem to have forgotten the $100,000 they claimed I owed them. But my suppliers all want me to pay for things I never even ordered. To top it off, there's a couple Bob and I used to know and their marriage is falling apart, and whenever I pick up the phone I have to wonder if it's the husband wanting a date. Then David still wants to marry me, and whenever I talk to my grandmother she pressures me not to let him get away."

Rebecca changed her voice. "Whatsamatter with you? So when are you gonna marry this guy? He has a Cadillac, he's already made his first million, and he'll take good care of you and Heather. You think guys like this come along every day? When are you gonna show up with a ring?"

"You're scaring me," I laughed. "You're too good an actress. You sound just like her."

"Oy vey, these Jewish women are all alike. Believe me, I catch it whenever I go home."

I asked, "Do you ever wonder if we're going to be like that when we get old?"

"Don't even talk like that!" she said with counterfeit severity. "Don't even think about getting old!"

"Well, back to the people who always want something," I said. "I have a question about Everett. I'm thinking about moving back into the Malibu house and Everett's lease has expired, but he doesn't act like he's moving. I wondered if you could give me any suggestions about how to approach him."

"Approach him? If I knew anything about how to approach him, we might still be married. Have you talked to him at all?"

"Sure; I see him every month when he drops off the rent, but he's still trying to get me to sell. Every time he hands me a check, he offers me a little more for the house. But his lease has expired, and it really is time for him to move out."

"Did you tell him so?" I heard an edge of uncertainty in her voice.

"I did, but he was like the tin man in The Wizard Of Oz – you know, the man that had no heart. We were out on the street in front of my store. He'd handed me the check and I said I wanted to move back into the house so I could be with Heather. 'You'd better look for something else,' he said, 'because I'm not moving.' I couldn't believe my ears. 'But you said Heather and I could move back whenever we wanted' I said – by now tears were running down my face – and he said, 'That was then, but this is now. Besides, you're wrong about the lease; it hasn't expired, and I'm not leaving.' And before I could think of what to say next, he said 'Look, I can't stand around talking about it now. I've got to get back to work – I know you have your problems, but I've got problems of my own.' And he got in his car and drove away, and I had to go back into my shop with mascara running all down my face."

"Oh JoAnn, I'm so sorry. I know what you're dealing with; now you can see why our marriage fell apart. When it comes to business, he's like a machine. And he never rests; everything is business to him."

She understood, and now my tears came gushing out. She listened patiently as I poured out the whole thing that had made me battle depression for the past few weeks: I couldn't live with Heather because I needed someone to look after her; I didn't have room for her and a maid in my apartment; I wasn't sure I could afford a bigger place because I wasn't sure what would happen with the business; I couldn't find trustworthy people to run the shop.

But I bounced an idea off her. I'd been thinking of buying another car, something fun to drive. "Maybe a sports car or a convertible," I explained.

"Do it," she said without hesitation. "You need to do something for yourself. You said you're working twelve hours a day? And when do you ever take a break? Do you want to end up like Everett?"

That got me laughing, and soon she started too. Then she started singing my favorite Janis Joplin song: "Oh Lord, won't you buy me a Mercedes Benz."

I chimed in, "Dialing For Dollars is trying to get in touch with me." We joked around for another half hour, and by the time I hung up I wondered what I would do without Rebecca. I was depressed when I called her, but now my face was wet with tears of laughter.

Just for fun, I looked at the want ads and there it was, the exact car I wanted: "1967 Mercedes-Benz 250SL, chocolate brown convertible-hardtop with tan leather interior. Excellent condition. Private party, one owner."

Impulsively I called and arranged to see the car. I took one look, and had to drive it. I wrote the check on the spot without thinking about whether I could afford it. I knew the check wouldn't bounce; that was all that mattered.

Then I called David. "You said to call you if I needed anything," I reminded him, "and I wondered if you have time take me to pick up my new car. "

"I'll make time. When would you like to go?"

Soon we were in his Cadillac. "A Mercedes!" he said. "I'm impressed. So this must mean your business has really taken off now that you've got the new machine?"

"Well, first of all, it isn't a new car; it's used. I haven't become a millionaire overnight. I still have to watch my spending. But I'll be okay, and you're right – the new machine did help."

A smile of satisfaction spread across his face. "I knew it would."

We both laughed, and now my guard was down. Suddenly, without thinking, I started pouring out the troubles I had had with Vinnie and Ray. "I really thought they could run the business and I could find a way to move Heather back in with me, but it all fell apart and I've had to start over."

I glanced at David and saw a faraway look on his face, the very reasonable and sincere look that came over him when his mind was taking what he had heard and turning it into a sales pitch. I needed to change the subject. "Hey, if you see a place to stop, I'd like to buy some gum."

He snapped out of it. "Whatever you want – there's a liquor store over there; they probably have gum."

We went in. David bought the gum, and on our way out a grubby man by the door stepped up to me apologetically and mumbled, "Can you spare a quarter? I've been down on my luck." He had the same defeated look I had seen on the people lined up at the jail.

"Here's a dollar," I said, handing it to him. Everybody seemed to want something, but for once I could give someone more than what he asked for. Without a word David opened the car door for me, then he got in his seat and we drove away.

"I never give to these guys," he said softly. "He'll probably spend it all on booze."

"It's only a dollar," I shrugged, "but you're probably right. Still, I always wonder what makes these guys end up like this. And who knows? The way my business is going right now, maybe I'll be the one bumming quarters by the door of the liquor store."

"Listen to this!" David said playfully. "You act like you're on the brink of bankruptcy while we're going out so you can pick up your Mercedes. Does this sound like anyone who's about to start having to bum quarters outside the liquor store?" If Rebecca's shtick had been Jewish mothers, David's was the Jewish patriarch.

"I guess you're right," I laughed, but I'd done it again. I was talking too much about personal things and making myself vulnerable.

"But since money is so tight," he continued, "maybe I'd better take you to dinner as soon as we get your car."

I wasn't expecting this, but I looked at his face. Where would I find anyone else so kind and so helpful? "Well, it really is sweet of you to run this errand for me," I said. "And dinner would be nice…"

So we got my car and I followed him to the restaurant. Whatever we talked about, somehow the conversation always came back to my struggles with the business and my desire to have Heather live with me. I kept chiding myself for walking into a trap, and sure enough, out it came:

"You know, it really would solve everything if you'd just marry me." He used his warmest voice and looked straight at me with his sincere brown eyes, and I almost tumbled in. "You and Heather would never have another worry as long as you live. You could keep your business if you want it, or you could sell it – you wouldn't need it anymore…"

It was sweet and I knew he meant it, but I also knew that once he closed the deal, everything would change. I thought about what Rebecca had said about businessmen who are like machines, and I had seen it already. Now I foresaw dinnertime conversations about sales projections and financial targets; I thought about country club membership and the numbing conformity that would go with it; I thought about life in the world Aunt Hazel had always reached for. Suddenly I was very tired.

We finished our dinner and I needed to go home. "I hate to have to leave so early," I said, "but I've got to start work early tomorrow."

He paid the bill and escorted me to my car. "Just remember," he said, holding the door for me as I got into my Mercedes. "Take your time. I'll be waiting for you."

I drove out and headed for home, but I was restless and the car was unbelievably fun to drive. When I reached Topanga Canyon, I impulsively turned right and ended up at the Topanga Corral.

I had never thought the day would come when I would go into nightclubs alone, but now I was thankful for the solitude. It was packed and I could look around and have instant friends or lovers, but tonight I chose to be alone and danced the set by myself.

The musicians took a break and I decided to go for a ride. It was warm out. I rolled down my windows and turned the stereo up full blast. I headed up the canyon and got on the freeway. There were only three other cars on the road: two that were far ahead and one that was way behind me. Then the car behind me caught up and started to pass. It was a red Corvette, but the driver matched my speed and motioned that he wanted to race.

I had never raced a car and I didn't know how fast mine would go, but I floored it and in seconds was up to140 M.P.H. I never got to open her all the way up because I was closing in too quickly on the cars ahead. The Corvette was far behind – I wondered if I had outrun him or if he had chickened out. I smiled to myself, knowing I was going to enjoy this car.

I drove home. Maybe I was being a fool. It really would solve everything if I married David. But was that what marriage was supposed to be, just a way to solve problems? It hadn't been like that with Bob. David wouldn't have raced the Corvette, but Bob would. He loved to race. He would have loved this car.

Twelve

THE DIARY, MY BEST FRIEND

Friday night rolled around soon and I got a call from Cyndi. "I'm free," she announced breezily. "There's nobody in my life anymore, and I can't just stay home on a Friday night! Wanna go out and find something to do?"

She picked me up around 9:00 and we went to all our favorite haunts. Everything was boring. "May as well go home," she sighed as she drove through Laurel Canyon towards Hollywood, but neither of us was quite ready to give up on the night.

Suddenly I saw a lot of cars parked on a side street. "Hey Cyndi, slow down – looks like a party." She hit the brakes. "See those two guys over there? Let's ask what's happening."

She drove up to them and now that I could see them, I wondered. One was tall, thin, clean cut and grey-haired – old enough to be my father. The other was my age, with scraggly hair down to his shoulders, his eyes twinkling as though he were enjoying a private joke. I put the window down. "What's going on?" I asked.

"Party time!" said the older one. He bent down so he could get a good look at both of us. "I'm Walt and this is my friend Wally, and we'd like to invite you to this party," he announced as Wally came over to the window and looked inside.

I turned to Cyndi and shrugged. "We've got nothing to lose. Nothing else is happening."

"I'll park the car," she said. A moment later we were walking up the steep driveway with our new friends to a large brick house atop a hill. We wandered from room to room, and it was the typical party scene with rock music blaring on the stereo as a haze of marijuana smoke drifted from one dark room to another. There were two kinds of hippies: those who had class, and those who bent over backwards to prove they didn't. So it didn't surprise me to see people sniffing coke and drinking. But as soon as I saw disheveled people draping their legs over the arms of the sofas and chairs and resting their feet on the coffee table, I knew it wasn't my kind of crowd. They were too cool to use ashtrays; they dropped their cigarette butts into unfinished drinks or empty beer cans.

Within minutes, Walt was ready to go. "I've already invited a few of my friends out to my place." He shrugged. "You're welcome to come too. I won't try to give you directions, but if you want, you can follow me in my car."

"It's fine with me," I told Cyndi. "I haven't seen any interesting looking men here. And these guys really do seem nice."

"Yeah, they don't seem threatening, but they're not my type at all. Still, who knows who might be at their house? Let's go."

His house had been built for Ginger Rogers at the top of Sunset Plaza Drive. The view was breathtaking as we followed Walt down the estate's long driveway; at every turn we saw another constellation of city lights sparkling far below us. At last we arrived at a beautiful two-story house, and he took us inside and showed us around.

"I give parties almost every weekend," Walt explained as he led me into a large room with a dance floor. "Sometimes I have an open party. Four or five hundred people show up – I tell my friends to put the word out, and who knows where they all come from? I like to be the disc jockey."

As I got to know Walt, I learned he and I had something in common: he had been widowed recently. "It's crazy," he sighed. "I surround myself with people, but the loneliness never quits. How do you replace…?" and the words caught in his throat and tears filled his eyes.

Instantly I was in tears too. "I know," I said. Here was someone who understood.

For the next few months, Walt's parties became my hangout. One night he hosted an English rock group and the house was packed. I went out to the front porch for air and watched people coming and going. A long Mercedes limo pulled up; the driver opened the door and at first I saw nothing but blonde hair, short skirts, and long legs as six girls spilled out. Then I saw that they all were fluttering around a dark-haired man handsome enough to be a model. I wondered who he was. The six girls were all trying to cling to him, and he seemed oblivious to them.

He tried to catch my eye as he walked up the stairs towards the house. What's he looking at me for? I thought. He already has six women chasing him; he sure doesn't need me. I turned and looked the other way. It was fun to be aloof towards men, though in this case I couldn't help being curious. He continued to try to get my attention and finally cornered me in the kitchen.

"My name is Tom," he announced. "Who are you?"

I never answered. Two blondes in his entourage crowded him and I ducked under the taller one's arm and got away. He didn't need me and I wasn't in the mood to compete with the blondes to try to talk with him. Anyway, it was time to go home.

Tomorrow was a big day. I needed to shop for a new outfit and go to my 10-year high school reunion. The kids with rich parents had always snubbed me and had kept me out of their clubs. But how many of them had made it on their own? It would be fun to drive up in my Mercedes and be as outrageous as possible. I decided to go to the reunion with the one openly gay guy in our class. We teamed up with another couple and all dropped acid before we left.

We arrived early and parked near the entrance. Everyone else drove up in Fords, Chevys, and Volkswagens. I made sure they noticed me in my Mercedes. But many didn't recognize me. People were gawking at me and whispering to each other, "Who's that?"

I began to realize why they didn't recognize me. I was a blonde now and wore sexy clothes that accentuated my shapely figure. Most of all, I now had the self-confidence that had eluded me in High School. It's all in the attitude, I thought as I realized how eager I had been to impress them ten years ago. Now I didn't care.

The evening passed quickly, and in a way I felt I had made a triumphant comeback of sorts – I had become richer even than a lot of the rich kids. But though everything had changed, nothing was different. I hadn't connected with them ten years ago, and I didn't connect now.

Walt had gotten it right: even if you surround yourself with people, the loneliness never quits.

It was warm the next morning. I put the top down and drove to Walt's. A few of us sat on the lawn and smoked joints and listened to Wally strum his guitar and sing.

As I was leaving, a red Corvette screeched around the driveway and the driver flagged me down. It was Tom, the guy with the blondes who had cornered me in the kitchen, and now he blocked me in. He had a slightly cocky look on his face, as though he were daring me not to be impressed with his good looks, his car, and his elegant clothing. "Where are you going?" he asked.

I thought I'd throw him off. "Are you writing a book?"

"Maybe," he said, not missing a beat. "Let's have dinner tonight and discuss it."

"I'll think about it," I said, as though there were a chance I wouldn't say yes.

"All right. We'll meet at the Troubadour at 9, after you think about it," he said. "I'd better get your phone number."

I gave him my number and drove down to the beach.

Now that the fun of the cat and mouse game had worn off, I was depressed. I wanted Heather back but couldn't fit her into my apartment, and where else could I go?

Restless, I called my attorney. He wanted me to go after Vinnie. I couldn't decide if this was the right thing to do. Everything was in chaos. I never knew what new disaster would arrive with the next phone call or the next piece of mail. The pressure was getting to me. I could see why people drop dead at 35 from stress-related illness.

It was overwhelming. As the afternoon wore on, my restlessness began to border on panic. I needed someone to talk to. I called David, but he wasn't in. I called my old boss, Nate; we had an on-again-off-again relationship and he was someone familiar.

"JoAnn!" he exclaimed. "Great to hear from you! What's going on in your life?"

"Well actually, I just needed someone to talk to and I thought of you. Do you have time right now? Or maybe you're in the middle of something...?"

"No, go ahead – let's talk."

So I started pouring it out. "Well, you've been in my store when Ray and Vinnie were working there. Making a long story short, I had to let them go – it turns out they were really bad news – and now I'm realizing I really had it made when they were there. All I had to do was pick up my check every month and get on with my life, and I was getting ready to move Heather in with me again. Of course that was all a mirage; they were crooks. Now I'm stuck: long hours in the store, a pile of past-due bills, an accounting mess nobody can clean up ..."

"Whoa! Slow down!" Nate interrupted. "I'm hearing too much too fast, and I can't keep up with it. I've got an idea: why don't you come over so we can talk about all this face to face?"

So I got in the car and drove over to Nate's. He was waiting for me and opened the door. "So it's JoAnn the flower child," he said, looking me up and down. I was still wearing the same jeans I had worn to sit on the lawn and listen to Wally's guitar.

"What do you mean?" I asked as I went inside.

He laughed. "I never know what to expect when I see you. You might tell stories of going out on the yacht the Kennedys chartered, or about a spur-of-the-moment drama as you cashed a check at the bank. You can be glamorous one day and a hippie the next, and somehow they're both the real you. I love the variety."

I ended up spending the evening with him, and the word "love" kept coming up. At one point it slipped out that he had gotten rid of his date so he could be with me. Several times he said he loved me. It was probably just my mood, but I didn't believe him – right now, I wasn't sure I could believe anybody who said, "I love you" – and for some reason, I felt not better but worse by the time I got home at midnight.

I stuffed myself with chocolate cake as I got ready for bed, and my mind kept running back to my business and its challenges. I realized I was starting to see through men. Attorneys Brunson and Gaston had both said they would "take care of me". They always said it charmingly, but I wasn't fooled. It was an ongoing battle to resist their advances, some subtle and some blatant. Was there a man anywhere who would see me as a person?

The phone rang at 1:00 A.M. "Hey baby, where are you?" Tom asked. "I waited for you at the Troubadour till midnight but you didn't show."

I'd forgotten all about him.

"Sorry, but I got hung up and couldn't make it," I said, "and I'm not feeling too good."

"Then come over to the Rainbow Club and I'll buy you a steak and you'll feel better," he countered.

I was full of cake, and I didn't really need a date or a steak at this hour. What I really needed was sleep. "All right, I'll be there in 15 minutes," I said.

The Rainbow Club was nearly empty by the time I pulled into the parking lot. I walked in and saw Tom sitting in a corner booth. I threw my purse in the spot across from him.

"What'll you have to drink, Hon?" he asked in a gentle voice. I was expecting him to try to put me on the defensive for making him wait, but he was tender instead and it disarmed me.

"Bloody Mary."

Tom waved for the waitress authoritatively and she came right over.

"Double Bloody Mary, and one more of these," he said lifting his glass, "and a nice New York Steak. Tell Danny to cook it just like the lady wants it…how do you want it, baby?"

"Medium rare."

I was intrigued: in the few times I had seen him, I had noticed something different in the way he carried himself: seemingly immune to the charms of the blondes at Walt's party, elegantly concerned about my needs as we sat in the Rainbow Club, and now commanding but gentlemanly as he ordered for me without even needing a look at the menu. "Who are you?" I asked.

"I'm just a guy who's tired of the Hollywood scene. I just gave up my apartment and put all my stuff in storage."

"Where are you gonna go?" I asked.

"To Europe – you wanna fall in love and come with me?" he asked.

"You're crazy," I said. "You don't even know me."

"Well, what better way to get to know you?"

We started to get to know each other while we ate. Tom said he'd had managed a few actors and some well-known rock groups. Now he was burned out. I told him about myself and said I needed to get home early so I could get a few hours sleep before I had to open the store in the morning. But one question led to another. The restaurant closed and we moved to Tom's car, still talking. Suddenly I realized the sun was coming up. I never got home that night. We went to Barney's Beanery for breakfast, and then I had to go straight to work.

The next evening I had a date with Shane but I wanted to see Tom again, so I faked a headache and cut the date short with Shane around 10 p.m. This gave me a few more hours with Tom.

The next week was a big turning point. Tom and I fell madly in love and he wanted me to move in with him. He seemed to have resources, so I laid it on the line. "I'll need a house with plenty of room for Heather and me, and I have to have a live-in maid because I have to spend so much time at work.

Things happened fast. He canceled his trip, rented a house, and hired the maid. He made a few calls and soon had taken an executive position at Holiday Inn. "On the side, I'll still manage a few rock groups," he said, "but only the ones that don't give me a bad time. Of course, most of them are pampered spoiled brats."

So it was time to move in, but how would we transport all of Heather's things? "Between your Corvette and my Mercedes, we still don't have a real trunk," I pointed out.

"There's always a way," he said, and he went to another room to use the phone. A few minutes later he returned with a smile and said, "It's all fixed up. I've hired a Mercedes stretch limo. We'll have all the room we need."

It was a thrilling and happy day for all of us. A famous architect had designed the house, and Tom couldn't wait to show me the basement. "I've been around and I'm not easily impressed," he said as he steered me down the stairs, "but you won't believe your eyes. It has a full bar and is designed to look like a cave."

I didn't believe my eyes, all right. It featured a gaudy pool table trimmed in gold fringe. To me it was an eyesore, but he was excited about it. "Very nice," I mumbled, trying hard to sound like I meant it. And why shouldn't I mean it? He was entitled to his basement; I was excited about Heather's beautiful room with its elegant flowery wallpaper. And I fell in love with the rest of the house and its rich wallpapers, fascinating nooks and crannies, and lavish moldings.

Within a few weeks I was falling out of love with Tom. I couldn't understand myself, but now that I had everything I wanted, it wasn't what I wanted after all. What was wrong with me? I called Rebecca and poured it all out. "I was starting to think it was men I couldn't trust, but lately I'm starting to think I can't even trust myself," I confided.

"Don't be hard on yourself," she replied. "If the chemistry isn't there, what can you do? Besides, you're talking like a married woman. Who says you have to stay with Tom for the rest of your life?"

"Maybe, but I can't help feeling like a rat. He's done so much for Heather and me; he's given us everything I asked for, and yet now I feel like I'm just going through the motions. I can't keep faking it. I think he's trying to settle down all of a sudden."

"Oh, goodness. But maybe he thinks that's what you want?"

"Not at all. All I want is to be able to live with Heather. To tell the truth, I'm already starting to go out with other men."

"And what's wrong with that? Okay, Tom's gotten a house and a maid, but does that mean he owns you? It sounds like Heather's the person you want to live with, not Tom."

"I'm sure you're right," I said. "I've talked to Everett again about moving back into my house in Malibu. He insists that his lease lasts until May. 'The best idea is for you to sell me the house and get another one,' is all he said, then he left me with the words, 'Think about it'."

"JoAnn," she said, "I'm so sorry." I noticed something. She was always the first to tell me marriage didn't mean anything anymore – it was just a piece of paper – but then she still acted as if she were responsible for Everett's actions, even though they had been divorced for more than a year.

"But here's the thing I can't get away from," I said. "I feel like something inside is broken. I get everything I want, and then it turns out I don't want it. Who knows? Even if Everett changed his mind and Heather and I went back home, how do I know I wouldn't regret it within a month or even a week?"

"Don't be silly. Do something fun – find another man – you'll bounce back."

But I didn't bounce back. My depression deepened. In the past, I'd always been able to break out of it by working hard or partying hard – there always seemed to be something out there that would make the pain go away. But now I wondered if there was anything to live for, except Heather. It didn't seem to matter what I wanted; as soon as I got it, I discovered I was as empty as before.

Within a week of my conversation with Rebecca, I found an apartment in the same building where Bob and I had lived before we bought the house in Malibu. I ordered the phone and turned on the utilities. The next day I scribbled Tom a note while he was at work. Then I rented a limo for Heather, the maid, and our things, and I gave the driver the address of the apartment. I drove over in my car to meet them, and the maid had us settled in and was cooking dinner by sunset.

I had left my new number with Tom and he called as soon as he got home from work and pleaded with me to come home. I told him I couldn't. He went to pieces and now I was the one like the tin man, heartless.

The apartment was cramped, but we managed to squeeze in. The maid looked after Heather when I went to work, but I would come home so stressed that every little thing Heather did wrong would cause me to explode. I felt so guilty I would cry myself to sleep every night because I'd been so unkind.

Shane asked me out every day and stood me up every night. A crazy thought shot through my mind: what if he was married? I had assumed he wasn't, but did I really know? I could come right out and ask, but what would I do if he admitted he was? Marriage was still sacred to me, but it might be better not to ask. It was less trouble just to accept his explanation that things were flaring up at work.

My emotions became my accusers as the days passed by. You're neglecting Heather. You're letting your business fall apart. You'll never make it alone. You'll never find anyone to replace Bob. You'd be better off dead. I knew to resist that one; who would look after Heather? But the accusations would continue. If you were gone someone would look after her, and then she'd be better off...

These thoughts kept coming at me and I couldn't drive them away. But one night I tucked Heather in bed and settled into my usual lonely night routine. My pressures all seemed to close in on me at bedtime like a thick cloud of bats. Often I was finding it hard to get to sleep, but I had learned to have a glass of wine a few minutes before bed. I lay down but couldn't sleep; thoughts kept coming. *Whenever you look after Heather you neglect your work, and vice versa. How are you going to keep going?*

An hour later I was still awake, so I took a sleeping pill. After another hour I took another and drank a little more wine. Eventually sleep came.

Sometime just before dawn I woke up with a start and smelled something burning. A chair had been pushed against the furnace and was smoldering. I quickly put the fire out and sat down on my bed. I realized I could have been killed because the only door out of my third floor apartment would have been blocked and I wouldn't have been able to reach Heather.

I shook my head trying to get rid of the drugged feeling and thanked God for keeping us safe. *How can I want to die one moment, and hold on to life so dearly when faced with death?* I asked myself as I made my coffee. *I must really want to live,* I thought as I heard Heather stirring in the other room.

I went around in circles for the next year. My mood swings deepened; I fell in and out of love; I often did outrageous things for a laugh. I tried one thing after another to get my business in order, and nothing seemed to work.

My friends and I took it for granted that we would all move from one sexual partner to another, but I began to notice that we were becoming more decadent. People began to invite me into three-way sexual relationships. Gay or straight, nothing was taboo. I began thinking I needed to move – I needed to get away from the crowd I was in.

By now, my diary had become my best friend, the only one I could talk to about what I was really feeling. This is how I was living:

OCTOBER 16, 1973 – Oh God, what do you do on a Sunday afternoon when all you want to do is kill yourself? I'm so lonely God, so down and so unhappy…Why is the world so lonely? We really are, God. Please help us all…

Somehow I got through the day. By the time the sun set I couldn't stand it any longer so I got on a plane and flew to San Francisco to spend the night with a guy I knew. I needed the diversion. It's a good thing I have a full-time live-in maid again.

NOVEMBER 2, 1973 – I thought I fell in love twice in the past few weeks and those guys are already history. One dumped me after a few days, which sent me plummeting into depression until a friend showed up with a pound of coke she had just smuggled out of Colombia.

We spent many hours enjoying her stash, and then I met a guy named Dean and spent a week with him. Problem was, whenever I went anywhere with him I'd see guys that looked more appealing, so I knew he wouldn't be around long. But he was an artist, and used a grocery bag to make Heather a great Halloween mask. She was a little afraid of it at first, but after we put it on she thought it was funny.

I told Dean I didn't feel good and went by myself to Walt's Halloween party. I dressed up like a rag doll and had a great evening. I met Rafael, a friend of Johnny's, who was dressed like a Catholic priest. I don't know where he got the costume but it really looked authentic. He kept throwing his robe up in the air and he was completely naked. That guy is something else.

My moods were like a poodle that had gotten off its leash, running senselessly wherever it wanted. I had everything going for me, but I never knew when a random happening would send me into depression.

One day I saw a lumpish middle-aged woman dragging herself up the stairs to a dingy apartment. It hit me: was I really any better off than she was? I drove a Mercedes and she probably took the bus. I was young and pretty and she was old and dumpy. If her phone ever rang it was probably someone boring; if mine rang it was probably a man who had money and good looks. But so what? I was as lonely as she was; and even if I had more money than she had, I probably had more to worry about than she did. At least her life was predictable.

As for worries, the economy was going crazy. A gas shortage had led to talk of rationing, and I wondered if I should sell the Mercedes. Meanwhile I got nervous about the bank. I had $60,000 in a CD and decided to convert it to cash. The bank manager was obviously upset; they didn't have the cash on hand and he had to set up a special delivery by armored car. It took them forever to count it, and then it didn't look like much when I threw it in my safety deposit box.

I was ready to sell Everett the house if he would pay me $10,000 more than the appraisal; then I could look for a small place to rent in Topanga Canyon. But the more I thought about it, the worse the idea seemed. What would I do with another $110,000? Put it in the safety deposit box? It wouldn't do me any good there.

But my moods had nothing to do with what was going on around me. In the midst of all this uncertainty I could be euphoric:

November 17, 1973 – I feel incredibly together today. Gary came over last night and we dropped acid. It was a good trip. Shane came over tonight and brought a couple of steaks. I told him I was in love with Gary and didn't want to be involved with anyone else. He was sweet and understanding and wished me the best.

Today I am in love with life. Contentment, serenity and peace are with me. I cherish these moments filled with love.

It's a waste of time to be unhappy, no matter what is going on. I should kick myself in the behind any time I'm not thinking as clearly as I am today.

It was never a problem to think clearly for a day or two; it was harder to keep it up. Things were never what they seemed. Life was full of surprises.

One night I took a drive through Topanga and stopped at the Center for dinner. I felt lonely eating by myself, and saw a couple of girls sitting near me who looked as if they couldn't afford a meal. I felt sorry for them and offered to share my dinner. They said they weren't hungry, but asked if I wanted to join them.

One of the girls at the table was Rachel. She looked like an artist: thick wavy black hair, olive complexion, a lot of big dangling jewelry, jeans and an exceptionally eye-catching tie-dyed top. It turned out she owned the Pleasure Dome on the Sunset Strip. It was a large high-priced boutique catering to rock stars, groupies, and movie people. "This top I'm wearing is one I've made myself and the jewelry is from my store. But I get to design things a lot more stunning than this when I custom make something for someone who needs something special for the Academy Awards and has a great body. I design it all myself and make the patterns, and I have a staff of seamstresses. My head seamstress and I make sure each piece is a work of art."

You never knew who was who around here. I realized I didn't look like a business-owner myself, dressed in grubby blue jeans and a tattered shirt. We had a good laugh about it, and they invited me to go to the Corral with them. I followed them in my Mercedes, and afterwards I visited Rachel at her house deep in the Canyon.

Her house looked like Rachel, exotic and artistic. It had a beautiful black lava rock pool, and she had decorated the house with things she'd collected from all over the world. Each item had its story. It made me start thinking about travel again.

But I noticed one other thing about the house: books everywhere. There were bookshelves full of books in a few rooms, but this wasn't enough. In every room there were stacks of books all over the place. "I don't think I've ever known anyone who's done so much reading," I said.

"It's what I do to unwind," she replied. I couldn't imagine unwinding with a book, but maybe it wasn't any different than watching TV at bedtime.

A few nights later I was at a party with Rachel and ran into a high school friend, Deanna. We caught up on old times, then she said the magic words: "I've been thinking about making a trip to Mexico, but I don't plan to go alone."

"Mexico? That sounds interesting. I've been thinking about making a trip myself, but I haven't decided where to go. What's in Mexico?"

"I like to go to Puerto Vallarta," she said. "Everything's there. We'll take a bunch of people – rent a big house – we all share expenses, and it costs next to nothing. Why don't you come along?"

"I'd love to, if I can bring my three-year-old daughter." I said.

"Sure, bring her along!" she said enthusiastically.

A few nights later Rachel and I went to the Saloon; it was a smoky bar full of 50-year-old men trying to score on all the young girls. "This is a real bore," I said. "I'm ready to get out of here as soon as you are."

"Then let's go," she said, heading out the door. On our way out I ran into a handsome guy dressed all in white. I looked up into his face and it was Tom, staring at me. I almost fainted. I said hello warmly, and he responded like an iceberg.

We went outside. "What was that all about?" she asked.

"Oh, just a guy I was seeing a year ago," I replied.

"Are you okay?" she asked, instantly protective. "He didn't seem very friendly. He wasn't giving you a hard time, was he?"

"Not at all," I said. If anything, I felt a bit guilty about the hard time I had given him. For Heather and me, he had given up his plans, rented a house, and hired a maid. And what had I given him? Nothing but grief. A lot of men had said they loved me and some had even said they wanted to provide for Heather, but who else had cared for us like that?

I wanted to change the subject. "Hey, did I tell you I'm thinking about a trip to Mexico?" I said. "I ran into my old friend Deanna at the party the other night. She's planning a trip to Mexico and invited Heather and me along. Do you think you'd want to join us? I'm thinking of going."

"Not my style," she said matter-of-factly. "But you go if you can get away. I'm sure you'll turn it into an adventure."

I called Deanna and said Heather and I would go. "Great!" she said. "We're getting quite a crowd. And don't worry about Heather; there'll be other kids for her to play with."

I made sure Andy was okay to run the business while I'd be gone. "I'm sure I can keep up with everything, but when will you get back?" he asked.

He sounded nervous, but maybe he needed reassurance. "I don't know at this point," I replied, "but Mexico isn't far away." There really wouldn't be a good way for him to get in touch with me, but I couldn't imagine why he would need to.

I went out with Gary and told him I'd be gone. He too wondered when I'd be getting home, and he took it in stride when I said I didn't know. I could read this two ways; maybe it meant our relationship was so deep we understood each other perfectly, or maybe it meant we would both find it easy to find someone else.

Or maybe this was just two sides of the same coin.

So the day came for all of us to pile in our cars and drive to Mexicali, where we caught the train to Puerto Vallarta. We had our kids with us; some of the locals had brought goats and chickens. I was glad I had gotten our own sleeper compartment for Heather and me. She loved the train, and I was glad for a change of scenery.

Someone had found a house we could rent together. We didn't mind that it was run down – that made it picturesque – but we hadn't envisioned being isolated in the desert far from town. We could manage the walk if we had to, but it was dusty and the sun was hot. Before long we were looking for another place, and as soon as we found it I put up the deposit.

We moved in. There was plenty to do in Puerto Vallarta, but Christmas was around the corner and I started missing Gary. I called to see if he could come down for a few days. "I'm realizing I may not be cut out for communal living," I said. "The people are fine, but it's Christmas. I need something less like a zoo and more like a romantic getaway."

He arrived the next day and we asked around until someone told us about Yelapa. It sounded perfect. You couldn't get there by road; it would take at least two hours to get there by boat. It was totally unspoiled: they didn't even have hotels. Instead, there were a few thatched huts available for rent on the beach.

We took one, and I fell in love with it. "I feel like we're stranded on a desert island," I sighed with contentment.

Within a few days, Gary had to return home. We took the boat back to Puerto Vallarta and went on to the train station. As we said goodbye, I told him, "I'm so glad we found Yelapa."

Thirteen

LIVING IN A JUNGLE HUT

I returned to the routine in our big house overlooking the city: going out every evening to the night club scene with "The Beautiful People"; always waiting for the next influx of weekly tourists; trips to the beach every day; drinking frozen daiquiris and smoking pot; falling in and out of love. Then one night I met Armando at a nightclub and he asked, "Do you want to come live with me in Yelapa?" Soon Armando, Heather, and I were on the boat.

He sounded rich. "My home is a villa in Paradise," he said with a smile, "but my business takes me to Vallarta every day – I have to commute by water taxi. But business is good; I have a maid who cooks and does the laundry."

The villa was a grass hut with no doors, no windows, and no electricity – electricity hadn't made it to Yelapa yet. If I got up in the dark I had to remember to slip into my Huaraches and light a lantern so I wouldn't step on a poisonous spider on my way to the outhouse. If we wanted hot water for a shower, Heather and I would search for wood chips during the day and put them in a container that looked a bit like a diver's tank; somehow it warmed the water.

I loved it. It would have been terrifying to live in Beverly Hills with no locks, but here I felt safe. Our hut sat on the side of a cliff with a view of the bay. Armando went to work in Vallarta every day, and then I had to use sign language to communicate with the maid. She would cook our meals of rice, beans, eggs, and tortillas whenever we wanted. She washed our clothes on the rocks in a stream where all the locals gathered each day to do

The view from our hut in Yelapa.

their laundry. Armando paid her a few dollars every week.

Life was simple. Most of the people in Yelapa didn't speak English, so Heather and I stayed to ourselves most of the time. We never ran out of things to do. Days melted into weeks. Armando didn't always get back at night; sometimes business ran late and he missed the last water taxi.

I wasn't sure if I believed him, but what difference did it make? Heather and I were content. Then one night Armando got back from Vallarta, late and drunk. "One woman can never be enough for a real man," he babbled, "but I want you to be my number one woman. You'll always be first, the one who will stay in my home."

So that's your trip, I said to myself. It was one thing to suspect, but quite another to know that he had other women. Maybe I'd been kidding myself about the whole thing. I took another look at this place I loved so much. He had acted like the richest man in the world when we met, but what could it cost him to rent this little grass hut? He was feeding us beans, tortillas, and eggs; he was paying a maid a few dollars a week to do our laundry and sweep out the hut every day. How much could it cost – maybe as much as $300 a month? As far as that went, how did I know the hut didn't belong to another of his girlfriends?

I knew it was the whiskey talking, but I let him babble. I decided I'd live with it as long as I was having a good time. Three days later, we left for L.A. I didn't mind leaving Armando, but I looked back on Yelapa with longing. It was safe, serene, simple. And Heather and I had been together again.

The flight to L.A gave me plenty of time to think. What if I moved to Yelapa? Maybe I could give Armando another chance; if things didn't work out, I could always find my own hut to rent. But Heather and I had been together. Wasn't that why I was working so hard, trying to keep the business going? We could live on next to nothing if we went back. Maybe it was materialism that had been keeping Heather and me apart.

By the time we touched down in L.A. I decided to get my things in order as quickly as I could so we could hurry back to Yelapa. I called Rebecca as soon as I got home and we went out for dinner.

"That was quick!" she exclaimed. "You haven't been home even 24 hours, and already you've made up your mind." The same words coming out of anyone else's mouth would have sounded like scolding, but coming from Rebecca it sounded like admiration.

"It was a simple decision," I explained. "First I left Yelapa and the sun was shining on the beach. I got home to grey skies in L.A. – it seemed like a sign – and immediately I felt the demands of our materialistic lifestyle. Ever since I went to Yelapa, I've been on a natural high. It's like going back to a simpler day and time, without the materialism and the crazy pressures we all live with."

"I wondered why you didn't want a joint," she replied. She took another long drag on hers, as if to underscore how strange my behavior had become. "But what are you going to do about all your connections here? What about Gary? And what about your business?"

"I haven't figured out the business yet, but I've talked to Gary. He said he's disappointed, but what does that mean? He seems to think relationships should go on forever. But why should they?"

"That's right," she agreed. "Who made up the rules, anyway? Maybe romance turns sour because people try to hang on too long."

"As far as that goes, so what if it lasts only six hours?" I said. "It sure beats hanging onto a sour romance because you're afraid of being alone. Look at me: I've been in love so many times I've lost count."

"Same here," she laughed. "I think we're in love with falling in love. And speaking of falling in love, you seem to have fallen in love with Yelapa pretty fast. Are you sure you want to make this move?"

"Absolutely."

"Well, I never would have taken you for the type to live in a grass hut without electricity, but it's your decision and I'm behind you all the way. What are friends for?"

I met Everett for lunch and we agreed on a price so he could buy the house. "You've made me the happiest man in California," he said with a big smile. "And what's this place you're moving to?" I launched into an enthusiastic description but noticed that he didn't seem interested. "Yeah, great," he added as we shook hands on our deal. "Whatever turns you on…"

I was at the store a few days later and Nate came in. I was used to seeing him in expensive suits, but today he had jeans, a T-shirt, and a Dodgers baseball cap. Nate had become a Dodgers fan? His ears had disappeared in a thicket of hair, and his moustache was so long I wondered how he could get food into his mouth. Ordinarily I would have dropped what I was doing and let him sweep me into his day, but I felt so together that I realized I didn't need to cling to him. So I was aloof, which didn't seem to bother him because he was stoned. He left a few minutes later.

I congratulated myself for passing a test. For the first time in years, I felt no need to cling to men. I could stand alone. Something about being in Mexico had given me new maturity and a new love for life.

Of course, it was easy to contemplate being alone. I had Gary here and Armando in Mexico.

That night, Julian invited me out, Johnny had a party, and Rebecca wanted me to go out dancing. But more than anything in the world I just wanted to cook dinner with Heather and relax, which is what we did.

Johnny thought I was crazy. "I don't know what happened to you in Mexico," he said. "Did they give you some new kind of mushroom? What have you been smoking?"

"No, it's nothing like that," I laughed. "The lifestyle was simple. I felt free."

"But why would you want to live in a grass hut in the jungle, with all you could have here? I don't get it."

"That's my point. What all can I have here? Diamonds? Does it really matter whether it's five carats or just a chip? Does it feed you or keep you warm or love you?"

"That's fine, JoAnn." A patient tone always came into his voice whenever he wanted to end a conversation. "I don't get it, but I don't have to. It's your life."

He really didn't get it, and neither did anyone else. They were all trapped in materialism, and it slanted their view of the world.

It was time to simplify. Days sped by rapidly as I stayed busy finalizing everything. It was a happy time. Armando called me from Vallarta; it was good to talk to him. Then I started going to nice places and meeting new friends. It was good to be out of the bar scene.

I gave each of my friends a favorite purse and gave away most of my clothes. I had met a lot of people who talked about the need to be less materialistic, but I hadn't met many who followed through. It felt good.

I arranged to trade my Mercedes straight across for a custom Dodge van. When I realized the owner of the dealership wanted my Mercedes for his personal car, I talked them into adding several custom features: a bed with storage space for clothes, oriental carpets that covered floors, walls, and ceilings, and color-coordinated throw pillows.

Then I paid cash for property in Antelope Valley, though I never went out to see it. I invested $30,000 in gold stock and it doubled in value almost immediately. Instead of feeling elated, I found the economy's fluctuations more disturbing than ever.

All through January I was more purposeful than I had ever been. I was proud of myself for not changing my mind, not even secretly. It was a natural high, and it carried me into February when I finalized the sale of my house to Everett. I had a lease at my apartment, but I managed to find a way to be evicted so I wouldn't have to pay any more rent. The last thing I had to take care of was to pick up the new van I had ordered. And it was only then, as I drove to the dealership, that I wondered: what on earth am I doing, moving to Mexico to live with a stranger?

By the time I picked up the van, I had decided not to go.

My natural high evaporated. I had been proud of my strong sense of purpose, but it had all collapsed like a house of cards. Now I felt stupid and unable to make decisions.

I let Armando know I wasn't coming back and he didn't even ask why. He'd probably met someone else.

Now I would have to find a place to live. It was a strain, but Johnny let Heather and me move back in with him. I went out to look for another apartment and ran into Jan, who had been my neighbor when Bob and I were first married. We chatted for a few minutes and she said she had become an accountant. "Oh really?" I asked. "I need an accountant. I've tried several, but they all say the same thing – everything's in too big a mess to straighten out."

"That's crazy!" she replied. "I never heard of anything like that. Don't worry, JoAnn; it's just a matter of sorting out the paperwork and then clearing up one pile after another, until it's all in order."

"Is that all there is to it?" I asked. So I had been right all along: if I could just find the right person, everything would fall into place. "You make it sound simple. All I know is I'll give you half ownership of the business if you can."

"I'll be there," she said.

So at least I was going to get my business in order. As I kept driving around and looking for an apartment, I realized I didn't like the van. I talked to dealers and looked at the want ads, and quickly realized I'd take a big loss if I tried to sell it. What could I do?

But what if it was stolen, and I could collect the insurance money?

I called a few of Bob's old friends – he had hung out with a rough crowd – and I found someone who said he'd take care of it for $200. "Not right away," I said. "Give me a couple of weeks. I want to be out of town when it happens."

"Good thinking," he agreed. "I'll wait for you to give me the go-ahead."

Meanwhile, I'd gotten into a relationship I wanted to get out of. I had met Gene at one of Walt's parties. He was witty and charming, and we went out for drinks the next night. That's when he told me he had been married for 18 years. Against my better judgment, I agreed to go out with him again. He took me to dinner and tried to paw me but I pulled away. "I can't do that," I protested. "Marriage is sacred to me. I don't want to have an affair."

But marriage wasn't sacred to Gene; he was an important movie producer and he was used to having starlets throw themselves at him. Why should he want me? It was crazy, but I kept seeing him. He was sweet and I loved his emotional stability. We had leisurely breakfasts in nice restaurants and long drives in the afternoons. He wanted to get me an apartment but I refused to be kept by a married man.

Then Rachel came up with the answer. "I've decided to go to Mardi Gras and Anita will be with me." That was her eleven-year old daughter. "Would you and Heather like to come along?"

"Sure, we'll go," I said. This would solve everything, getting me away from Gene and putting me out of town when the van disappeared. Besides, I'd always wanted to see Mardi Gras. "How soon are you leaving?"

"Next week."

I had to get ready as fast as I could. My business was $6200 in debt with bills piling up the week before I left, and Jan hadn't been able to get things in order after all. She had quit after only two days. So I ran things myself, putting in six days of hard work and long hours, and the cash came in to cover the debt. And just before I left, I called Bob's friend to say I'd be leaving and to arrange his $200 payment.

We flew to New Orleans. Rachel had booked rooms in a five-star hotel and we could watch the Mardi Gras parade from our hotel balconies. I liked this; it didn't feel safe on the streets, especially with our two children. But Anita enjoyed playing with Heather and was old enough to be a baby-sitter, so they were able to amuse themselves in the safety of the hotel room and Rachel and I could go out.

We met two men, Carl and Mark. They were clean cut, conservative, and well dressed. They had come just to see what Mardi Gras was like. "I'd heard it was wild," said Carl, "but it's too wild for me." So he and Mark invited Rachel and me to go with them to jazz clubs, Cajun restaurants, or places where we could hear down-home blues. We also went to a few graveyards to try to find the scene from Easy Rider. They had to leave before we did, but we exchanged phone numbers and Carl mentioned that he had been thinking of taking a break in L.A. "Maybe I'll see you there."

When they left, Rachel and I decided to rent a car and explore. We drove further and further out of town, and as we got out into the bayou we found the accents harder and harder to understand. "I don't know about you, but this place is giving me the creeps," I finally told Rachel. "I think we were safer with Carl and Mark."

"I think so too," she said. "I don't like the way the men are looking at us. How far out of town are we?"

We were closer to Lafayette than New Orleans. "Let's go to Lafayette and see if we can drop off the car there, and then we can fly straight home," I suggested. We stopped at the first phone booth we saw and I called the rental agency in New Orleans. Rachel stood outside the phone booth and listened to my side of the conversation.

"Yes, we have a branch in Lafayette," said the rental agent, "but you rented the car in New Orleans and you're going to have to return it to New Orleans." I turned on the charm, but all the sweet-talking in the world couldn't make him back down. "I didn't make the rules," he offered as though he wished they were different, "but that's the way it is."

Rachel had heard my end of the phone conversation. "I guess we'll just have to make the three hour drive back to New Orleans," she sighed as we got back in the car.

Sometimes I worried about Rachel. She was too serene. The one thing we had in common was that we both tended to sink into depression. But she would accept things passively, and found it remarkable that I always found a way to fight back. We had talked about our differences often, and agreed that we were good for each other. Her serenity helped me calm down. But whenever I thought life was unfair, my ability to find imaginative ways to fight back always seemed to inspire her.

"I'm not licked yet," I told her. "Look for a gas station and pull in." She did, and I found an attendant. "What would you charge to fix this car so it won't run?" I asked.

"So it doesn't run?" he asked. He couldn't have looked at us more strangely if I had asked him where I could catch the bus to Mars. "Why would you want that?"

"Never mind why," I said. "How much?"

He shook his head mournfully. "I guess I could disconnect a starter wire for five bucks." Rachel looked on silently, but her eyes were starting to twinkle.

Within minutes it was done and I called the rental agency again. "Now the car died," I complained. "At least we managed to roll into a gas station, but now it won't even start. I turn the key and nothing happens."

The guy on the other end really blew up. I could tell he smelled a rat, but what could he do? We left the car in Lafayette and changed our tickets to fly home from there.

"That wasn't so hard," I told Rachel with a smile. "Five bucks at the gas station, a phone call for a taxi, and now we're on our way." We settled into our first-class seats and the jet took off. Soon they brought out sandwiches. "This is first class?" I snarled, and I turned to Rachel. "My sandwich is dried out! How's yours?"

"It's a bit dry, but it's fine," she said.

"Send it back!" I urged. "We paid for first-class. We don't have to put up with dry sandwiches!"

"No, it's okay," she replied. "It's only a sandwich – how good does it have to be?" So while she ate, I tried to get something else. The stewardess did what she could but I really didn't have any other choices. I gave up on the sandwich and she brought out one drink after another.

"Nothing to eat," I murmured, "but at least the booze is free."

"I'm happy with whatever they want to give me," she said. "We've had a good trip, our girls have had a good time together, and now we're on our way home. I'm content." She sat back and closed her eyes for a moment, and then she turned back and looked at me. "I don't know whether to be thankful or worried," she said. "Your scheme at the gas station saved us hours of backtracking – and I really am thankful. But sometimes I worry about you, JoAnn."

"Worry about me?" This was puzzling. "What on earth for?"

"It's the schemes you always come up with," she said. Her smile looked tolerant but her eyes looked troubled. "I have to admit I'm probably a little too quick to roll over and play dead. But what about you? The schemes you come up with seem to take a toll on you."

I laughed. "It would have really taken a toll on me to have to drive that rental car all the way back to New Orleans just because some yokel in a back room somewhere thought that's how the business should be run."

"I know," she said with a sigh, "and I really am thankful that you came up with something." She laughed again. "I never know what you'll come up with!" But then a tone of deep concern replaced her laugh. "But it's you I worry about. How long ago was it that you wanted to leave everything and live in a hut in Mexico? I just get the feeling something in you is getting real tired of it all. I can't help it; I worry about you at times."

"It's friends like you that keep me going," I said. But her words had struck a nerve; it would be easy to collapse in tears. I reached for something funny. "Meanwhile, there's a mechanic in a gas station who's going to look like a genius when he manages to get the rental car going again."

"I can just hear him!" Rachel said with a broad smile. Then she imitated his drawl. "I can't tell you how it happened, Sir, but somehow a wire must have worked its way loose..."

We laughed about memories from the trip for the rest of the flight. The free champagne helped.

I got home and the van was gone, but I couldn't collect on the insurance right away. The police had to search first, and they called a few weeks later to say they had found it. "Somebody torched it," they told me. "There's nothing left but a shell." The insurance check arrived soon after.

That was one business deal taken care of, but there were others. I still had to decide where to live and whether to rent or buy. I still had to decide what to do with my business.

I had been to court and won a $28,000 judgment against Di Carlo, but I was afraid he'd kill me if I tried to collect. He didn't even know about it yet. The attorney had found a way not to serve him the papers but to get someone to verify that he was served. I told Brunson to hold the judgment; I had ten years to collect on it. Just because none of us could see how to collect right now didn't mean we wouldn't come up with something later.

I was good at getting things to go my way, but for some reason I couldn't shake off my depression. I would find a bit of paradise, whether drugs or another guy, but I would always come crashing down to earth in a few days or hours. What a joke…

David had sent me to a shrink once when we were together. The shrink had hypnotized me, but all he could find out was that I wanted to die. It cost a lot of time and money, and he had no answers – just, "Come back for another appointment next week."

Sometimes I would hear Heather whimpering in the other room. What could I do but embrace her and tell her everything was going to be okay. Was I lying to her? Nothing was okay. Would it ever be again? I didn't know. I loved her so much. I wanted to comfort her but my inadequacies haunted me.

I began to wonder if something was seriously wrong with me.

I needed another car, and Johnny talked me into buying a Porsche. "Of course you hated the van," he said. "You're cut out for something fun. Remember how you loved the Mercedes? You're going to love the Porsche even more."

"But I don't know how to use a clutch," I protested.

"You'll learn," he said confidently. "You may stall once in a while at first, but then you'll get the hang of it." I dreaded hills, and stop-and-go traffic was murder. I never did quite get used to it, but at least I could get around. And once I got it in the right gear, it really could be fun to drive.

I went to Rachel's store one day and was admiring some leatherwork I hadn't seen there before. "Who's the artist?" I asked.

"Oh, JoAnn, you would have to ask about him," she sighed. "I've been a little hesitant to tell you about Garrett, because I'm afraid of what will happen if you get together."

"What do you mean?"

"I don't know what to tell you. You and he are both crazy in the same ways." She shook her head and laughed. "I guess you'll see."

"But what does that mean?" I persisted. I had a feeling there was more she wasn't telling me.

She shook her head and laughed. "You're both outlandish and outrageous and very creative, and you're both your own worst enemies. But something tells me you're going to look for him until you find him, and then I guess we'll all see what happens."

When I walked into his shop in Marin County, our eyes locked for a moment as we surveyed each other. Then I looked around. I saw leather suits, vests hats, bags – everything was one-of-a-kind, a work of art. Then I noticed several young women who seemed to belong in the shop. I would learn that they were his seamstresses and that some lived with him at the house where he had his other workshop.

He stood out wherever he went. He was tall, with thick wavy brown hair and an in-your-face attitude; he always wore buckskin with fringe or one of the leather coats he had made. The only thing I didn't like about him was a snakeskin bag he always carried, but otherwise I was crazy about him. He was so unpredictable I never knew what would happen next. Heather and I moved in with him. If Garrett and I went out, one of the seamstresses would baby-sit Heather.

He drank a lot. More than once I saw him under the table in a bar after he had downed a fifth. Often the rest of us would be under the table too because we had tried to keep up with his drinking.

But he was also insanely jealous and possessive. One night, one of his friends was passing around some really good cocaine and I took it. Garrett started screaming at me. It scared me so badly I took off with his friend and Garrett came over to the guy's house, burst into the living room, and tried to drag me home. I was afraid to go with him so I spent the night, talking to the guy. When he went to bed, I curled up in a stinky blanket on the sofa. I felt like an outcast. I had to go back to Garrett's the next morning because Heather was still there.

I felt ashamed and humiliated as I walked in the front door. Garrett was sitting on the couch. "I waited up all night for you to come home," he said, "and you need to know this – I've never waited up for a chick before."

Things were really strained between us, and I needed to get away for a break. I called Rachel and she had the answer: "Wes is here!"

"Who is Wes?"

"He's a friend from way back. He lives in a Greyhound bus, and he's driving to New York. Here he is – why don't you talk to him?"

So within a few minutes I agreed to go to New York with him. It sounded like a great adventure.

Garrett didn't want me to leave, but we had gotten into a power struggle and I couldn't stay. I got my things together and loaded the car to leave. "So this is really the way you want it?" he asked.

"I don't know," I said, faltering for a moment before my resolve kicked in again. "But my mind's made up – I'm on my way."

"Well, I want you to have this," he said as he handed me an Indian necklace. I knew it was special to him. We both cried as I pulled out of the driveway, and we were both too stubborn to be the first to suggest if or when I might come back. We really were both crazy in the same way.

It took several hours to drive to Rachel's. By the time I arrived, I had thought about traveling with Wes. Who was this guy? Did I really want to trust my life and Heather's to a total stranger? I decided not to go.

Two or three weeks later, Rachel called me. "If you've had second thoughts about Wes, he's back in California," she said. "He's in San Francisco for the Grateful Dead concert." It turned out he was their manager, living with his daughter in the bus that served as a mobile office.

So I took Heather to San Francisco to meet them. Heather hit it off with Wes's daughter and wanted to ride the bus to the concert. So we decided to go to the Dead concert at Berkeley. "It's fun, Mommy. I've never gotten to play in a bus before."

"Just follow me," he said, adding with a laugh, "You shouldn't have any trouble keeping up with a bus in your Porsche."

It sounded good, but I hadn't thought about the hills. Wes took off and I followed closely behind the cumbersome bus as it made its way through the crowded streets, weaving in and out of the late afternoon traffic. Suddenly he went up a very steep hill. We paused at a stop sign and I couldn't control my car. I'd never been on such a steep hill and panicked as I tried to work the clutch. Wes turned right and drove on as I rolled backwards further and further down the steep street.

Finally, a man came up to the window and asked, "Do you need help with your car?"

"It's my first time using the clutch on these hills," I said miserably.

"I thought so," he said smugly. "I taught my old lady to drive with a clutch on these streets – almost turned my hair white," he said with a grin. "But if you want, I can get you to a spot where it's downhill almost all the way out of town."

Should I let him? Was it safe to let a stranger take the keys to my car and drive me to who knows where?" I looked at him carefully. His blue eyes sparkled with laughter, and his moustache broadened his smile. "I suppose I could use some help," I said nervously as I got out and went around to the passenger seat. He got in.

"The only problem is that my daughter is on a bus I was trying to follow, and I couldn't keep up with it. I'm supposed to be right behind her. They're on their way to the Dead concert."

"Whoa – bummer – wish I could go!" he said. "I'd take you there myself, but then how would I get back to my car?"

"Yes, but I really should be trying to catch up," I said. A bit of panic had crept into my voice. Where was this guy taking me? We'd already made some turns, and we had kept going up hills. "I don't even know your name!" I added.

"Wes!" he said with a grin.

"Wes!" I said, "I can't believe it! That's the name of the guy driving the bus!"

"Sounds like a sign to me," he said with a smile. "Well, if I were you, I wouldn't worry about it. Things have a way of working out! There you were, stuck in traffic, and suddenly someone came to drive you to safety. Who knows – maybe I'm not a man at all, but an angel that was sent to help you out."

"That would be great," I said. "Then you could find a way to catch up with the bus."

"Wish I could, but really I'm just a man," he laughed. "And I need to get going, but first I'll show you how to get out of these hills." He gave me directions, and thank God they were simple. All I had to do was cross the Golden Gate Bridge and head towards the safety of the flat familiar streets of Marin County.

He got out and glanced back at me. "I never even got your name."

"JoAnn," I replied.

"Take care," he said, and he was gone. There really are some nice people in this world, I told myself.

Where could I go? I decided to go back to Garrett's, and I walked in as though I had never left. Garrett was inking a design on a leather jacket, and he looked up at me for a moment, said nothing, and then went back to his work. Both of us acted as if we had never split up. Nonchalantly I went to the phone. There was no way to call Wes, so I called the police and explained the situation. "I'm sure everything will work out all right," said the woman at the police station. "We'll probably hear from your bus driver before the night is over. Why don't you call back in the morning to check?"

It was a long night. I anxiously waited for the sun to come up so I could call the police department, and they had good news. When Wes had realized we had gotten separated, he had called the police. They were able to tell me the cross streets where his bus was parked, so I could find him. Garrett drove me to San Francisco to meet Wes. As for Heather, she had had so much fun on the bus that it was hard to pry her off when it was finally time to say goodbye.

After a few chaotic weeks at Garrett's, I decided to go visit my sister Marie and her husband Ron, who lived in San Jose.

Ron had a day off, so the three of us took a ride through the Santa Cruz mountains, and I fell in love with the towering redwoods. We stopped in Boulder Creek, a little town not far away and in the heart of the mountains. I peeked in the window of a real estate office, and saw cabins for four to ten thousand dollars. One thing led to another. Soon a realtor was taking us to see a farmhouse on three and a half acres.

It looked like a storybook picture as we drove down the long dusty driveway and saw the house peeking through the trees. The house was part logs and part shingles, with a big front porch. We got out to walk the property. We heard a bell jingling in the cool spring breeze; it went with a cow that trotted down the hill to greet us. Everything about the place said "home."

I looked at my sister and Ron; their eyes were as big as saucers. I knew it was their dream house, so I bought it so we could all live there. This would be my chance to get out of L.A. and have the stability of a family life.

My sister, Ron, and the kids moved in after escrow closed, but things didn't work out. I'm not really sure what went wrong. I had an addition built so we could have separate quarters, but they bought another place and moved out while the workmen were completing the project.

The house was isolated and I didn't like being there alone, especially for the first few days as I waited for my things to be delivered. Should I get a dog? A shotgun? My things arrived eventually, and Ron came over to help me move them in.

The home life I had hoped for never materialized. I enrolled Heather in a Montessori school down the road and I still visited Garrett occasionally, but my mood swings continued. My loneliness increased and I was so isolated that sometimes I cried out to God for help, if there was a God. Sometimes I screamed as loudly as I could, hoping He'd hear me.

I felt I was on the brink of losing my mind. One day I dropped Heather. I didn't want to, but I couldn't stop myself. It was as if another person lived in me, someone I couldn't control. She was cold, hard, ugly. I was afraid she was taking me over.

By fall, I was living with an artist. We were invited to a Halloween party, and we put on our costumes in Santa Cruz and flew to L.A. I was a belly dancer and he was a 17th century earl in a pink ruffled shirt, pink tights, and an insane looking mask. I loved watching the prune-faced old ladies as we walked by. It was a rush to blow people's minds.

At the party I met Craig. Busted for selling a pound of cocaine to a narc four months ago, he was now facing three to five years in prison. I felt sorry for him and didn't want to leave him alone. But I had to go back home to Heather. She had stayed overnight with a babysitter.

If it had been fun to wear our costumes on Halloween, it was even more fun the next morning as we flew back to Santa Cruz. I picked up Heather, took her home, and called Craig. "I'm thinking about coming back to L. A.," I told him. "I've got a good lawyer and I'd like to introduce you to him. I think he can get you off. My only problem is that I'll have to find a babysitter for Heather."

"That's easy," said Craig. "There's a wonderful lady nearby who runs a day care center, and she loves kids. Often she lets them stay overnight. I'll show you where she lives; you can take Heather there and check it out for yourself."

So we packed up and I took Heather to L.A. I asked around, and we found the day care center. I noticed the children all seemed happy there. So did Heather; immediately, she ran off to play with them. I moved in with Craig.

Then I put Craig in touch with Shane. He listened to Craig's story and said, "From what you've told me, I'd say you have a 100% chance of going to jail with your present attorney; with me, I'd say 40%. But I have a friend who's an attorney; he plays golf with the judge. If he'll take your case, and I'd say you have an 80% chance to get off." We contacted the friend, and he said he would need $10,000 up front to take the case.

Where could we raise $10,000? We talked to Craig's wealthy aunt and uncle, but they refused to help. I wondered if I should lend him the money myself, but I talked with Shane first. "I know how it feels to want to help out," he said, "but how long have you known Craig? Sure, he's likeable; but what do you really know about him?"

Craig really was likeable. He always had good dope and he was fun to be with. Late one night, a friend dropped in with LSD he'd just picked up from a chemist. We dropped it at about 2:00 a.m. and contemplated hitchhiking to Denny's for breakfast. Instead, Craig ordered a limousine and I called Johnny at 6:30. "Wake up!" I announced when he picked up the phone. "It's me, and it's time to make the coffee – we're on our way over!"

"JoAnn, do you know what time it is? It's 6:30 in the morning." He sounded a bit fuzzy. He wasn't quite awake yet.

"That's what I'm trying to say – it's time to make the coffee. You'll see the limousine pull up in front of your place. I'm with Craig – you haven't met him yet, but you'll like him. He's a lot of fun. See you soon!" And with that, I hung up.

Johnny and his girlfriend Julie were ready by the time we arrived and we drove her to work. I had the chauffeur deliver fireworks to one of Garrett's old girlfriends, and then we went to the Old World for breakfast.

We dropped some more acid after breakfast and snorted a bunch of coke. We got so stoned we ran out of ideas. "Just drive anywhere you like," we ordered the chauffeur. "We don't feel like making any more decisions." After 12 hours, we had him take us home and collapsed in bed.

"Yeah, he sounds like fun," said Shane, "but I'm still asking how well you know him. What if he has a dark side you don't know about? Are you prepared to lose $10,000?"

"Not really." Shane had gotten to know me pretty well; when he put it like that, there was no way I was going to loan $10,000 to somebody I barely knew.

"I didn't think so," Shane continued. "So if you're determined to help this guy, use your imagination. I'm sure you'll come up with something."

Fourteen

MY HOLLYWOOD HILLS GAMBLING PARTY

We came up with a plan as soon as Craig introduced me to his friend Lance. "His Dad owns a bunch of hotels in Vegas," he told me. So when we discussed how to raise the money for Craig's lawyer, naturally we decided to have a gambling party. Lance had the connections to get roulette wheels, slot machines, and so on. He and I agreed to be the bank and we each put up $7500.

One of Craig's customers had a large, beautiful house, and that's where we held the party. We discreetly invited about 400 people. I smoked some angel dust early in the evening and was having such a good time that I didn't pay much attention to what was going on with the money. But I knew we were doing well; I saw piles of it.

Around 4:00 a.m., Nate was lecturing me about the risks I was taking when someone shouted, "Police!" People started escaping out of the doors and windows. I stepped outside and saw helicopters with search-lights overhead. Not for me. I didn't really want to jump fences and trudge through the mountains in the dark. Besides, I didn't want to miss the excitement inside. I was stoned, and it looked like fun.

The police burst through the front door, brandishing rifles. "All right, everybody – in the foyer!" they commanded as they moved through the house. "Right now! Hands behind your heads! Everybody! In the foyer!"

It was an unforgettable sight. The guests obeyed and gathered in the spacious marble entryway. They looked like something in a surrealistic painting: formal attire, hands behind heads, elbows sticking out like wings. The officers kept shouting directions, and several on the balcony and circular stairway kept their guns trained on us as though we were dangerous criminals.

It was too late to escape, but it wasn't too late to get rid of our drugs so we wouldn't get busted for possession. I was directed to sit down and the guy next to me furtively stuck his stash under my rear. I was mad

enough to choke him. I kept my eye on the officers until they looked
away, then I slipped it quickly into a planter. I saw Craig throw his
dope into Kaitlyn's lap and she was the first one arrested for possession.
What a rat, I thought. This is the guy I'm trying to raise money for?

We were all frisked. Rafael and Rick were handcuffed, along with
many other people. We all had to wait in the foyer to be interviewed.
What was I going to do? Sooner or later, someone would find my purse
with coke in it. Just then, a cop came into the foyer, waving my driver's license with one hand and the vial of coke in the other and calling, "JoAnn Dejoria? Where is JoAnn DeJoria?" I didn't respond. I
didn't look like the innocent picture on my license any more; maybe
they wouldn't make the connection.

A few minutes later they moved me into the living room for question-
ing. "What is your name?" the officer asked.

"Mary Stevens," I said calmly.

"What are you doing here?" he asked.

"Officer, I'm so frightened," I said, looking as innocent as I could. "I
was invited to this party with my friends and had no idea what would be
going on. We got here just before you showed up."

"Are your friends here?" the officer asked.

"I don't know what happened to them," I answered. "They seem to
have disappeared and abandoned me." Now my eyes filled with tears.
"I just want to go home!"

It sounded so convincing I almost believed my own story. I was
among the first they released, and I walked serenely out the front door.

But I was running by the time I passed a patrol car, and a voice called
out to me. "JoAnn, how did you get away?" I couldn't see his face in
the dark, but I recognized Rick's voice, curdling with the injustice that
he was under arrest and I was getting away.

But I'd never get away if a cop overheard him calling me JoAnn.
"Shut up, you jerk," I hissed as I passed the car, and I ran towards the
first moving vehicle I saw. Who was in the car? I didn't know and I
didn't care. I waved; the car stopped; I opened the door and jumped in.
I just wanted to get as far away as I could as fast as I could.

The police stopped us about five minutes later on Santa Monica Blvd.
They searched the car and found a few joints but let us go. They seemed
to be looking for money, not drugs.

I got back to Johnny's. It was late but I couldn't sleep. I was upset with Craig; I wondered if I would ever see my $7500 again; I couldn't be sure the cops wouldn't use my license to track me down. I went to the freezer and got into my wedding cake – I had kept it in Johnny's freezer for a few years – and sometimes when I was really upset I would cut off a little piece and eat it. I ate a few pieces and closed the door.

I scribbled as much of the story as I could in my diary before my few hours of fitful sleep. I woke up with my insides tied in knots. Even the weather seemed to be upset; a cold hard rain was falling, unusual for California. I wrote more in the morning. Writing always helped me sort things out.

The first call was from Johnny, and he was excited. "You made the news! I read the article in the *Herald-Examiner*."

I went out later and got the paper so I could clip the article and save it. They hadn't had to send reporters; the editor had firsthand information because he had been at the party. He had left with a few lawyers just a few moments before the police had arrived. The article is on the next page.

I tried repeatedly to reach Craig, but couldn't get through. What's going on? I wondered. He's never been hard to reach before. Why hasn't he tried to call me? Surely he isn't trying to avoid me. But no, that didn't make sense. Why would he be avoiding me?

Several people called and told me they had seen Lance stuffing money into his pockets before he took off. Apparently, he got away with the crowd that escaped and took a wad of money with him.

Then Shane called and asked me to meet with Tyler, the lawyer who had asked for the $10,000 retainer before he would represent Craig. They had talked to people who claimed they had seen Craig stuffing money into his shirt before he escaped.

"You're making it sound like Craig's running off with the money," I said, suddenly sticking up for Craig. "Things were happening pretty fast last night. There's got to be a mixup of some kind."

"Have you talked to him?" Shane asked. He said it gently but his question was going somewhere, and he wasn't about to back down.

"Well, no; I can't seem to reach him, but I'm sure I'll hear from him soon. It really was a crazy night," I explained. "He's probably playing it safe and hiding for another day or two."

"You're right about that; he seems to be hiding. But the more we learn about this guy, the more we're finding that he's really bad news. Several

Los Angeles Herald-Examiner, Sunday, December 1, 1974

Police Raid Hollywood Hills Party

Hollywood Hills home, 8818 Thrasher, where police raided "Jet Set party" early Saturday.

Police vice officers Saturday raided what they called "a Jet Set gambling and cocaine party" at a luxurious Hollywood Hills home taking eight persons into custody as an estimated 150 others fled out windows and doors.

Jeffrey Duffell Russell, 25, identified by police as the owner of the house at 8818 Thrasher Ave., was held on a booking of operating a gambling house. Seven others were held on possession of cocaine bookings.

Raiding officers said they confiscated two roulette wheels, six blackjack tables and two ounces of cocaine.

"This had all the earmarks of an organized gambling operation," said police Lt. Dan Cooke. The raiding party also seized an estimated $10,000 cash they said was spread around the house and large numbers of $20 chips bearing the logo "King's Crown, Las Vegas."

Long after the pre-dawn raid, police said they were still unable to identify all of those arrested.

William Schell, Larry Shulman and Miguel Rodriguez, ages and addresses unknown, all went free on $1500 bail shortly after being booked for possession of cocaine, said police.

The Herald-Examiner learned the party got underway about 9 p.m. and that an estimated 400 persons came and went between 10 p.m. and 2 a.m.

Arriving guests were greeted by uniformed valet parking attendants. Doormen posted inside a metal grill work checked guests names against a master list and in some cases demanded identification, said the sources.

Dealers distributed cards from large gambling shoes at three blackjack tables in a downstairs living room while partygoers crowded around a spinning roulette wheel in an adjacent dining room, sources said.

It was also observed that heavier bettors were receiving free drinks while others were paying for drinks at a bar in an alcove off of the living-room.

Two sergeants and 10 uniformed officers entered the house at approximately 4:30 a.m. Police first mistakenly attempted to enter a house across the street, said a neighbor.

When the gamblers saw the uniformed officers, panic spread through the house, and an estimated 150 persons fled through rear doors and windows, police said.

One woman, later booked on possession of cocaine, was found nude by police in an empty bathtub, said authorities.

people claim they saw him stuffing money into his shirt before he got away, and we've got to make sure we get your money back," Shane said.

"Money? Right now that's the least of it," I said. "I care about Craig. The money will sort itself out later." But my words trailed off as I was digesting the ugly picture of Craig that was starting to emerge. Fact: I had seen him toss his stash in Kaitlyn's lap and now she was facing charges for possession. Fact: other people had seen both Lance and Craig grabbing the money and escaping. Fact: I had been trying to call Craig all morning and couldn't reach him. Was he simply hiding from the police, or was he hiding from me? Why was I determined to believe the best about Craig? I had never felt so betrayed.

Suddenly I saw Shane differently. He didn't have it in for Craig; he was simply trying to protect me. I had let my feelings for Craig stop me from asking the hard questions I should have been asking all along. But Shane was helping me put two and two together.

Shane gave me a moment to think before he spoke again, and again he was firm about Craig but gentle with me. "We're really disgusted with this guy," Shane continued. "Of course, if Craig comes up with the $10,000 now, that'll show us that he really did stash quite a bit of money. In that case, Tyler is going to see to it that he gets the maximum sentence. Who knows? Maybe Craig wasn't frisked."

I met Shane later at a classy bar and we sat with our drinks on plush sofas and chairs. I put my feet on the coffee table. "We've got to track down Lance," he said as he slipped his arm around me, "and I've brought you the card of a good private detective. You need to hire him."

"There's something I forgot to tell you," I said, taking the card and glancing towards the entrance. "Garret might meet me here."

"Garrett? I thought he was in Marin County."

"He's moved here," I went on. "Some businessman is backing him and got him a house in the Hollywood hills, and we found a great spot for his shop on Rodeo Drive. He's hit the big time; Barbra Streisand just bought one of his coats."

As I finished talking, I saw Garrett coming in. Our eyes met and his greeting drowned out all the other sounds in the bar. We motioned for him to join us. He plopped down on the sofa and put his feet on the coffee table too, crossing my legs with his own.

Shane immediately stretched out his legs and put them on top of Garrett's and mine.

There was a light-hearted tone to it all, but also an undercurrent. Garrett and Shane both knew about my involvement with each other, and without words they were staking their claims.

They couldn't have been less alike: Garrett in platform shoes, glitter socks, twice-patched blue jeans, embroidered shirt, hand painted leather jacket, and carrying his snakeskin bag; Shane in Gucci shoes, black suit, and tie.

We brought Garrett up to date on what had happened at the gambling party. "Creative problem solving!" said Garrett. "Only problem is, it creates more problems than it solves. We'd better have another drink!" he roared enthusiastically, as though we were celebrating.

"Not for me," said Shane. "I've got to drive home." Then he turned to me. "I could solve everything. If you'd just marry me, I could work everything out." Then his voice became playful. "A Beverly Hills lawyer is quite a catch."

"Ha!" Garrett countered. "How about a successful Beverly Hills designer? She'd be better off with me," he teased.

But if possession is nine tenths of the law, Shane had the closing argument. "I've been waiting for her to marry me longer than you have," he said to Garrett. And with that he left.

"I can't be here long," I told Garrett. "I've got to go to the babysitter's in a few minutes to pick up Heather. We're trying someone new, so I can't be late. If things work out today, she's going to stay with her until I get things sorted out."

As it worked out, I didn't have to watch the clock. Suddenly they had to evacuate the bar; someone had phoned in a bomb scare. "It's just as well," I said to Garrett as we walked out. "I have to go get Heather."

The new baby-sitter was Sofia, Rafael's mother and a teacher for the Head Start program. "Heather was fine," Sofia said when she answered the door. "We're all set for tomorrow."

Heather chattered all the way home. "I'm going to start school tomorrow!" she announced.

"I know. Are you excited about it?"

"Yes, I am!" she said, and she poured out stories of new friends she had met and games she had played. We got home and I tucked her into bed. "I can't wait for the sun to come up," she sighed happily as I turned out the light, "because then I can go to school."

I felt lonely as I went to bed. Heather and I would be separated again. I longed to give her a home, a daddy, even a Christmas tree, yet it was unfair to keep her with me when I was so unstable. I wanted normality, whatever that was, but instead was drowning in a sea of booze, drugs, and aimless days.

I got up to take something for my stomach. My fear of being separated from Heather again had made me feel nauseated. Even now when I was in one room and she was sleeping in another, I missed her. What would it be like when she went to stay with Sofia?

Still, I couldn't get around it. Heather needed children to play with and a regular routine – two things I simply couldn't give her.

I got into the frozen wedding cake again before I went back to bed. I finished all of it but one last rose, a dollop of rich frosting. I saved it for later.

I hired the detective the next morning. His team had names like something out of a B-movie – "The Eliminator" and "Fat Bob" – and I had to take them for a drive to show them where everyone lived. But it wasn't a movie; it was real.

Later, Shane called to say Craig came up with the $10,000 for Tyler. He reaffirmed their plan for Tyler to go into the judge's chambers and ask for the maximum penalty. "I still can't believe the way he messed with you," he said.

Now that Heather was gone, I left Johnny's and rented another room in Laurel Canyon. It belonged to Simone, who was leaving for Mexico with Rafael, and the house had a huge swimming pool on seven acres. Seven other people lived there; I had already met four. I didn't want to live alone – not with the mess with Craig and Lance. Besides, other people might help distract me from the deep loneliness that was settling in now that Heather and I were separated again.

Early the next morning, the detective woke me with a phone call, asking a bunch of questions. "We think we've found Lance," he said, "but we need you to go with us so we can get a positive ID." This meant I had to drag myself out of bed, get dressed, and sit in the detective's car, waiting to see if Lance would step out of the door.

"A few of my muscle boys broke into his place last night," he told me as we sat beside a house. Nothing was stirring. "He'd completely cleaned it out – only thing they found was a few maps of Mexico. But he must really think we're suckers to fall for that one."

The morning fog in my brain hadn't lifted yet, but even I understood what he meant. "I guess if he were really going to Mexico he would have needed the map," I said.

"You got it. It's the oldest trick in the book. Meanwhile, one of my boys talked to an informant. The guy said Lance just spent what he called 'a lot of money' to buy two pounds of cocaine. And it turns out his Dad owns a couple of hotels in Vegas and – get a load of this – he was indicted for criminal activity last week."

We sat in the car, sipped coffee, and watched the house. "But you can't be too careful with this guy," the detective droned on. "He's bad news…" I started tuning it out; I'd heard this same story about Vinnie. But at least we were tracking him down.

After two long hours passed and we didn't see Lance, I went home. One of the girls who lived in the house was in the front room, and I introduced myself. Her name was Melinda, and we quickly discovered we had a lot of mutual friends.

"I can't believe you know Garrett!" she gushed. "Did you ever meet Paige? She used to live in the room you have now, but now she's living with Garrett." Now Melinda's eyes widened and her face turned serious. "She's an out-and-out witch. I don't mean it as a put-down; I mean that she's really involved in witchcraft."

I wasn't surprised. I had seen her large collection of books about witchcraft at Garrett's; they had been living together before I had moved in. And I had met her a couple of weeks ago. Rafael had taken me to Garrett's and Paige was there. We all went out to a concert together and then to dinner. I didn't sit at Garrett's table; Paige was furious that he had invited me along. She tried to get him to leave, but he wouldn't. So she started screaming that she would hitchhike home. Garrett didn't pay any attention, and at 2 a.m. she walked out to make good her threat. We went back to the house and sat on the porch. Paige was already home; she came out and told Garrett that if he didn't come in the house she wanted him to take her to the airport. He ignored her, and I enjoyed tormenting her. Somehow we eventually ended up at his dining room table drinking wine and laughing till sunrise. This was how I had met Paige.

Melinda continued. "There was one night when Paige got a bunch of spirits flying around. One of the girls was so freaked out that she packed up and left that night. Her rent was paid ahead, but she never came back, not even to get a refund."

I laughed. "It might be exciting to see spirits – even better than watching TV."

"It's no laughing matter," said Melinda. "You don't want to mess with Paige, or she'll put a spell on you."

"I'm not worried about it," I replied. And I really wasn't.

A couple of weeks passed. At four o'clock one afternoon, Lance called. The connection was bad; it sounded like long-distance. He started screaming. "I'm gonna kill you! You, John, Craig, and Shane – somebody with a knife just ripped off $4000 from Cody!"

It made no sense. "Who's Cody?"

"You know who he is – he's my partner!" He kept screaming threats and I tried to reason with him. Eventually he calmed down for a few minutes. "Fact is, there wasn't any money to escape with at the party," he lied. "We were way in the hole." I told him people had seen him and Craig stuffing their clothes with money before they left. He began screaming again. "I don't have to put up with this! If you don't get the $4000 back to us by 10:00 p.m., you're dead. Don't go to your car; it might blow up. Don't go outside; you might get shot."

"Call Shane!" I screamed as I slammed the receiver down. I was shaking, more from anger than from fear.

But I was the one who called Shane. He listened to the story then said, "I wouldn't worry about it. Usually people don't threaten you if they're really going to do something. Either they talk about it, or they do it."

A few hours later the phone rang again. It was Cody. "I've talked to Lance," he said, "and we've decided to shine on the $4000." Apparently Shane was right.

"That's great," I said, "but what about my $7500? Return the rest of my money, and the heat will be off. And while you're at it – I'm not afraid of your death threats. You want to blow me away? You'd be doing me a favor!" I slammed the receiver down again.

And it was exactly how I felt. My days were meaningless and my nights were unbearably lonely. I was going nowhere. Several times in the past few weeks I had gotten so down I would pound my head against the wall. Why? I wasn't sure. It was like the time when I had dropped Heather: sometimes it seemed someone else living in me would take over.

Fifteen

ARREST IN MEXICO

It was the week before Christmas. I was living a contradiction, surrounded with people yet unable to shake a deep loneliness. I was drifting from one event to another, all seemingly unconnected. But these two weeks would bring an unexpected change to my life; later I would look back and realize I should have seen it coming. Here's what I wrote in my journal one night:

December 20, 1974 (During an acid trip)
I'm writing to nobody trying to reach somebody. Oh no, the telephone keeps melting when I try to call somebody. Oh help, all that effort and I got the service. Nobody is home and I can't stay on the ground.

My insides want to come out. I'm so lonely. Somebody, please help me. Nobody wants the pile of garbage; everyone wants roses. I'm so cold but the news said it was 90 degrees. It was hot till the acid came on. It's just my lonely soul freezing.

What was wrong with me? Shane and Garrett both said they wanted to marry me, and all I wanted was to have a normal family life – the smell of bacon on a Sunday morning, a walk on the beach with a husband and Heather, time to draw pictures in the sand. But whenever I reached out, it always seemed nobody was there. It was easier just to lie in bed. What would happen if I never got out of bed again?

We went home. My friend Lorraine called and insisted I meet her at a party. "I've got a new boyfriend – you've got to meet him!" I got there, took one look at him, and oh no! Was he an old lover of mine? I wasn't a hundred percent sure I recognized him, but I felt really awkward. I decided to pretend he was a total stranger and I was meeting him for the first time.

A few minutes later he cornered me in the kitchen. "JoAnn, what's going on? You're acting really weird, like we don't even know each other."

"I'm thinking about Lorraine," I told him. "You're with her now – why tell her about us? Besides, it's over."

"It doesn't have to be," he said. Oh no, I thought, here we go again. "Don't get me wrong, Lorraine is cool. But you and I could really get something going."

"Not now," I replied. "I've gotta go." I managed to escape from the kitchen and get into a crowd of friends where I thought he wouldn't try to bother me again. But he kept following me all over the house. Several times he said, "Let's slip. The party can go on without us." My mind began to close off and finally I ran out. I screamed my head off all the way home.

I called Garrett's when I got back and Paige picked up the phone. "Whoa!" she said. "What's happening? You sound really out of it." Normally she sounded jealous, but this time she sounded worried. "Why don't you come over?" I did, and she served Garrett and me a snack in the dining room while she and her brother ate in the den.

"You know I love you," Garrett said as soon as she left us alone. "Let's run away and get married."

"Impossible," I sighed. I had two businesses here; he had moved his business to Beverly Hills and it was just starting to get on its feet. It was no time to run away and start over.

"Come on," he wheedled, "You know you love me as much as I love you." It was true, but this was no time to talk about it. Paige was just one room away. What if she walked in?

"I can't talk about this right now," I said. I heard movement in the other room, and the door swung open.

"Just getting a beer," said Paige cheerfully, passing through to the kitchen. Garrett was slumped down in his chair, staring glassily into space as though he and I hadn't been talking at all. I was annoyed; he was overdoing it. Did he really think she would believe he had been sitting there in a stupor, as though he and I weren't alone in the room? She came back with the beer and shut the door behind her when she left.

Now Garrett leaned back across the table and looked me in the eye. "Really, JoAnn. Why not? What are you waiting for?"

And this is how the conversation went on – Paige kept coming in and out, Garrett would have one personality when she was in the room and another when she wasn't, and I felt as if a vise was slowly tightening on my head. Paige had to know something was going on; she kept finding reasons to come through the dining room. Finally I couldn't take any more. I jumped up and ran out, not even bothering to say goodbye.

I was crying when I got home, but our neighbor Jay saw me get out of the car. "Hey JoAnn, come on over! I've got some really good weed!"

It was what I needed. I crashed a few hours later.

Bob had been gone for more than two years now, and this would be my third Christmas without him. Where was my life going? If only I could get used to being alone! But however hard I'd tried to be strong, I couldn't seem to function without a man. I'd gone from failure to failure, not because of a shortage of men, but because I always managed to find the wrong one.

Life had made sense when all I had to do was take care of Bob and Heather, but I couldn't go back to those days. Without anyone to cook for it didn't seem worth the bother to prepare a meal. I wasn't eating much; the sun would go down and I'd be ravenous, but I'd end up going without. Who wants to eat alone? I'd gotten in the habit of nibbling snacks at home, and I rarely bothered with a real meal unless I went out with friends. But then I would get mad at myself for not being able to be alone.

Still, it was just as well that I wasn't doing a lot of cooking. More than once I'd forgotten to turn off the stove. The smell of something burning would bring me to the kitchen and I'd realize what I had done. But what would have happened if I'd been out? I was like an old lady; my memory was undependable. Sometimes I couldn't remember what had happened a few days or a few hours before. I needed help. It wasn't safe to be alone.

My next outing began with a call from one of Bob's old friends, Duff. He was with his girlfriend at the International Hotel and invited me to meet them. Girlfriend? What had become of Allison? I decided I'd find out when I saw him; if nothing else, it would do me good to get out of the house.

"Yeah, Allison and I are still married," he shrugged as he glanced toward his girlfriend, "but this is my old lady – you know how it is." She was Allison's opposite, slouched on the sofa, sultry and pouty with an unkempt mass of honey-colored hair, obviously in her early twenties but already showing the signs of drug burnout. She and I managed to ignore each other for the rest of the evening.

I was really stoned on coke – the detective had given it to me – and my teeth were grinding. Duff could tell I was messed up; he tried to give me more coke to help me relax but I didn't want it. So he offered me the next best thing: heroin cut with coke. I was reluctant. I'd never heard anything good about heroin, and I'd never tried it.

Whatever he gave me relaxed me all right. Whenever I tried to move, I thought I'd throw up. I tried to leave several times but was too sick. I fell in and out of sleep all night. Around 10 a.m. a couple of guys showed up. They were flying into Colombia to pick up some coke and bring it back to the States. "You'd be welcome to come along," they said with a grin. It sounded exciting and I was tempted, but I still wasn't feeling well. I decided to go home.

So which was better: to stay home alone or to go out with friends? Both were perilous, and both were pointless – but not when I could be with Heather. On my way home, I went to Sofia's, picked up Heather, and took her to the beach. She dipped her feet in the water and ran into my arms, giggling as we snuggled. Nothing mattered but Heather. We made a sandcastle and got soaked when a big wave surprised us. The sandcastle washed away and Heather looked up innocently. "It's gone, Mommy. Did it go to be with Daddy?"

I hesitated. "Maybe," I answered. I scooped her up and went back to the car. We had dinner and I tucked her in bed.

Heather woke me up the next morning. She was sitting on the bed and was gently touching my forehead. I spent the morning with her. She was so precious! But by the time we had eaten lunch I was ready to take her back to Sofia's because I was so depressed. I was still throwing up after Duff's heroin cocktail. I cried for much of the afternoon – I couldn't have found words to tell why I was crying – and couldn't seem to get control of my mind. I told myself I wasn't the only one; all my friends were lonely and bored.

But I had a business detail to take care of: I had to meet Lance's partner Darrell at Richo's Restaurant. He insisted on searching my purse for a gun or a tape recorder. "This is like something out of a bad movie," I grumbled as I passed my purse across the table to him.

"Just playing it safe," he replied as he pawed through my things. We talked, but I felt I was wasting my time. It was impossible to know what to believe. The latest rumor had it that Elise, the girl who lived in the house where we had the gambling party, was a known drug informer working off a drug bust.

I left Richo's realizing I'd never get to the bottom of what had happened at the party. Everyone had a story to tell; everyone insisted everyone else was lying. I decided to drop the detective and take my losses. The party was illegal and I would have to take responsibility for it. Chalk it up to the school of hard knocks.

But there was one thing I knew for sure: it was a great party.

Garrett took me Christmas shopping, and we spent the day looking at lynx coats. I almost bought one but Garrett stopped me. "They did a lousy job making that coat," he told me. "I can make you one that looks better than that. Come on; I know where there's a place that sells hides." Off we went, and there I decided I liked bobcat better than lynx.

Shopping always wears me out, and we stopped at a bar for a meal. One drink led to another and soon we were both really drunk. In a moment of inspiration, I told Garrett I would marry him. I thought it would make him happy, but he exploded. "Do you think I'm crazy?" he demanded. "You're so freaked out you can't even think straight, and to top it off we're both in a drunken stupor."

Drunk as I was, I could tell he was right. I drove him home at 2:30 a.m. Paige came out the door to scream at us when we drove up. "I think I'd rather go home with you," he said, "at least until this blows over."

But by now my drunkenness was wearing off. "No way; you're on your own," I said.

"I'm the town fool!" he muttered as he slid out of the car and I took off.

For Christmas Eve I was invited to a party at the home of one of the Byrds and his wife – I'll call them Ricky and Laura here – and they asked a few of us to come early for dinner. We waited a few minutes for one of the actors from Easy Rider, but he didn't show up so we decided to eat without him.

As soon as we finished eating, he arrived. So we decided to punish him for being late: we all sat and stared at him while he ate his turkey dinner. It was hard to keep a straight face; he wolfed his food down nervously, glancing from one of us to another.

Dinner ended and the party guests started arriving. The actor redeemed himself – he had brought some great pot, and soon we all were high.

The actor and Ricky decided to call my answering machine and sing me a Christmas song. There was a guy named Aaron who backed them up on keyboard; he had played with several well-known bands. He was tall and so good-looking he could have been a model. Our eyes kept meeting and soon he was trying to pick me up. I laughed it off but he kept coming back. I had to admit he was attractive, but I really didn't want to get involved with anyone else right now. So the more he persisted, the more I treated it like a joke.

As the night wore on, I began to realize he wouldn't take "no" for an answer. Musicians can't believe anyone would turn them down. At one point he picked me up and tried to carry me out of the party, but he had to put me back down because he couldn't maneuver through the crowded room. He waited for the party to thin out, and tried again. This time I let him.

I woke up at his place near Malibu Lake at sunrise on Christmas morning. I didn't hang around; I wanted to get out to deliver Heather's presents. She was excited and looked beautiful in her new Christmas dress. It was fun to watch her open her gifts.

But I'd promised Aaron I'd come back that afternoon, so I put Heather in the car and drove back to Malibu. I rang the bell several times but Aaron didn't answer the door. I couldn't believe he was standing me up! I tossed rocks at his screen, and still he didn't answer. Last night he couldn't leave me alone, and now he was blowing me off. I was furious! I found paper and pen in the car and left him a nasty note.

I took Heather to the beach and we went for a long walk. I was too churned up to enjoy it. I drove her back to Sofia's and tucked her in bed.

I started back home, alone again. My depression had been a light fog when Heather and I had walked on the beach and now it was growing thicker and darker with every mile. I was supposed to go to Rachel's for dinner, but I realized I didn't feel up to it. I got home and called her, but never got a chance to tell her I wasn't coming.

"Have you heard from Aaron yet? He's been looking for you everywhere."

I was upset, but the serenity in Rachel's voice soothed me. This had happened many times before. "Looking for me?" I answered, surprised that my own voice sounded as calm as it did. "I went to his house this afternoon – I thought he was expecting me – and nobody was home."

"He had to go out. Didn't you get his note? He'd left a note on the door."

"What note? I never saw a note." A ray of light was trying to break through the clouds, but I wasn't convinced yet.

"Well, he told me he got your note and realized his must have blown away." Had he told Rachel what I'd written to him? Even if he had, it would be just like Rachel to pretend he hadn't. "As soon as he saw your note, he knew you hadn't seen his. He's been frantic ever since, trying to find you."

So I ended up eating dinner at Rachel's, and Aaron arrived later to pick me up. He picked up a guitar and sang to me, tender romantic songs that washed away the afternoon's misunderstanding.

It was hard to tear myself away from Aaron the next day, but I had to fly to Santa Cruz to take care of some business. A few months earlier, I had needed to rent out my house but hadn't wanted to stay in Santa Cruz to show it until I found a tenant. So Kent, the artist I had gone to the Halloween party with, offered to show the house for me. In return, I was giving him free rent until a paying tenant moved in.

It had seemed like a good deal at the time and I didn't mind paying a few weeks' utility bills. But weeks had stretched into months, and now I had gotten a $375 phone bill with charges for a lot of calls to England. What was going on?

Kent met me at the airport, and as soon as we met we started hassling. How many people had asked to see the house? "Ah, it isn't that simple," he explained. "It isn't easy to sell art in Santa Cruz. But I've sold a little, and I've been trying to save some money for the first month's rent and a security deposit."

"But how many people have you shown the house to?" I interrupted.

"Well, nobody yet," he said. "What if they decided to move in? Where would I go? Until I get my money saved up, I can't afford to show the house."

When we arrived at the house I discovered his girlfriend had moved in with him. I said I expected them to pay some of the bills they'd run up, but they said they were broke. Suddenly they had to go out. I was tired from the trip and the arguments, and I went to the bedroom for a nap. Ron and Marie would show up as soon as Ron got off work.

I must have fallen into a deep sleep. A car in the driveway woke me up. As I walked to the door I noticed my answering machine was blinking. I played the message – it was Aaron. I wanted to call him right away, but first I had to answer the door.

Kent was back. "We've talked it over," he said, glancing at his girl-friend. "Fact is, we're blown away that you're asking us for money. That wasn't part of our agreement. I was supposed to stay here rent free until your place was rented."

I shut the door on him, locking it with a loud click. I moved quickly to nab some of his paintings; maybe I could find a way to sell them to cover the money he owed me. He must have guessed what I was doing; he flew through a side door and knocked them out of my hands. We struggled and he started choking me, but we heard a car coming up the driveway and he let go. Ron and Marie came to the door. "I was just leaving," Kent said to them; he was trying to sound nonchalant but he was breathing too hard.

"You're right you're just leaving!" I shouted. "Get out of my house and don't ever come back!"

He drew himself up, looked me in the eye, and said, "I'm really sorry it had to end like this. I wouldn't have moved in at all if I'd realized that you'd become so commercial about the whole thing." Then he turned to Ron and Marie as though I weren't even there. "I don't know what's going on. She was trying to lay a trip on me about money, and suddenly she went wild. I just want to get my things and get out of here peace-fully."

While they talked, I went into the kitchen and filled a pot with ice wa-ter, waiting for just the right moment as he carried his things out of the house. He peeked through the screen for a final goodbye and I nailed him, and then gleefully shut the door in his face. I laughed as he walked back to his car, dripping wet and shaking his head in disbelief.

Marie and Ron left and I walked out on the porch and sat down on the swing. My hopes had been shattered once again, and I felt devas-tated. The sky filled with mysterious clouds as a howling wind blew in a storm. I bundled up and strained my ear to listen. It seemed as if the wind had voices whispering to me, but I couldn't quite make out the words.

"I wish you could talk to me and tell me what to do," I said as the tears poured down my face. "Oh God, how I need someone to tell me what to do."

The rain started coming down and I went inside and built a fire. I was certain that I didn't want to live in the house, so I called a realtor and asked if she could possibly come right away. I ended up listing the house and imposing upon her to drive me to San Jose airport. It turned out they had no flights available for L.A., so I took a cab to San Francisco International and arrived home about 10 p.m.

I sat on my bed and looked around the room. The walls and 10-foot ceiling were painted a soft white, and the hardwood floors were well worn after many years of traffic. It was depressing. What had made me feel the need to take pieces of broken glass and glue them to the wall? The drug memorabilia, psychedelic posters, black lights, and filth buried the charm of this once beautiful master suite.

Thunder roared as lightning lit up the many windows and danced across the window seat that looked out on the distant mountains and valley. I noticed the message light blinking on my phone and listened to see if anyone interesting had called.

"JoAnn, get over here right away. We're all going to Mexico and Aaron wants you to come with us," Laura shrieked with excitement.

My depression lifted and I quickly returned the call. I was on my way out the door in a few moments. Rain was coming down in buckets as I headed towards Malibu, and the steep driveway and sophisticated security system made me wonder if I'd ever manage to get in. But at last I did, and soon we all got very stoned on half an ounce of cocaine. We played Monopoly all night, and at 9 a.m. we collapsed in bed and slept until dinnertime.

After a delicious lobster dinner at Nantucket, Ricky and Laura decided to go back home. Aaron and I headed for Mexico.

We stopped in Carlsbad to see Duff and Allison. They had moved down there right after Bob died. It was good to see Allison, but I had mixed feelings about Duff. He and Aaron really hit it off and the three of us did a lot of coke. Like a prude, Allison wouldn't touch the coke and went to bed early. Aaron and I left soon and arrived in Ensenada about 2 a.m. in a pouring rain. We checked into a motel and headed for Hussongs, the local hot spot.

I lost count of how many tequilas we drank. The music became a dull drone as we clung to one another, dancing between drinks. At sunrise we left Hussongs and wandered into a seedy little bar around the corner. I was too drunk to be frightened but it obviously was not a tourist place.

I went into the bathroom and got so dizzy I lay down on the filthy floor, unable to move. Eventually, Aaron came in and rescued me. He made me feel safe and warm as he picked me up and carried me outside. He sang me beautiful love songs and I snuggled into his arms.

Suddenly, Aaron put me down and slowly backed away from me. He was very drunk and had a hard time focusing. He put one hand on my shoulder and lifted my face towards him with the other as he wept like a baby. "I'm in love with you and I don't want to be," he said. "I don't want to be."

Then he turned and began yelling at passersby. This was crazy; now I was going to have to rescue him. "There's a restaurant over there," I said, taking him by the arm and steering him towards the door. "I think we both need coffee."

But it didn't help. Even in the restaurant he continued to shout at strangers like a crazy man. Police cars pulled up outside and Aaron grabbed my arm. "We're getting out of here," he said hysterically. "They're not putting me in jail."

The police tried to get our attention by honking their horns as we quickly walked out of the restaurant. I kept my eyes down and we jumped into the Porsche.

Aaron tried to outrun them but they cornered us and ordered us into the back of the squad car. I felt helpless as I watched one of the cops follow behind us in my car. He seemed to have as much trouble with the clutch as I did.

Aaron acted like a madman and tried to swing at the cops. When they got us out of the car and forced us inside, Aaron grabbed the Chief of Police and punched him in the nose. I couldn't believe my eyes. About 20 officers jumped on him and dragged him behind closed doors.

Nobody in the office could answer any questions; I asked one after another but they all just shrugged and laughed as they said, "No Ingles." I could see they weren't going to lock me up so I went outside and sat on the steps. I shivered in the early morning chill as I watched the sun peek through the soft gray clouds. I was barefoot and tried to remember where I'd left my shoes. People walked by, carefully ignoring me. Now I know what a bum feels like, I thought as I tried to warm my hands.

The morning dragged on and the sun rose higher over the dreary neighborhood. I went back inside and tried to reason with someone but again they all shook their heads, shrugged sadly, and said, "No Ingles."

They seemed to regret the language barrier when they spoke to me, but laughter twinkled in their eyes when they looked at one another.

I wasn't surprised that one of them learned English within hours. About 3 p.m. I tried again, and now the same man behind the counter said, "You pay $50 fine and we release señor and car." Immediately I handed him the money. I was exhausted and nervous as I waited for them to release Aaron.

About an hour later, I heard a lot of commotion and Aaron cursing like a madman at the policemen and people working in the office. He was beaten up and still out of control. He was screaming threats as they escorted him towards me, telling all the ways he was going to get even. They ignored his words and steered him into my arms; I calmed him down. "It doesn't matter right now," I soothed. "Let's just go."

We went back to the motel and fell asleep. Aaron held me tightly. As we drove home late the next afternoon, he was in too much pain to drive. I was happy because he apparently was too drunk to remember what he had said about being in love with me.

It was New Year's Eve but we were too tired to go anywhere, so we took a hot shower and lay down about 10 p.m. and smoked a joint.

"So what do you think you'll be doing next year at this time?" Aaron asked.

I was pretty stoned and gazed out the window remembering all the times I wanted to die.

"I don't know," I admitted. "I'll probably be dead. I've really been thinking a lot about killing myself lately."

Aaron's Latin blood seemed to boil as he jumped out of bed and said, "I'm leaving."

"Why?" I asked, startled at his attitude.

He grabbed his shirt and ignored me, so I threw a bottle of wine at the wall. He never turned to look back as he walked out.

I found my keys and chased him down the hill, but he ignored me. I knew his car was in Malibu so I waited a few minutes and drove down Laurel Canyon looking for him. "Aaron, please get in the car and stop acting like a baby," I begged. "I'll drive you to Ricky and Laura's."

"I'll drive," he said, and I got out and let him. I took the passenger seat and pleaded with him, but he wouldn't speak to me. His face had turned stony.

When we got to Ricky and Laura's, he couldn't get the car up the driveway because he'd burned out the clutch driving 70 m.p.h. in first gear, trying to outrun the police.

Aaron let it roll backwards into the street, roughly jerked up the emergency brake, and got out. He left me sitting there. By the time I got the car into the driveway and followed him into Ricky and Laura's house, Aaron was leaving. He hadn't said a word to anyone. I smoked a few joints and drank champagne before I left and headed back home.

The car hassled me all the way back to Laurel Canyon and finally conked out a couple of miles from my house. It was about 4 a.m. as I walked the rest of the way home. I felt numb inside and wished I were dead. Why had Aaron walked out on me? Why wouldn't he answer me? It was hard to find my way as I walked through the darkness on winding roads, and the headlights of the cars that passed every few minutes blinded me. Suddenly it hit me that this walk in the dark on a winding road was what my life had become.

Eventually I made it home and fell into bed, waking up at 2 p.m. the next day. I looked back at the events of the past few days, and somehow the memories had scrambled and none of them made sense. My next diary entry says it all:

January 2, 1975
Happy New Year you fool! Well, I'm at Mt. Sinai hospital in the nut ward. It caught up with me and I'm having a heck of a time keeping it straight...

It would take several phone conversations over the next few days to reconstruct the events that led to Mt. Sinai.

Sixteen

LIFE INSIDE THE MENTAL WARD

Rachel was the one who could tell me how I had gotten here, because she was with me every step of the way. She and Carl had stayed in touch ever since Mardi Gras, and now he was in L.A. She told him, "I'm worried about JoAnn. She's been depressed lately and I haven't heard from her. I think I need to go to her house and see if she's okay." Rachel had her own battles with depression, and often read psychology books to try to overcome it. She had seen all the signs that I too was dangerously depressed.

Carl came with her. Rachel let herself in the house in Laurel Canyon where I was renting a room, and Carl followed a few steps behind. She found me sleeping in a bed full of candy and cupcake wrappers, potato chip bags, empty wine bottles and dirty dishes, with "Dark Side Of The Moon" playing and replaying on my stereo. She turned it off and woke me up, and I started crying uncontrollably. "Come on, let's get you cleaned up," she said as she helped me to my feet. "We're taking you out to dinner."

"Go without me; I'm not hungry," I protested.

"No, you're going with us," she said as she glared at the trash in my bed and steered me toward the shower. "You need some real food, not just the junk you've been eating." Somehow she got me dressed, and though I kept insisting I wasn't in the mood to go out, she wouldn't take no for an answer. We went to dinner.

But nothing they said or did could stop my crying. It had begun when they woke me up, and it continued nonstop as we sat in the restaurant.

"How about if Rachel and I take you to Tahiti with us?" Carl asked, trying to cheer me up.

"I don't think I'd want to spoil your trip," I said. "I'm just so bummed out."

After dinner we went for a ride through Beverly Hills. I was in the back seat of her plush white Mercedes convertible and began to feel like I was shrinking. It seemed as if I was going to be five years old again and I was freezing inside. It was like that when I got really lonely. Even if I sat in front of the hottest fire, I'd still shake from the cold.

I began to panic. "Rachel, stop the car! I'm shrinking!" I screamed.

She slammed on her brakes and held me like a baby. After I calmed down she drove me to U.C.L.A. to see if they could help me. I thought I would freak out if anyone looked at me when we pulled in the parking lot. I kept looking down at the ground as we walked into the hospital. Maybe if I didn't look at anyone, they couldn't see me.

I vaguely remember talking to a shrink while Rachel contacted Shane. "There are two ways to go here," he said. "You can commit yourself, or I can have the state commit you, and if the state commits you it'll be a whole lot harder to get out." I realized I'd better commit myself, but even that was impossible right now because they had no room in their Psychiatric Ward. They explained the alternatives to Rachel; I couldn't keep my attention focused and wasn't really listening. By the time we left, the one thing I understood was that I needed to come back in the morning and see if I could commit myself then.

I felt extremely depressed as we drove through Westwood until I spotted a "31 Flavors" sign.

"Rachel, I want an ice cream," I said. Somehow, the cone made me laugh and between that and a Valium, I made it through the night.

Rachel insisted I sleep at her house and the next day she took me to Mt. Sinai where I committed myself.

I doubt that I could remember these days at all if it weren't for my diary. Here's a fragment; it speaks for itself:

January 2, 1975
...That's the basis for everything that's wrong with me...LONELY... LONELY. I feel like I'm a problem and don't want to bother anyone. I feel like I'm in the way and if I had one wish it would be for eternal rest.
It's hard for me to think. I probably really cracked up when Bob got killed but have kept it under control until...Oh, who knows?
I think I'd rather be pronounced D.O.A. than be here in the nut jail, but there is part of me that wants to live. There is a part of me that is so full of life.
They did let me call Heather tonight. Her voice sounded so small. "When are you coming, Mommy?" she asked in her tiny innocent

voice.

Oh my little angel, I wish I could hold you right now.

"Where are you, Mommy?" she questioned.

I wish I knew where I was. I love my little Heather so much. I'm so sorry my sweet baby that my heart is breaking cause I'm not strong enough any more...

Life in the mental ward was no fun at all. The day began with someone waking me up, making me go to the bathroom in a bottle, and then taking blood samples.

I tried to go ask a question but people were everywhere, like yellow jackets that suddenly swarm when they smell the food at a picnic. I thought I'd explode if I couldn't go hide. I couldn't stand looking at any of the people there, patients or staff, and I couldn't stand it when they would look at me. People would come to me with questions I couldn't answer. I looked for a place to get away.

I couldn't sit in a corner; they'd find me. I tried to hide in my closet, even if it was uncomfortable; that didn't last long because they found me and made me go out into the lounge. The problem was that I had no way to lock my door. "You don't need a lock," one attendant said. "You're not allowed to stay in your room anyway." He seemed to make it his personal mission to hunt me down if I found a way to be alone. "Come on," he would say as though he were inviting me to a party. "It's time to get out and mix with people..." Fun, fun.

At every turn I ran into absurd rules. I took a cracker into my room and tried to eat it; a nurse came in and ordered me out. "No eating in your room..."

I wished Heather were here – well, not here; but I wished we could be together and go out and run on the beach. Instead I was herded into group therapy, a lot of games and charades that were supposed to get us in touch with our feelings. We all knew it was a joke. I spotted a cute guy sitting across from me and later had a fantasy date. We pretended we went to the laundromat and got an ice cream cone. He was trying to kick junk and his folks had lots of money, so they'd put him in here.

After group therapy I had a private consultation with the shrink. He took a lot of notes, and as our session ended he said, "No visitors for a few days, but after that I'll reevaluate." So I knew I had just a few days to get my act together.

We all had to take sedatives three times a day, and someone had to watch us to make sure we swallowed them. In spite of the pills, there were a lot of fights and bad vibes. At supper, a girl knocked over all the plates and chairs before a few orderlies managed to subdue her. People were always pacing like animals in a cage; I never knew when I would hear the next blood-curdling scream. Meanwhile I felt like kicking and screaming myself, in spite of all the drugs they had given me.

I wanted to be with the guy I'd met in group therapy and I tried to sneak into his room. The guard caught me and said I'd be put in solitary if I didn't behave. Solitary? First they didn't want me to be alone; now they were threatening me with solitary. Who was crazier, the patients or the staff? I went directly to my room and fell asleep.

"Time to get up!" said the attendant with a cheery voice as he jerked the covers off me in the morning.

"What do you think you're doing?" I demanded.

"Rise and shine! It's almost time for breakfast!"

I cursed the air blue and got up. I was furious; nobody had ever gotten me up this way.

A really crazy lady came into my room and asked, "Can you see me?" She wasn't making an appointment; she was afraid she had become invisible, and she'd been asking everyone this same question ever since I'd gotten here. I hadn't had my coffee yet and didn't feel up to dealing with her question, but I decided to settle it beyond all shadow of doubt. "Come here," I said, trying to hide my impatience as I steered her into the bathroom. "Let's clear this up once and for all. Look into the mirror. What do you see?" She peered into the mirror wordlessly for a few moments. "See? There you are," I announced.

She stared for a few minutes more, and then she stepped out into the hall. "Can you see me?" she asked the first person she passed.

Is this what they thought I was like? I wondered how anyone could get better in a place like this. I finished dressing and went to breakfast. I had just gotten seated when someone came up to me, looked at his watch, and said, "You're late. You're going to have to learn to be on time…"

Hatred and anger roared out of me like lava out of a volcano. I jumped up screaming curses, and with one sweep of my arm pushed all the trays off the table. Immediately a bunch of guards and orderlies pinned me down and shot me up with a bunch of drugs.

I calmed down later and realized I was making a mess of things. The shrink said I couldn't have visitors until after a few days, and already I had two strikes against me: sneaking into the guy's room the night before, and now my tantrum at breakfast. And I knew he'd hear about it all; whenever anyone did anything out of the ordinary, some functionary was standing there with a clipboard, writing notes. It wasn't like baseball; three strikes and you're out. I wondered if I'd ever get out; three strikes might keep me in forever. I was really going to have to get my act together.

Aaron called. "You know, JoAnn, our time together was really beautiful," he said, "but I need to let you know it's over. The important thing now is for you to get well. I really want you to be happy when you get out."

Out? Out where? I was so lonely I was ready to run away with a 20-year-old junky.

I phoned Shane. "I'm ready to get out of here," I said. "I've been ready ever since about ten minutes after the door shut behind me…"

"I know it's hard," he said, "but you need to be there. You really haven't been yourself lately. You need to get well."

"Are you kidding?" I asked. "Have you ever been here? You stay here for a few days. Between the piddly little rules and all the real nut cases here, I bet you'd go crazy yourself within a few days. Anybody in his right mind would be figuring out how to escape…"

"Bad idea, JoAnn." He was trying to sound gentle, but there was something cold and distant in his voice. "You need to stick it out until the doctor says you're ready to be discharged."

He was probably right. I would fade in and out of confusion. Sometimes my thoughts would dart this way and that, like a cloud of flies. My thoughts might be clear for a while, then a dark fog would move in. It was hard to focus, but in the rare moments when I did, they would numb my mind with pills and shots, as though chemicals could kill my pain. Anybody could see this couldn't work. I could tell it was crazy when they were the ones doling out the shots and the pills, yet I had spent a few years using my own drugs to try to accomplish the same thing. Bizarre.

I felt awful…really awful. I wanted to kick holes in the walls and scream, and choke myself or anyone who got in my way. But I talked to the doctor on my third morning and he approved visitors. I called a few friends, and they showed up right away. Rachel and Laura brought me a radio and some blouses because I was running out of clothes. Garrett and Barbara brought me a beautiful belt, and JillAnn and Peter brought me a chunk of hash.

That night I called Heather, and Sofia told me she wasn't going to be able to watch her much longer. Oh God, what will happen to my little girl? I've got to get out of here. Who will take care of us?

A week passed. My thoughts were getting a little clearer, but I still felt lost. The doctor let me go home one night on a pass. Nate picked me up and we had a long talk. As always, he said a lot of things that made sense, but the bottom line was that he thought I needed to stay in Mt. Sinai as long as it took to get well. "That's easy for you to say," I replied, "but you might not be so sure if you'd ever been inside."

He shook his head sadly and turned the tables on me. "And that's easy for you to say," he said gently. "But these doctors are professionals. They know what they're doing. Please, JoAnn, give yourself a chance." I couldn't argue with him; he really cared.

But I didn't make any promises. In a way, I couldn't see much difference between things outside and things inside. I figured the doctors and nurses knew the whole world was crazy, but they were just trying to cover it up. No wonder we called it "getting your act together" – it was only an act. Deep down, we were all crazy.

Two days later my birthday rolled around, and by then I was starting to understand why I was inside with the crazies instead of outside. I spent about half an hour trying to arrange a ride to see Heather and it exhausted me so much I could hardly move or think. This wasn't normal, was it?

Gone away minds are hard to find.

In my exhaustion I jotted down a few notes to discuss with the shrink: "Dress up, confusion, responsibility, play, too many decisions, dolls, 5 years old, hold my hand." I hoped I would remember what it meant.

A few days later I wanted to sign myself out and got really upset with the doctor because he said no. "Don't even try," he said. "If you go down that road, I'll have to get a court order to have the state commit you, and then you'll really have a hard time getting out. Please don't push it; I don't want to have to go that route." He was trying to sound concerned, not authoritative, but either way it worked out the same. He looked down at the paper I'd handed him. "Now tell me again about Bob's death…"

It wouldn't do any good to be angry; I simmered down. Little by little I told about my feelings as he coaxed them out of me with his questions. Faces were familiar, but I didn't feel that I really knew anyone. The whole world felt like another planet and sometimes I hardly recognized Heather. Often I felt numb towards everyone. Between his questions and my answers, it emerged that I had created an imaginary shell to live in, a shell that would protect me from pain.

"This is good," he said as we finished for the day. "It's helpful if you write things down when they occur to you. If it helps, write a letter to a good friend. You don't have to send it; the important thing is to write it down and get in touch with your feelings."

So I would take time to write. Maybe it would help get me out. I sat down to write, and since I didn't have to show it to anybody, I let it come pouring out:

Dear Ricky and Laura:
The alligator dropped in for tea. As he ate a chocolate cloud he blew away with a singing parrot. Although the moon was dripping with diamonds the gold peeled off the sun. Foxtail and Leopold took me sailing on snowflakes while the cannons blew bubbles over our heads.
Alas, we stopped in the center of an atom to pick up a raindrop which melted and then we went to bed on some autumn leaves which conveniently scattered themselves in the field of clover where Cricket and six fireflies live on very warm nights…

It went on and on. It probably wasn't what the shrink was looking for, but it was fun to write. Then as I met the shrink day by day, I began to pick up on what he really was looking for. Was I hurting? Yes, I could admit it. Was I angry? Sometimes. I began speaking his language, hoping that if I said what he wanted to hear he would let me out. Maybe he knew exactly what I was doing. If so, he probably reasoned that it was what any sane person would do. He released me by the end of the month.

I don't know what I was supposed to get out of being in Mt. Sinai, but if nothing else it opened a fountain of writing. It felt strange; nobody in my family had been a writer.

Meanwhile, I still wondered what was wrong with me. Maybe conning my way out of the hospital hadn't been a sign of sanity after all. I'd be up one day and down the next, taking whatever pills I could find and wondering why my moods swung so unpredictably.

I still contemplated suicide a lot. Should I simply slash my wrists? It seemed too gruesome, but when my self-hatred was strongest I felt I deserved it. Or maybe I should take every pill I could find down to the beach about midnight and bring along the bottle of expensive wine Bob bought for my 21st birthday. I'd get really drunk, take all the pills and let the sea carry me back to him. Bob, I miss you so much. I've run away from facing up to the fact that you're dead, then I feel like a melting snowflake and cry for days. I'm so angry and my insides scream... Why??? Why did this happen to me???

The urge to die came hundreds of times during the day and thousands of times at night. I hated it when the sun went down.

My friends had a birthday party for me and Aaron showed up. He was really drunk and abusive and wanted to stay with me. I was a fool and fell for it, but he was gone in the morning and left me feeling cold and numb. I should have listened to that little voice inside me that said, "Don't let him stay; resist him."

Did I love Aaron? I really didn't know. I wondered if I fell for some of these guys because I saw something in them that reminded me of Bob.

I wrote a little more of the fairy tale.

> The wall opened up and man walked out. "What's wrong young lady?" he asked, stepping towards me.
> I was startled and wondered what the huge box with ringing red lights might be. I didn't say a word.
> "What are you doing in here?" he asked in a stern voice.
> "I don't know, but I'd sure like to get out," I replied. He became more sullen with a curious look on his face as he frowned...

By now, my diary really had become my best friend. It never bothered anyone and was always ready to listen. I could tell it all my problems and not take up anyone else's time or energy. But sometimes it seemed a personality other than my own did the writing, someone forceful who nevertheless had a mysterious and delicate side.

Soon after my release from Mt. Sinai I went back to Santa Cruz to try to rent my house. It had been up for sale but nobody had bought it, and now I was having trouble finding a tenant. My water source was a spring, which had seemed quaint when I bought the place. But the water was non-potable, and sometimes the spring went dry. Prospective buyers and tenants didn't find it quaint; they thought it was a lot of work.

Meanwhile I had found a place for Heather. Carolyn had visited me in the hospital and suggested that Heather live with her family for a while to give me a chance to get well. Her husband had been one of The Byrds.

I went through the mixed feelings I had whenever I had to find a home for Heather, and I wrote about it in my diary. Then I added a line I can't explain. I don't know why I wrote it, or if it was one of the lines written by another self:

> Then I'm going to meet a really rich funky guy with an earring in his ear and who drives a Lamborghini, and we're going to fall madly in love.

It was a foolish bit of fantasy, and I wondered where the idea had come from.

First I drove to Albion to drop Heather off at Carolyn's. It was a big farmhouse, filled with the smell of fresh baked cookies. Carolyn was excited; she had just gotten a new wood stove and made the cookies. Within minutes of our arrival, Heather was bundling firewood with the rest of the kids. It was as if a time machine had taken us back to a simpler era when people had built their own fires and baked their own bread. I could tell Heather would be happy here.

When I got back to Santa Cruz, I ran into my friend Kari and she invited me to go out on the town one night. We stopped by a friend's house to see if she wanted to come with us and I saw a beautiful silver Lamborghini in the driveway.

A few people were sitting around an old oak table in the dining room and I wondered who owned the car. One of the guys had piercing blue eyes and long black hair. He wore a torn velour shirt, old blue jeans, and an earring. He was very soft spoken and intelligent and I was instantly attracted to him. Wouldn't it be funny if he owned the car? I thought. But no, he isn't dressed like someone who could afford a Lamborghini.

We left for the club a few minutes later and I watched him climb into the Lamborghini. He was alone.

We arrived, but the club was packed. We never even went inside. We took one look, turned around, and left. Disappointment swept over me as I watched him drive off.

A few days later my friend Kristi came over; she sold stuff at swap meets and had offered to help me price a few things I wanted to sell. I looked out the window when I heard the car in the driveway and it was the Lamborghini.

My heart pounded as I went to the door.

"Hi JoAnn, this is my friend Stephen," Kristi said with a cheerful smile as they walked in.

We spent about an hour putting tags on all the things I was getting rid of. Stephen stood in the corner silently and watched my every move; I grew more and more nervous. What's wrong with me? I wondered. I'm as nervous and giddy as a teenager. I went to the kitchen for a glass of water and he followed me in.

"Want some?" I asked dumbly, feeling like I'd stumble over my words if I said anything else.

"No, but how would you like some magic mushrooms?" he asked.

"Yes, I'd love some," I said. I did my best to sound calm; my heart was beating so fast I was sure he could hear it.

"Give me your phone number and I'll call you later," he said as Kristi walked in the kitchen. I took one look at her and clammed up. Was she his girlfriend?

She must have read my mind. "It's okay," she laughed. "We're just friends. I'm very happily married and have four kids."

"Very happily married," Stephen echoed. "So I'll call you tonight."

But I was still uneasy. Would he really phone? I stood on the porch and waved goodbye.

I was staying at my sister's house and we ate dinner about 5 p.m. The evening dragged on as if invisible weights were slowing the clock. The phone rang and I jumped, but it was for Ron. What if Stephen was trying to call and getting a busy signal? Would he call back? I sat on the couch wishing Ron would hang up, but his conversation seemed endless, and each sentence tortured me.

Finally, Ron hung up and they went to bed at 9 p.m. My sister and her husband were such early birds! I turned on the TV but couldn't concentrate, so I lit a joint and tried to focus on anything but the phone. After a few good hits it rang. I grabbed it. "Hello?"

"This is Stephen. Would you like to come over for some mushrooms?" His voice sounded playful.

I got directions and left my sister's house as quickly as I could. I smoked a couple of joints on my way to Stephen's, hoping they would give me courage.

Stephen was friendly and easygoing, and he made me feel comfortable. He built a big fire and fluffed some pillows behind my back, handing me a joint. "I'll give you the mushroom and you're welcome to take it with you if you'd rather not stay and share your trip with me."

I realized he was being considerate so I pretended I was thinking it over, though I had no intention of leaving.

"I think it will be fine to take it here," I said.

It was a beautiful evening and a fantastic mushroom trip. In the morning we woke up and I snuggled in his arms.

"How would you like to go somewhere wonderful for dinner?" he asked.

"Where?"

"Hawaii," he said as nonchalantly as if it were the corner coffee shop.

In no time at all we were on a 747 flying over the Pacific Ocean. Our time together was a wonderful fantasy and I never wanted it to end. We spent ten days in Hawaii, and then headed back for Santa Cruz.

Stephen didn't want me to leave, but I had to go home to check on the store. I stayed for a few more days and left for L.A. reluctantly.

I was home a few days when he called.

"There's a ticket waiting for you, flight 129 PSA," Stephen said confidently.

I dropped everything and went back to Santa Cruz. I had missed him so much I felt relieved to know we'd be together in a few hours. I fell head over heels in love with him because he treated me so well.

After a few weeks, Shane called and said I had to come back to go over some problems in the shop. I hated leaving and promised Stephen I'd get back as quickly as I could. Before I left, Stephen took me to a doctor because I thought I might be pregnant. The test was negative but a few days later I still had symptoms, so I went to my doctor in Beverly

Hills. This time, the test was positive.

I called Stephen when I got home.

"Stephen, I had another test and this time it's positive," I said.

"Well, I'm not the father because I can't have kids," he said coldly.

I hadn't been with anyone else for a long time.

"You're a liar," I screamed and slammed the phone down.

A haunting pain grabbed me as I fell on my bed and sobbed uncontrollably. A tempest of emotions tore through me for the next few days: fear, anxiety, hatred towards Stephen and other men I'd been involved with. For a few hours I would feel like a victim, then I would feel like a fool. I decided to get an abortion, and then I'd get my tubes tied so I would never have to face this humiliation again.

I told Nate what I was going to do and he took me to the hospital and brought me to his place to take care of me until I was well enough to go home. He was another puzzle in my life, but at least he was always there when I needed him.

I wasn't in any hurry to get back in touch with Stephen, but I still loved him and I couldn't quite let go either. His memory caused me terrible pain. How could he be so cruel? How could he lie? But it wasn't just me; I had seen him lie to others. It was the one thing I didn't like about him.

I confided in Nate. "I've finally learned that I can't trust men. Oh, you're different – you've been a real friend. But once romance gets into the picture, friendship goes out the window. After Stephen, I'm going to be much more cautious next time – if there's ever even going to be a next time."

"You never cease to amaze me," he replied. "You've gone through so many phases since I first got to know you. And yet underneath it all, you're always JoAnn – always working hard and playing hard, always getting into an impossible scrape and always coming up with an unexpected way to get out of it. Whatever you do, you pour yourself into it."

Seventeen

AUTOMATIC ART AND WRITING

Johnny and Julie were getting married. Heather and I went to Rhode Island to be part of the wedding, and we stayed with Julie's parents in a magnificent Victorian mansion on the ocean. This house had about 30,000 square feet with 14 bedrooms and 9 baths, and people were coming and going all the time. Heather and I each had our own rooms, but it was wonderful to be with her. We could walk on the beach and be together for meals. I loved to hear her laughing with the other children out on the lawn. I savored the normality of this family's life, and wished it were mine.

One night a bunch of us dropped acid and stayed up all night, fishing off the private dock. The sunrise was breathtaking; I loved the serenity of the lake and the tall trees reflecting in the water. But a few minutes later, I stepped inside and met another reality. I looked in the mirror and my reflection became a kaleidoscope of faces. I was terrified as a multitude of women took turns moving to the forefront. I clasped my hands over my face to get rid of them and ran from the bathroom.

I had brought my diary with me, and I grabbed it and wrote:

> Who are all these people? What do they want of me? I see so many
> faces in the mirror...which one is me? God, where am I? Each
> face seems to be taking away part of me. Certainly all these faces
> in the mirror can't be me.

So I was stepping back and forth between two realities. Julie's family made me feel at home, and everything wholesome in me came alive when I was around them. But when I was alone or on drugs, my dark side took over.

Nights were empty. It felt unreal to be alone at twilight. Sometimes dawn would come and sleep hadn't taken me away. I would watch the stars fade and hear the birds chirping about the new day. Another night gone, little or no sleep. Another day dawning, and for what? Where was I going? Where had I been? I would look back at my nightstand covered with pills, cigarettes and stale gin, and then I would fall back into my pillow crying because I was still alone.

One really good thing had come out of my stay at Mt. Sinai: writing. Of course I had already been in the habit of writing my diary, but at Mt. Sinai I had started writing my fairy tale. I loved to be in my room with my paper and pen. I couldn't figure out why, but when I was writing I didn't feel alone.

Maybe I didn't feel alone because I really wasn't. What if that was it? What if all the faces in the mirror were real? This would mean I was never alone, so why bother being lonely? I knew there was at least one besides myself. Whenever I wrote, I felt someone else living in me, someone I couldn't control. It had taken me 28 years to face the fact that she was there. Had she been there all my life, or had she come in only recently? And if she had come in recently, how had she come in? It was a lot to think about.

Writing was putting me in touch with this other identity. Was she another me, or was she someone else? I didn't know, and I wasn't sure which of us was doing the writing. Sometimes it seemed to be my other self because she thought of things I would never have thought of. Then at other times I knew it had to be me. Maybe we took turns.

This wasn't the kind of thing I could talk to anybody about, but writing helped. If nothing else, I could get everything down on paper. Then I could look at it later and try to make sense of it.

I wondered about something else: who had written the line about Stephen – that I would meet a man who wore an earring and drove a Lamborghini? I remember writing the words down and then immediately wondering where they had come from. If I had written it, what had made my improbable words come to pass? And if someone else had written it, how had she managed to take control of me and pen what I wrote?

It was good to come up for air once in a while, doing something conventional like eating pancakes and eggs for breakfast with Julie's family. Even if it was for just an hour, it was good to feel normal.

Heather and I left Julie's parents' house after the wedding because Brooks, a friend of Johnny's, invited me to stay at his place on a beautiful riverbank across the bay. He was half a generation older than me and had a 17-year-old daughter, Terry. Brooks was like the big brother I never had, and we had a platonic relationship. He made a living promoting hairdressers and fashion designers. Some had become quite famous.

He was planning a big fashion show in Rhode Island with Halston, Giorgio, and others, and I jokingly asked him if he could put Garrett in the show. "Sure, why not?" he replied.

"You're kidding," I said.

"I'm not kidding. I trust your judgment. If you're willing to recommend him, I'm willing to give him a chance.

So I called Garrett. "I'm with a guy who promotes designers – we're just friends." Garrett could be insanely jealous. "But he's putting on a show with a few big names, and I told him about you. Now he wants you in the show." There, I'd said it. I braced myself for his reactions.

"Oh yeah? What big names?" Garrett sounded skeptical.

"I don't remember them all," I said, "but I do remember Halston and Giorgio. There are others; they're all people everybody's heard of."

"Don't gimme that," he said. He really sounded disgusted. "Don't try to tell me that after all this time you've been away you're in a platonic relationship with some big shot that wants to feature me in a big show. Where's the show gonna be?"

"Providence. It's the capital of Rhode Island."

"What are you jerking me around like this for? Do you really think I'm gonna drop everything I'm doing to fly all the way to Rhode Island with stars in my eyes, thinking I'm gonna be featured in a show?"

His cynicism could be maddening. "Garrett, why do you have to be your own worst enemy? I'm telling you, it's for real. What do I have to do to convince you?"

"Ha, that's easy. Maybe you could fly back to California and marry me. Who knows, maybe if you were here in person I'd find your story more believable."

"Don't be crazy," I said. "I don't know what I have to do to convince you that it's for real. Don't throw this opportunity away; it's your big chance."

So we went round and round. Garrett was slow to believe he was going to be in a show with all these famous fashion giants, but after a long argument he said maybe he did believe me. Then as we finished talking, he asked me again to come home and marry him. Now it was my turn to think he was joking, and he had to talk me into believing he was serious.

I didn't answer him on the phone, but I seriously considered his proposal for the next few weeks because of the security of knowing he loved me. He really loved me.

I decided that as long as I was so close to New York City, I owed it to myself to go. I had never seen anything like it, but I sat on the bus and wrote my impressions in my diary: garbage in the streets; people talking about nothing, yet to them it was everything; kids and old ladies sitting on upturned garbage cans in the center of Harlem at 2 a.m. – what were they doing out so late, anyway? I couldn't imagine walking through this neighborhood, let alone calling it home. It was strange that my being on the bus made me feel safe in such a scary place.

Through the window I saw brightly colored signs promising dreams and excitement – Chance! Prizes! Bingo! – but the signs hung on grimy run-down buildings, a few of which couldn't have looked worse if they had been bombed. It's like the men I've known, I thought. A lot of promises, and underneath it all just a shabby and crumbling life. Brooks was a welcome exception. He really was nice, and platonic was nice. It was a relief not to have to deal with the romantic angle.

But now it was time to leave the safety of the bus and find a cab to take me to my hotel. I got off and felt like a salmon swimming upstream as a crowd of people tried to push their way on. Some looked scary, some were frail, some smelled terrible, and some were obviously crazy. I made it to the curb and realized I wasn't the only one trying to catch a cab. Finally I caught the prize and got in. "Barbizon Hotel," I told him.

"Yeah, lady," he said. I clutched my suitcase as the cab took off with a jolt. I was starting to have a love-hate relationship with New York. The city was exciting, and some of the people were nice while others could win an Academy Award for rude and crude. Insane people seemed to be on every corner and in every alley.

I checked into the Barbizon and went out to explore the city each day, walking a few blocks and taking in the sights. I was crossing a street as I explored, and a gust of wind caused rubbish and leaves to swirl about. I felt something hit my ankle, and I looked down. It was a Tarot card, the five of pentagrams. The card was well worn, and I wondered if fortune-tellers somewhere in the city had sent it to me as a message. A strange sensation like an electric shock went through me.

I saw an art store, and went in immediately. I bought art paper, ink,

If I Tried To Find
The Words I Heard
Blowing On The Breeze,
By The Time I Explained Them
They Would Be Blown To Eternity.
All I Can Tell You
Is I Can't Tell You
Because We All
Hear A Different Message
In The Breeze,
So Don't Listen To Me
Cause I'm Just Blowing
In The Breeze.
But If You Want To Walk
By My Side In Silence......
Maybe We Can Hear.

and a Rapidograph pen. I went back to my room and began to draw. Strange letters came out and began to spell words. When I would go out after that, I would see them all over the buildings and in the clouds. They were alive, and always in motion. It was like an acid flashback, but I wasn't on drugs. I knew the art was supernatural, and wondered why I had been chosen. Maybe in some strange way, Garrett and I had birthed a child. He always outlined his work with a Rapidograph pen.

I returned to Rhode Island for the fourth of July weekend. Brooks was throwing a big celebration and the house was full of guests. Two of the guys kept flirting with me and even though they were cute, I ignored them. Chance! Prizes! Bingo! Ha! I didn't need it.

By 2 a.m. we were having such a good time that we decided to drop acid together and go to the beach. We were still there as the sun was coming up, and Christopher disappeared because he could tell Paul was finally winning me over. He returned a few minutes later with a tray filled with coffee and fresh fruit. A neighbor stopped by and took Paul and me for a speedboat ride. The chilly morning wind made me shudder and Paul put his arms around me to keep me warm.

The party ended and everyone went their separate ways. But a few days later Paul called. "I'm all alone here in New York," he said. "Why aren't you here?

One of his friends chartered a plane and I left the next day. Paul was a well-known hairdresser with a salon in New York. We really hit if off. Heather was with me, and Paul's son was her age so we brought them to the park every day.

At first it was great, but after a few weeks the city got to me. How could anybody live there? I decided to return to Rhode Island, and as soon as I arrived I knew I had done the right thing. It was refreshing to return to the cool breezes blowing off the river and to hear water rippling by.

Then Garrett called. "How's it going?" I asked. "Are you getting your things ready for the show?"

"I haven't even started yet," he announced.

"Haven't started!" I was shocked. "Why not? This is a huge opportunity…"

"I'm not going to start working on this fashion show until you come home," he interrupted. "I refuse to cut one piece."

I couldn't believe my ears. "Garrett, this is your big chance! Why won't you get started? You've got only six weeks before the show." Already I was mentally walking through the calendar, picturing the steps he would have to take to get ready.

"JoAnn, if you don't come home I'm not going to start," he insisted. "I need you here."

Eventually he wore me down and I said I'd call back. I hung up and went straight to Brooks. "What should I do?" I asked.

"JoAnn, go to California." I was frantic, but he was matter-of-fact. "I've been through this kind of thing before. It's the artistic temperament. You can leave Heather with Terry and me," he said. Terry was his 17-year-old daughter and Heather loved both of them.

"Oh Brooks, I'd have to stay the entire six weeks because he's a big baby," I said. "If I don't, he won't get the stuff done."

"Most artists are," Brooks assured me. "Believe me, artists couldn't be artists if they didn't do something tiresome from time to time. Just get on the plane and everything will be fine."

The night before I was going to leave, I was reading Heather the fairy tale. I'd finished quite a bit of it while I was in Rhode Island and had added a few drawings, including a picture of Strawberry Jan, the main character. I had drawn her one night in the dark, and it had been as if the drawing had flowed out of the pen.

As I read, I heard laughter from the next room. "What is that story you're reading Heather?" Brooks asked.

"It's a fairy tale I started writing when I was locked up in the loony bin," I replied. I was embarrassed that he'd overheard it.

"My goodness, child, you could make a fortune," Brooks said. "You're really talented. Is it finished?"

"Almost." I said. He thought I had talent? This was a shock. I'd never imagined I would ever show it to anyone, other than reading it to Heather at bedtime.

"When can you get it done?" he asked, talking to me through the wall.

"I think I can finish it while I'm at Garrett's."

Now he came into the room. "JoAnn, I'd love to promote the fairy tale. It would really be a challenge – something I'd enjoy doing – if you would like me to," Brooks said.

I didn't know what to think, but I called Paul to check up on the idea because Brooks had been his promoter. "You must really have something if Brooks is impressed," he said. "You can trust his judgment. But here's something else to think about: have you gotten it copyrighted?"

"It never occurred to me."

"I didn't think so. I have an attorney here in New York. Can you see him before you go to California? I really recommend it." So I postponed my flight for a day and went to New York to get the copyright.

When I arrived in San Francisco, it was midnight. Garrett was waiting for me, clad in his wolf coat with the big snake bag slung across his shoulder. I threw myself into his arms, then we chattered about the fashion show all the way home. We went inside and I saw a very pretty girl with short dark hair, sitting at the kitchen table.

"This is Monica," Garrett murmured, waving one hand towards me and the other towards her while he looked somewhere else. She had kept her large round eyes trained on Garrett as if I weren't even in the room, but now she forced herself to glance up at me. "Hi," she said.

"Hi," I replied. We were both acting as if it weren't a big deal to meet each other, but the atmosphere was thick with the unspoken. I went into the other room and I could hear them talking for a few moments, then I heard the door close as she left.

Garrett walked into the room. "Who's the chick?" I asked, still trying to sound nonchalant but not quite carrying it off.

"What's it to you?" he snapped. "Do you expect me to sit around here by myself waiting for you to decide to come back to me in between your romances?"

I hadn't bargained for this, and I suspected things could get really ugly really fast. "Aw, never mind," I said. I didn't have it in me to argue. One look at Monica had told me I had been a fool. He had said he loved me and he wanted to marry me, but did I really expect him to wait for me? Now that I heard the words spoken aloud, I realized how crazy my expectations had been. But it didn't matter whether I was reasonable or not. It still hurt.

"Never mind what?" he challenged as he went out the front door. The screen door banged behind him. I heard a car door, and then the engine started and I heard the car go down the driveway. He was gone. I knew he was going out to meet Monica.

I hadn't expected to be alone, but at least for the moment it would give me time to sort things out. Why did he want me to come back if he was involved with someone else? Other girls had never been a problem before. I would come back and he'd send them away immediately. I had never paid any attention to them; there had never been any reason to. But I had a feeling this one was different, and I began to burn inside.

The next day we went to the grocery store and had a terrible fight. Garrett put the groceries in the car and I started throwing them out the window. Garrett just sat there, not saying a word. He really knew how to infuriate me. I was so angry I got out and slammed the car door as hard as I could. Garrett methodically backed over a whole bag of groceries I'd tossed out, and then he peeled out and left.

I needed a ride back. I called the house and got one of Garrett's seamstresses. "Barbara, can you come and pick me up?" I asked.

"Where are you?"

I told her and she showed up in twenty minutes and drove me to the house. Garrett arrived three hours later, cool and unruffled as though nothing had happened. "Well, let's go get the leather for the show," he said calmly. Did he think I'd been waiting meekly for my opportunity to go with him? Dream on, big boy.

"You go get the stupid leather yourself!" I screamed.

"Now dear, just calm down," he said. He was using his sweet and tender voice. "I'll take you to Sausalito for a wonderful dinner afterwards."

I screamed back at him and he kept replying sweetly. In a few minutes he wore me down. How could I fight with someone who was being so nice? Soon we got in the car and left.

So I stayed on with Garrett and days melted into weeks. Monica showed up only occasionally. After the designs for the show were laid out and Garrett talked to Brooks several times, the light suddenly went on and he realized he really was going to be in the show. He began working feverishly. And for some reason, he started picking fights with me and became crueler than ever.

One night he got drunk and shoved me down. He said some really mean things and when I began to cry, he laughed. The harder I cried, the louder he laughed. It was like a nightmare and I became very frightened. Suddenly I became very quiet, and he left.

What was going on? Was he trying to get me to leave? The more I thought about it, the more sure I was that this is what he was after. He hadn't really wanted me in California; he was just trying to make sure about the show. I had a hard time accepting this because Garrett had always been so loyal to me, whatever my ups and downs. No matter what I had done and no matter how long I'd been away I could always move back in with him. There had always been security in Garrett; but now I realized it was gone.

I packed my bags and Barbara took me to the airport; I flew to L.A. to stay with Johnny and Julie for a few days. Rachel and I went to Ricky and Laura's one night and I brought the fairy tale.

Ricky looked everything over and went in the other room to get his guitar. He sat down and began to compose a song. "I haven't been inspired in so long," he said excitedly. "I want to call my next album for Columbia, 'Strawberry Jan Is Coming.'" Then he took us all out to dinner to celebrate.

It was good to be home again and to be reconnecting with old friends, but things started getting confusing. People would say something one moment and then deny it with the next breath. I started taking a tape recorder with me wherever I went so I could record conversations and phone calls. At first it seemed to make people nervous, but I started calling the tape recorder "Herbie" and that was all it took to make people relax. I had to do something, and this was the only way to keep things straight. But which was weirder: that I even needed Herbie in the first place, or that everyone took Herbie in stride as soon as they learned his name?

A lot of people got really interested in the fairy tale, and I couldn't understand why. I hadn't even finished it yet. One day as I drove down the street, Bernie, who does the artwork for the *Hollywood Reporter* and *Variety*, spotted me. He motioned for me to pull over in front of the Beverly Hills Hotel. I had *Strawberry Jan* in the car and showed him the drawings. "JoAnn, this is really good," he said. "I need your phone number. Can we get together later? I'd like to read it." I gave him a copy and took off.

That night he called. "JoAnn, I read the story, then called my agent right away. He just read it, and we would like you to come over so we can talk."

They both wanted to know how I'd written it, if I'd write with them, where the ideas came from, and so on. "No question about it; you've got talent. We need to get you into an office, putting in regular office hours and writing eight hours a day."

"Look," I said. "I don't know where the story came from. Maybe it's Bob writing through me; maybe it's someone else. All I know is I'm not a writer. It can't be coming from me; I don't know how to write or draw."

The agent went on. "Don't sell yourself short. You're a natural, at writing and at art." It was flattering, but I tuned it out. I was looking at Bernie, who was now silent and had a reflective look on his face.

The agent stopped talking, and Bernie said, "JoAnn, I haven't drawn in front of very many people because of what they'd think. I want you to know I understand where you're coming from."

"How?" I asked.

"When I draw, someone else takes over," he said. "I'll show you."

Bernie got a large drawing pad and a pen, and he hunched down as though his body housed a strange frog-like creature with quick movements and bulging eyes. His hands darted back and forth fiendishly as he drew. No wonder he didn't like people to see him work. Suddenly he snapped back to normal and held the picture up for me to see. It was a wonderful sketch of Frank Sinatra.

"Oh Bernie, you do understand me," I said excitedly.

They ended up picking my brain apart all night. We didn't leave until 10:00 the next morning.

I wasn't sure who had drawn through Bernie, but I was starting to think Bob was the one who was writing and drawing through me. Bob had started communicating with me through the I Ching, the ancient Chinese book of divination.

I asked the I Ching if it was Bob that was writing through me and I got the trigram, "Following." Did this mean he was still following me after his death, and at last had found a way to communicate with me from the world of the spirits? I might have been skeptical if I hadn't started receiving evidence from other people.

For instance, my friend Barry, a literary agent, read it and urged me to finish the story. He let his wife Marcia read it. I had known her for years, and she could see right away that Bob was trying to communicate with me.

I also noticed one of the poems I wrote was signed, "Love, Bob," and the signature was Bob's!

Rafael also believed it was Bob. He gave me a book, *The Other Side*, which tells how to get in touch with the dead.

So within a few days I concluded that I had been put in touch with my husband's spirit. It was very beautiful, and I cried tears of happiness and didn't feel lonely anymore. Bob was in my room; I just knew it. As for my writing, I realized I was writing some of the things, and Bob was writing other parts through me. This was going to be fun because we were in total communication and it was really beautiful.

I also had a premonition that I was going to die when all of this was over.

And was this just a coincidence? It was now the third anniversary of Bob's death, which meant it had taken him three years to find a way to communicate with me.

He had died three years ago, to the day. Suddenly I felt a compulsion to go to Malibu, and though I was exhausted I drove up to the house. Everett wasn't home, so I went into the yard and began screaming and yelling uncontrollably. I was possessed with the idea that I had to have my house back.

Still screaming and crying, I drove down the hill to call Shane. "You've got to do something to get my house back!" I screamed. "You're the one who knows the law – there has to be a way!" He said there was nothing he could do.

I went up and down the beach, looking for a hotel. They were all filled. Finally I gave up and started driving back to Johnny and Julie's. I was too tired. I had to pull over and sleep for a while.

Rafael was at Johnny's when I got home and I told him how much I wanted to sleep in Malibu because it was the anniversary of Bob's death. "Come spend the night at Simone's," he offered. "She lives on the beach in Malibu." So off we went, and we smoked a lot of pot and had a really good evening talking.

Simone reminded me that she and Paige used to practice witchcraft in the house I lived in, the one in Laurel Canyon. They used to play "The Dark Side of the Moon" in my room all the time and conjure up spirits. A chill went through me when I heard this; that was the same album I had been playing the night I had flipped out. I remembered Paige's long black fingernails, all her books on black magic and witchcraft, and the piranha tank she kept by the bed at Garrett's. "I'm a white witch," Simone explained, "but Paige practices black magic." That was why Paige was so mean and Simone was sweet.

"I definitely want to learn about white magic," I told her.

The next morning I walked out onto the balcony to breathe the fresh air and watch the surf. I smiled when I looked down because I stood right over the spot where Bob and I spent our last day together fishing.

"Thanks, Honey," I said taking a deep breath. I belonged in Malibu. This was where Bob was hanging out.

I went back to Simone's a couple of nights later with Kay and Rafael, and something really strange happened. I was lying on the bed half asleep, stoned out of my mind on some good pot, when I started to write a letter. It was automatic writing. Kay watched me. I closed my eyes until it stopped. It was a note from Bob; the first part was in my handwriting and then it switched to his! I threw the I Ching and it let me know that I was in touch with Bob again.

Eighteen

MULTIPLE PERSONALITIES

I had to move back to Malibu. My first step was to find an apartment on the beach. Then I bought another Mercedes, this time a two-door sedan.

Raphael kept raising a subject I didn't want to face. "How well do you know this guy, Andy, who's running your store? How do you know he isn't scamming you?"

Andy scamming me? It was unthinkable. "That can't be," I said. "We go way back. He and Bob were good friends."

"I don't know what it is, but something about this guy just doesn't add up. Hey look, I know I shouldn't be sticking my nose in your business, but I don't want to see you get hurt."

I blew it off the first couple of times, but Raphael kept bringing it up. Finally I decided to bring his suspicions to a head. "Who knows? Maybe you're right," I said. "Or maybe you're just being suspicious. But why don't we make a surprise visit and check the drawer? A few minutes of poking around should answer the question one way or the other." So we made a surprise visit at 3 p.m. and checked the drawer.

There was only $90 rung on the tape and $190 cash in the drawer. "What's going on with this?" I asked Andy.

He chuckled. "Nothing unusual. It's typical of the paperwork I have to straighten out at the end of every day."

Raphael and I left. "It's a classic scam," said Raphael. "The $90 goes into the bank and the cash goes into his pocket."

"No!" I protested. "Andy wouldn't do that!"

"Maybe you're right and maybe not, but there's only one way to find out. The next step is to go to the bank and see how much cash he's been depositing every day."

I may have been a business owner driving her Mercedes to the bank, but Rafael and I were also hippies in Beverly Hills. So we couldn't just conduct our business; we had to make a party of it. First we got stoned, and then we stopped at a convenience store for a few rolls of toilet paper. "Just a little something to give the bank a party atmosphere," I said. We got to the bank, parked the car, and strung the toilet paper all over the underground garage.

"Cool," said Rafael. "It helps the bank rise above its usual stuffy image." And with that we went inside. I had brought Herbie the tape recorder with me. We told a teller we wanted to check on the status of my business's deposits, and she sent us to a clerk who looked up the records and confirmed Rafael's suspicions: "There's no record of any cash in your business's deposits. Checks? Yes. Bankcards? Yes. But no cash."

We walked out of the bank, and I felt sick. I couldn't believe I'd been betrayed again. "Do you think we'd better go right back to the store?" said Rafael. "We should really go through the paperwork. Who knows what else we'll find?"

He sounded a little too eager, and I exploded. "No! I can't believe it's come to this! Andy's our friend. And now I have to go to the store and start digging up dirt and building a case against him? I won't do it!"

Rafael was wise enough to remain silent, giving me time to think. We walked back to my car and got in. Only then did he speak, and he didn't mention Andy or the business. "Paper's still there," he said, glancing around the parking garage. "And I didn't think of it until just now, but your car is the only one that isn't decorated."

"You're right," I said, looking around. "I should have papered my car too – it's too obvious. We must be more stoned than I thought." And as I backed out of the parking space I paused for a moment and looked Rafael in the eye. "You're right. I haven't been thinking straight. We need to go back to the store. I'm not looking forward to it, but we may as well get it over with." We drove back in silence.

The store was full of people and Andy was busy with them, so I was able to go into the back room, sit at the desk, and start going through the papers. I found a stack of unpaid bills in the top drawer and tax forms that hadn't been filed for the past three quarters. How could this be? Before I had left for Rhode Island, I had hired a C.P.A. to make sure the bills and taxes were paid on time. I could feel my anger churning in my stomach. I called my C.P.A., Len Holbrook, to make an appointment. His receptionist said he could see me later that day.

Then I called Shane and told him what I'd found. "Do you have a small tape recorder that will fit in your purse?" he asked.

"No just Herbie."

"Pick one up and hide it in your purse," Shane insisted. "Herbie isn't going to work."

So I stopped at a drug store and bought a small recorder and put the tape in. I slid it into my purse and went to Mr. Holbrook's office. The receptionist smiled at me cordially as I walked in.

"I have an appointment with Mr. Holbrook," I told her.

"Oh yes, he'll be right with you," she said.

Len was smiling broadly as I sat down. I reached into my purse as if I were looking for something and pushed the record button on my tape recorder.

"Len, how is Andy doing?" I asked.

"Andy is doing a wonderful job," he said.

"So you've been checking up on him and he's paying the state taxes and all the bills?" I asked.

"Yes, of course everything is being paid," Len said.

"That's strange, Len. I found a drawer full of overdue bills and the tax forms for the past three quarters."

"Oh you must be mistaken," Len insisted.

"I'm afraid you're the one who's mistaken," I said as I slammed the forms and bills on his desk.

"Well actually, I just found out that he wasn't taking care of this," Len admitted. He didn't seem apologetic; instead, he implied that I was a troublesome customer asking unnecessary questions about matters that a professional considered routine. I sensed he was trying to confuse me. *Stick to the subject,* I said to myself.

"What do you mean you just found out?" I asked. "What have I been paying you for?"

"What do you mean?" he said defensively and with a hint of aggression. *Don't back down,* I told myself.

"You know very well what I mean," I countered. "I have copies of letters I sent to you requesting you be sure to check the cancelled checks each month and be sure these things were being taken care of."

"Well, you can't expect me to do everything," he said.

"You're telling me I'm unreasonable because I expect you to do what you agreed to do when I hired you? Why didn't you tell me then that I couldn't expect you to do everything?"

The argument went on and on and was going nowhere. I stormed out of his office, got in my car, and turned off the tape recorder. I knew I now had the evidence that he was lying through his teeth.

I quickly drove back to the store, where Rafael was waiting for me. Andy was still working with customers at the counter, so while I told Rafael what the C.P.A. had said, I went through a few more desk drawers, the few that weren't locked. There I found that Len had been using my own personal money to pay the business's bills for the past four months. I had given him signature authority on my account before I left for Rhode Island.

I watched Andy hang the "Closed" sign in the door and called out to him.

"Andy, I want to see the books."

"What for?" he asked suspiciously.

"Andy, unlock this drawer now," I demanded.

"Well, if that don't beat all," he replied angrily. "Don't you trust me?"

"Andy, give me the keys," Rafael said, holding out his hand.

Andy threw the keys on the desk. "I quit," he said, and he walked out in a huff.

Rafael and I found more than $6,000 a month rung on the tapes with only $2,000 income listed on the books.

I also found concert tickets for Elton John and stacks of prescription forms for a local doctor. I called his office and learned that he had ordered 1,000 forms and had received only 300.

In the days that followed I found out the concert tickets were counterfeit and he'd done other shady deals. The store consistently brought in about $500 a day rather than the amount I'd been quoted of $150-$200.

Things began to unravel quickly. Andy had closed out my resale number with the State Board of Equalization and gotten his own.

A final notice arrived from the telephone company and the electric company. Meanwhile, the store landlord refused to renew my lease. Len Holbrook called and offered to buy the business. Then, a few hours later, Andy called and offered me $10,000 cash for it.

I checked with I.B.M. and found out that the $1,580 I'd sent to Andy to pay off their bill had never been paid. He had never paid them anything; now the bill was more than $7,000 and they were threatening to pull the machine if I didn't pay them immediately. I talked to their representative for a while, trying to get them to wait.

The State Board of Equalization told me I had to give them $1,000 immediately to reinstate my business license. I went to their office and waited in line for two hours so I could find an administrator to reason with. I explained that I was the one who had taken out the license and that I had never authorized Andy to close it out. But no, they couldn't reinstate the license. I would have to start over from the beginning, repaying the fees Bob and I had already paid a few years before. What could I do? I gave them the check and went back to the store.

I was putting out a fire a minute. Every day, past due bills came in from paper companies and other suppliers. Andy had opened accounts in his own name, telling companies he was the new owner. Then he would place a small order in his name and would pay those bills as soon as they arrived. But whenever he had to place a large order, he'd charge it to my account and never pay a cent.

To top everything off, I got a letter from the State Department of Employment that Andy had applied for unemployment insurance!

By day I was a hardheaded businesswoman but by night I was writing and illustrating *Strawberry Jan*. I wasn't getting much sleep; the best time to work on the fairy tale was between midnight and 6:00 a.m., cosmic time.

Sometimes I tried to tell my friends that at least one other personality was writing the story. Why couldn't anyone understand? I had no control over it. But they would get weird whenever I tried to talk about it. Shane said I needed to go back to Mt. Sinai. But couldn't they see? I didn't have any talent for writing or drawing. Obviously someone else was doing it.

Strawberry Jan was flipping me out at times. One night Laura had a party for Spanky to celebrate the release of her new album. Ricky wasn't there because he was on tour with the Eagles. I tried to mix with people but somehow I kept freaking them out and they were afraid of me. Things got so bad between me and a couple of the guys in the band that I left early and came home to ask the I Ching what was happening.

When I dropped the coins a bird hit my window. I went out on the balcony. The bird lay there trembling. I picked it up carefully and I could feel its heart racing as I brought it in the house. I set it on a towel and began to throw the coins again. The bird started throwing up. I moved it to the bathtub but somehow knew that it would die as soon as I got the answer to my question. I threw the coins and got my answer, and then I went to the bathtub to check on the bird. It was dead. I threw it over the balcony and into the sea at high tide.

At 4:30 a.m. Laura called me. "Abby!" she exclaimed. "I'm so glad you're still up. I need to talk to you."

"What's the matter with you?" I demanded. It wasn't a wrong number; I recognized Laura's voice. "But who's Abby? I don't know anyone named Abby."

"That's your new name," she replied. "Abby Normal. That's what I've decided to call you."

I laughed. "A new name, huh? Nobody's ever called me anything like that before."

"Maybe not, but somehow it seems to fit. Anyway, enough about that. I guess I'm calling partly to apologize, because I'm sorry I've been treating you so strangely lately. But there's an explanation. I don't know what's going on with *Strawberry Jan*, but whatever it is, it's scaring me out of my wits. And then tonight when you left early, it got me thinking and I realized how weird I've been toward you lately. So I wanted to call and say I'm sorry."

"That's so sweet of you," I said. I was touched that she had called to apologize, but I knew what had been scaring her because it had begun to scare me too. Several people had noticed that I was like a witch with the I Ching. They often asked me to throw the coins for them, or to read their fortune with my Tarot cards.

"Well, the point is this," she continued. "I really do love you, and I'd like to do something to help you with your book. So I'd like to come over to your place and pick up the manuscript, and I'll type it for you. You can think of me as your secretary!" She sounded as enthusiastic as I had sounded when I had gotten out of high school and gotten my first job.

"That would be wonderful!" I said. "I don't know how to thank you. When would you like to start?"

"As soon as you're ready," she said. "As far as that goes, I could come over to your place and pick up the manuscript right now."

"Right now? I'm ready." We got off the phone so she could drive over to my apartment. While I waited for her, I decided to replay our phone conversation; I always used Herbie whenever I talked on the phone. But something had gone wrong with the recording. There were no words, but only a strong heartbeat. It seemed the tape picked up nothing but her fear. When she got to the apartment I played it back for her. The throbbing sound of her heartbeat freaked her out, and she left right away. She never picked up the manuscript.

The next day, a guy came in the store wanting his money back because he couldn't get in the Elton John Concert with the tickets he'd gotten from Andy. "They took one look at that ticket and knew it was counterfeit – they said the ink wasn't even the right color! He couldn't believe it!" I couldn't believe it either. I told him Andy was no longer working here and he'd better take his complaint to the police department. He left right away.

I hired a new guy, Derek, to run the store. I wondered if I was doing the right thing. It had never worked out yet; what made me think it would work now?

I had talked to Shane about what had happened with Andy and had given him the tape of my meeting with Len. Now he wanted to meet me at noon. "You need to file charges against these guys," he said. "You've got an open-and-shut case."

"What'll happen to them?" I asked.

"It'll cost Len his C.P.A. license for sure, and then they're both looking at jail time."

Our visit was short. I couldn't bring myself to file charges against Andy. "I'll think about it," I promised as I got up to leave Shane's office.

"Yes, think about it," he said as he walked me to the door. "I'll be here. Get back to me when you're ready to move forward." It was annoying that he was so sure of himself; sometimes Shane could be really cut and dried. But what did I expect? For him, it was just two criminals; for me, it was a friend I might throw in jail.

I was really depressed as I walked to my car. I didn't have to go to work; Derek was taking care of things. I drove back to Malibu. How could I file charges against Andy? He and Bob had been so close that it was unbearable to think I'd throw him in jail, no matter what he'd done to me. And yet he had ripped me off. Why? Hadn't our friendship meant anything to him?

Impulsively I stopped at a phone booth and called him.

"Andy why did you rip me off?" I asked when he answered the phone.

A truck roared by and drowned out his answer, and I heard another truck coming. "Andy, there's so much traffic here I can't hear you. I've got to find a quiet spot and call you back."

I found another phone and called back. "I really want to know why you did it Andy," I said. "I trusted you and I care about you. I'm really hurt inside Andy. Why did you do it?"

"Now JoAnn," he said meekly, "the business wasn't doing good for a long time."

"Andy, I don't care about the money. Can't you see I just want you to tell me the truth? Shane wants me to turn you in to the D.A. Andy, I don't want to do that. Please tell me why you did it."

Tears began to fall. I cried the whole time we talked because I hurt so badly and felt sorry for him. He really didn't understand that I just wanted to know the truth, and ended up telling me it was a good little business and not to let it go. I hung up exhausted and drove back to the store to see how Derek was doing.

The first thing I saw was the guys from I.B.M. pulling my machine out of the shop because I hadn't paid the $7,000. I had gotten a backup installed, and Derek was trying to keep up. The phone was ringing constantly and customers were waiting in line at the counter. I stepped in to help, and I began to feel mounting pressure in my head as customers came in and out like huge waves.

Rafael showed up and came back into the office where I was talking on the phone. I brightened; it felt better just to have him in the store. But he gave me a cold look and said, "It's pay up time."

"What are you talking about?" I asked.

"You don't think I've been helping you for free do you?" he said. "It's for all that time I've put in to help you get free from all the ripoff artists. It's pay up time."

"How much do you expect me to pay?" I asked. I was reeling, but when he put it like that I could see that maybe I could give him something.

"I've figured it out. It's already up to a few thousand dollars," he said. "I charge $400 per day."

"Four hundred dollars a day?" I shrieked. "That's insane! Most people don't make four hundred dollars a week!"

"And most people wouldn't have seen through those ripoff artists," he assured me.

"But I never agreed to pay you for what you were doing," I said. "I thought you were doing it because you were my friend." I felt like an animal trapped in a cage.

"You're kidding," he replied as though I were the one saying something unbelievable. "At four hundred dollars a day, all of this week and all of last week add up to a couple of thousand dollars. Then there are a couple of days even before that…"

I didn't wait for him to finish his arithmetic. I leaped on him and began kicking and hitting him. I don't know where my strength came from, but one of the customers helped Derek pull me off. I think I could have killed him if they hadn't stopped me.

Rafael grabbed my car keys. "I'm gonna go to your apartment and rip up *Strawberry Jan!*" he sneered. I leaped across the counter and threw him down to the ground again. Derek pulled me off and got the car keys.

"I'll put a curse on you and nothing will ever be right for you again," Rafael screamed as he left the store. "You'll never be happy."

I threw myself into my swivel chair and turned my face to the wall, sobbing uncontrollably.

I could see Derek was shaken. "JoAnn, let me drive you home," he said. I was gibbering like a crazy lady all the way home. Sometimes I would cry; sometimes I would talk. But even I could tell my words weren't making any sense. Derek looked nervous as he drove, and he said as little as possible, always in a very soothing voice.

We got home. "Just give me a minute," I told him. "I've got to get my fingernail polish off." Why? I wasn't sure, but I knew I had to do it. I found the bottle of remover and tried to unscrew the lid and get the cotton on top of the bottle. I tried and tried, but couldn't get it to work. Frustrated, I gave up and lay on the floor. Something was seriously wrong with me. "Derek, you'd better call Nate and Shane," I said.

Nate showed up in a few minutes, and he and Derek drove me to the hospital. I was shaking uncontrollably. By the time we pulled into the basement-parking garage, I was speaking with a Spanish accent and another voice was coming out of the left side of my mouth. They took me into the hospital and Nate talked to the nurses on duty through the speaker, trying to convince them to let me in to the psychiatric ward.

The Spanish voice spoke with the doctor on duty because I couldn't find my own voice. It didn't take long for him to admit me. I was given a shot and fell asleep quickly. The next day I was called into the doctor's office as soon as I woke up.

"What is going on with you?" he asked.

Finding I had my own voice back, I answered: "Oh I just think about all the jerks and the problems and how complicated it is for me to keep myself from going off the deep end. Ha, it's probably the shallow end. As soon as I think I'm all right, I get this pressure in my head like a vise and I can't control it.

"It's like there are other people inside my body and I can't control them and I don't even know who they are. They just take over at will and leave me angry with them because I can't find myself again.

"Oh darn it…darn it. What is it? Who am I anyway? This is really boring." I stood up and gazed into space.

The doctor looked at me blankly and didn't say anything. I looked at him and smiled. "Do you think it would be wonderful to be a caterpillar or a gigantic hawk soaring in the sky?" I asked. "I remember one day I was sitting on a rock on top of a mountain. The wind was blowing really hard and I balanced myself perfectly, letting my body blow in the breeze. I felt just like a tree and it was a wonderful feeling."

The doctor changed the subject. "Let's talk about Strawberry Jan. She's here on your chart."

"Oh I can't talk about her," I said. "When it is time for her to come around she will, and she can talk for herself. It's really hard for me to explain and I don't feel like it now. I'm really tired."

"Okay, I think you should rest today, unless you have any questions or you have something you'd like to talk about," the doctor said as he wrote on my chart.

"No, doc, I'm all talked out," I said. "I do have one question though."

"What's that?"

"Are you really going to let me sleep today? The last time I was here, they wouldn't let me stay in bed during the day."

"Today we're going to let you rest," the doctor said.

So I spent the first day in bed falling in and out of sleep.

The next day I felt better and knew I had to get out of the hospital as soon as I could. If I could con them into thinking I was sane, they'd let me out, right? After all, it's what anyone sane would do, and the shrinks and I all knew it. So I went to see the doctor in the morning and something went right: it wasn't the one I had already talked to. I knew I couldn't let him know how confused I really was, or they'd keep me for a while.

I showed him the fairy tale and told him about all the business problems. "I haven't been getting any sleep, and between that and the pressure I must have flown out of control. You guys have been great – I slept most of yesterday and all of the last two nights, and you wouldn't believe the difference! Now I feel ready to tackle the project of selling my business – that's going to get a lot of pressure off my back – and I've really got to get on it right away." On and on it went, with assurances that I was going to start going to bed earlier and regrets that my business responsibilities made it impossible for me to plan to stay at the hospital longer – as though the Mt. Sinai Psych Ward was a five-star vacation resort.

But it must have been what he wanted to hear. Paperwork went from one office to the next, and I was able to sign myself out the next morning.

When I got out I called Shane. "JoAnn, this isn't good. You really need to give the program a chance. You've got all your friends worried; your business decisions aren't panning out; you tell me you can't sleep; you're like a time bomb..."

Typical Shane, always so cut and dried. "Lighten up," I giggled. "I thought you'd be excited that I was getting out so soon..."

"At the rate you're going," he interrupted, "you're going to need a conservator to handle your affairs. You've got the business; you've got Heather..."

"Heather's fine," I said firmly. "But now that you mention it, I do have work to do, and you're sounding like a broken record. I've got to go..."

Though I knew better, I couldn't bring myself to go back to the shop. I told myself it was okay; Derek was looking after things. I didn't want to go anywhere and I didn't want to call anybody. This wasn't like me; I wondered if it was an effect of Rafael's curse. I found it hard to go out of my apartment. I was afraid of people and didn't like them looking at me. I felt that if someone spoke to me I'd scream. I even hated going into the little store up the road; the man behind the counter had known me for years and I didn't even like to talk to him.

It was easier to stay home, drinking Southern Comfort and listening to Janis Joplin. I felt close to her. Southern Comfort was her favorite drink, and it became mine: something to prepare me for the morning coffee, something to flavor the coffee, something to wash it down. She had spent time with Stephen before she died – as close as I felt to Janis, maybe I should call Stephen again. I did, but he didn't answer.

What had it been like for Janis? What was it like to be a musician? I wasn't even a real writer or an artist, and the pressure was unbearable. I had written a poem, "Run Baby Run". Drew had put it to music and Spanky had told me she wanted to record it. Poor Janis. Poor me. I needed help.

Who could help me? I asked the I Ching and it told me, "Persevere. So I kept calling Stephen. I still couldn't reach him, but that shouldn't be a surprise. The I Ching wouldn't have said, "Persevere" if it was going to be easy.

Nineteen

$KICKED\ OUT\ OF\ THE\ IRS$

I had gotten out of the hospital, but there was no getting around it: something in me was broken. I was always tired, even when lying in bed or when waking up after twelve hours of sleep. I went out of my way to avoid people; even if I was hungry and had nothing in the cupboards I would postpone going to the store because I didn't want to face people.

I vaguely knew this wasn't normal, but I wouldn't get better in the nut house with doctors probing my mind and loonies wandering around, trying to figure themselves out.

The people who called or visited always seemed to want something, even if it was only for me to read their fortunes or to throw the I Ching. A few people wanted to buy my business but I was afraid I would make a mistake and I couldn't make a decision. It was getting harder and harder to pay bills and keep up with paperwork; the mail made less and less sense. If I called Shane for help, it always came around to his saying, "JoAnn, the real answer is for you to go back to Mt. Sinai." This always infuriated me. I'd played their game and they had let me go. Even the shrinks knew they couldn't help me.

But I was going to have to find someone who could. Heather flew back from Rhode Island by herself. It was good – really good – to see her. But I wasn't doing a good job of taking care of myself, and I knew I couldn't look after her. Once again, I'd have to find someone to watch her.

I was still using Herbie to keep track of all my conversations.

The I Ching had made one thing clear: that I should persist in trying to get in touch with Stephen. I kept trying to reach him, and eventually I got through. He dropped everything to come down and help me. He picked up Heather and flew her to Santa Cruz to stay with his brother and sister-in-law; he came back the next day, called his doctor, and got me admitted to a regular hospital.

At first they stuck me in a room with an old lady who never woke up.

I knew she was alive because she made horrible sounds when she tried to breathe, but she slept all the time. Her noises were so unnerving that I demanded a private room. They moved me.

Stephen was staying with his parents in Pasadena so he could visit me every day. He really was sweet.

After ten days they dismissed me from the hospital. Stephen took me home and cared for me. He cooked, cleaned, and took me to his accountant and attorney. They reviewed my business situation and turned it down because it was too much work. "Even if I could take the case," said the attorney, "I would have to hire two other attorneys to straighten it out."

No wonder I was so bewildered! People who were supposed to be in their right mind were telling me it was too much work? If they couldn't do it, how would I ever figure it out? The night before Stephen left, we stayed up all night drinking a pint of 151-proof rum. Somehow neither of us got drunk. We also smoked a lot of grass.

Around 3 a.m. we got into a very intense conversation about my pregnancy. He admitted he had lied to me earlier, just as I'd thought. "I had no idea it would tear you up as it did," he said, "and I've really felt bad about it. So I'm willing to make you an offer. I'm willing to marry you so we can adopt a baby to replace the one we lost. Then once that's taken care of, we'll get a divorce and we can each go our separate ways. But I'll take care of both of you."

I was furious. I'd never been so insulted. I was silent for a moment, lining up my thoughts so I could let him have it, but before I got a chance to say anything the phone rang.

"JoAnn, what are you doing? It's Garrett. Why aren't you in New York with me? I need you here!" It felt good to talk to someone who really wanted me, and I wasn't in a hurry to get back to Stephen. We talked for an hour.

I hung up and turned to Stephen. "That was Garrett," I said triumphantly. "He says he's in love with me, and he wants me to fly out to New York to be with him."

"I don't believe you," Stephen retorted. "I think you're making the whole thing up." This was a twist; he was the one with the history of telling lies. "I'll tell you what," he went on. "Pick up the phone and call him back, and this time tape the whole conversation."

So I did. As Stephen listened in he got upset and tried to grab the phone and cut off the connection. After I hung up, he listened to the tape and got weird because Garrett kept saying that he loved me and wanted to know why I wasn't with him.

Stephen ran out on the balcony and started to jump. I stopped him and coaxed him inside. He told me he didn't know who I was or who he was. I taped every bizarre word he said.

Suddenly, he laughed, said he was only kidding, and ripped the tape out of the recorder and threw it into the ocean. We drifted like strangers through the rest of the night and the next morning. He left for the airport before noon.

In the afternoon, I decided I'd go to New York just to get away from everything. When I called Garrett he said, "Well, I've got to bring you up to date. Monica just arrived."

"Monica?" I shrieked. "Why didn't you tell me she was coming?"

"That's the thing," he said sheepishly. "I didn't know myself. She just turned up unannounced, and now she's here. What am I supposed to do?" By now his voice was cajoling, and I knew he wouldn't ask her to leave.

I exploded with anger and slammed the phone in his ear.

I hurried to my closet, grabbed every piece of clothing he'd ever made for me, and ran onto my balcony. The tide was in, and I threw everything over the railing: coats, jackets, tops, dresses, and skirts. Most items would have cost a thousand dollars or more. It wasn't just leather; each piece was a work of art, hand-painted or trimmed with beads, feathers, or fur, and now they were all bobbing on the waves for a moment before they and Garrett sank out of my life. Somehow, I felt better, though I couldn't help wishing I could wash out to sea myself.

I collapsed on my bed and wondered what to do next. I called Shane; he said he wanted me to get another attorney and

Dressed in one of Garrett's creations

asked me not to call him anymore. He added that Stephen had already contacted him to find out how to get me committed. I hung up and dozed off.

I woke up to a horrible pounding on my front door. It was the Sheriff's Department. Stephen had called and told them I was going to commit suicide. I told them I was okay and they left.

Maybe this was a sign. Maybe I really was supposed to kill myself. I wanted to ask the I Ching, but I didn't have the energy. I went back to bed.

The next few days were a blur. I was still confused by the simplest tasks, still in love with Stephen, still afraid of being locked up in the nut-house. I got a letter from the I.R.S. but didn't understand it, so I put it aside and forgot about it. People were still offering to buy the business, but what if I made a wrong move?

One day I woke up longing for chocolate éclairs, ice cream, candy bars – I wasn't sure what. I lit a cigarette and waited to see what I really wanted. Suddenly I remembered the candles I had bought at the witchcraft shop in West Hollywood. I lit them and went through Alistair Crowley's book of magic to find a spell that would bring Stephen back to me. I found one and read it again and again. I finally went back to sleep, exhausted.

I woke up a few hours later and now at last I had the energy to ask the I Ching if I should kill myself. The answer wasn't clear.

Another morning I woke up to a beautiful day. I didn't feel up to it; I crawled back under the covers. A few minutes later I sat up to make a phone call and saw my reflection. My cheeks were starting to wrinkle. "The curse of growing old, old and lonely," I said aloud, lying back in bed changing my mind about phoning. I realized I would be thirty soon.

Maybe I didn't need anyone or anything but me and Heather. Maybe some day Prince Charming would come and take me away from it all. Maybe.

I forced myself to sit up and look around. The room was a mess. It would probably take fifteen minutes to straighten things up, but where would I begin? Just thinking about it wore me out. I smoked a joint and went back to sleep for the rest of the day.

At sunset I woke up and called Stephen. "I'm going to India," he announced, "but I'll drop by to see you before I go." Then a moment later he said he wasn't coming after all. He said he loved me; seconds later he said, "I never said I love you." He was taking Valiums and was starting to act like a crazy man. "It all started when I was visiting you," he explained, somehow shifting the blame for his craziness to me. "You freaked me out when I was there. Something creepy is happening with you – I don't know what it is, but it's really creepy."

I used Herbie and taped the whole conversation. After we hung up I played it again and again, trying to make sense of what Stephen had said. I wondered if Rafael's curse had somehow spilled over onto Stephen. In my own case, within an hour of Rafael's leaving the store I had felt things starting to happen. Now it felt like an evil melting over me, and everyone I was with.

Before I went to bed I threw the I Ching several times. It too wouldn't say the same thing twice. What was going on? It had never acted like this before.

I moved through the next few days in suspended animation. Life progressively got stranger. It was as if I was caught in a spider web of evil, and anyone who tried to help me in any way got caught in it too.

I called the store one morning and nobody answered. I kept calling, and finally at noon a stranger picked up the phone. "Oh, you want Derek? He isn't here right now, and I don't know when he'll be back. He got thrown in jail last night in Las Vegas…"

"Then who are you?" I asked. "And if Derek isn't there, how did you get into my store?"

"Oh, you're the boss? Don't worry; everything's cool. I'm Derek's friend, and he wanted me to open the store for him since he couldn't be here himself. He told me where to find the key…"

Outrageous! Maybe it was time to sell the store; I had a couple of offers. A larger business had valued it at $35,000 to $40,000 and talked about acquiring it; I asked the accountant Stephen had recommended to get in touch with them, but for some reason he couldn't make contact. And Derek had been telling me the business wasn't making any money; he was offering me $15,000 for it.

Meanwhile, the house in Santa Cruz sold, and then I cancelled the contract. The realtor got really mad, but I couldn't help it. I certainly couldn't handle moving my stuff out of there right now. These days it was hard enough just to get out of bed.

I rested whenever I could for the next week, then I went to Santa Cruz to see Heather. Stephen picked me up at the airport and he had gone downhill. His movements were a little too quick and a little too jerky, and there was a frantic look in his eye, as though something the rest of us couldn't see was distracting him. He took me to stay with his brother's family for the next few days. I settled in with them, and it was good to be with Heather again. I could see they had cared for her well.

Stephen came by the house every day, and I was really worried about him. He was driving me crazy with his habit of saying one thing one moment and then telling me the opposite a moment later. His moods were just as erratic; he would be sweet and considerate, then for no reason would become irrational and impossible.

Derek called. "I've got good news and bad news," he said cheerfully. "The good news is I'm out of jail and I'm back at the store. The bad news is that we're having problems – some of our checks have started bouncing."

"Checks bouncing!" I was horrified. "Why are you writing checks if we don't have the money to cover them?"

"Well, the bills are due so I need to put something in the mail. And normally there's enough cash flow to cover the checks by the time they arrive and someone manages to take them to the bank. But for some reason, cash flow has been a bit low lately, and that's why the checks are bouncing."

"You can't do that!" I screamed. "It's against the law!" As soon as the words came out of my mouth I realized how weak the argument would sound; we all broke the law every time we lit a joint, and I never had found out what he had been in jail for. But then I saw my angle. "Do you want to go back to jail? That's where people go who write rubber checks."

"Yeah, but like I say, it's never been a problem before; we always had the cash flow. You know, it's gotta be hard for you, trying to keep up with all this when you're so far away. Maybe it would take a load off your mind if I bought the business – I could give you $15,000 for it."

"Fifteen thousand!" I snorted. What a ripoff. "The other guys have offered thirty-five or forty thousand. Why should I sell it for fifteen?"

"Let's face it; they're dragging their feet. And with the cash flow down the way it's been lately, there's no way they're gonna fork over 35 or 40 grand. But it would be different if enough cash was coming in to keep the checks from bouncing."

"Number one, I'm not selling the business for fifteen thousand," I interrupted. "Number two, there aren't going to be any more rubber checks. I think the best thing to do is to close the store until I get back."

"Close the store? Are you sure?" he said. He sounded startled.

"Yes, until I get back it's the best thing to do."

"Okay," he conceded. "You're the boss. But don't forget my offer. I don't think you're going to get any more for the business than what I'm willing to pay." And with that he hung up.

"What am I going to do?" I told Stephen's sister-in-law. "I can't run the business, I can't find anyone else to run the business, and I can't sell it."

"Let's find out what to do," she replied confidently. She brought out the Tarot cards to tell my fortune. She studied the cards for a moment then announced, "If Stephen doesn't marry you, you're going to die."

It wasn't what I wanted to hear. "Well, if nothing else, the cards are giving a clearer message than I've been able to get from the I Ching lately," I replied. "But here's the next question: can the cards tell me how to get along with Stephen? That's the real challenge."

She shook her head and sighed. "You're right. Stephen isn't always the easiest person to get along with, and the cards can't give you any advice about that part. I'm afraid you'll have to figure it out on your own."

Too bad. The night before I was scheduled to fly home, we had a big fight and I told him to leave.

Stephen's brother and his wife were very kind and offered to keep Heather for me until I got my life straightened out. I decided this was the best thing to do.

But Stephen came early to take me to the airport the next day. "Make sure you pack Heather's things too," he commanded. "You're taking her with you."

"Why?" I protested. "Your brother and sister-in-law said they'd be glad to keep her for a while."

"I don't care," he said flatly. "It's time to completely sever all ties between you and my family. I can tell you don't really love me; otherwise, you'd be begging me to stay with you."

I packed Heather's things as he kept babbling. "Fact is, Heather would be better off if you put her up for adoption," he went on. "Look at the life you're giving her!" We got in the car and Heather snuggled into my arms. Stephen's monolog went non-stop all the way to the airport.

We got home, and a few days later I called to check up on Stephen. He was stranger than ever and I was afraid for him. I got someone to take care of Heather and I caught a plane. They seated me next to two Catholic priests; I asked them to pray for Stephen and me.

I landed in San Jose, rented a car, and drove towards Stephen's. On my way, I passed a Catholic Church and impulsively decided to go in. Maybe prayer was a good idea. The problem with Stephen seemed to stem from Rafael's curse, but I hadn't thought to mention this to the priests on the plane. So I found another priest in the church and explained what was going on. "Yes, I'll pray for you," he assured me. "There are prayers to break curses."

From there I drove to Stephen's. "What are you doing here?" he demanded when he saw me at the door.

"Stephen, I've been worried about you. You're not acting like yourself lately. I even met a couple of priests on the plane as I flew over here; I asked them to pray for you. Then I stopped at the Catholic church to ask the Father there to pray for you, and he said he'd be glad to come over and see if you're alright." Stephen's face was getting harder and harder, but I spoke as tenderly as I could, hoping to get him to soften. "I'm worried about you."

"How dare you!" he snarled. "If I need you to worry about me, I'll let you know. And if I need a priest, I'll call him myself. Get away from me!" He gave me a vicious shove that knocked me down the stairs as he shouted again, "Get away from me!"

He glared at me for a moment as I lay on the cold cement, completely stunned. I ached all over after tumbling down the stairs. Then he took off his shoes and threw them at me. I dodged them and he went in the house and slammed the door.

A few moments later the door opened again and a girl came outside to talk to me. I'd been through the jealous girlfriend routine before, but this felt different. Her voice was sweet but authoritative, like that of a family friend or a hired caretaker. "I'm so sorry about Stephen," she said, "but he's been going through a lot lately and he needs to take it easy. I really think the best thing for you to do is to leave; right now he doesn't need you upsetting him."

I drove back to the church and told the priest what had happened. "He never even let me in the front door," I told him. "Do you think you could call him?"

I waited while he made the call. Stephen refused to talk.

Exhausted, I flew back to L.A. I tried to sleep.

The next day I made myself open the shop. I lingered over the mail, trying to sort things out. I was desperate, and I really had to do something. Then I remembered hearing somewhere that the I.R.S. audits people. Maybe this would help. So I piled all my business records into five boxes, carried them out to my car, and drove to the I.R.S. office in Hollywood. I couldn't carry all five boxes at once, so I chose one and carried it inside, setting it on the counter. Then I took a number and plopped down in a seat, taking my place among all the other people waiting for their turn. They sat stonily, with blank faces.

Eventually a lady behind the counter called my number.

"I would like to see someone because I would like to be audited," I said calmly. I slid my box towards her, expecting her to reach for it eagerly. My words seemed to affect everybody in the waiting room; out of the corner of my eye I could see that they were now staring at me.

"Young lady, a citizen can't ask to be audited," she said. She looked at me forbiddingly, and she shrugged apologetically as she made eye contact with others in the waiting room behind me.

"Well, I want to be," I said firmly. I wasn't going to be put off.

She shook her head warily. "That isn't how it works." Her eyes were still scanning the room, as if I weren't to be taken seriously.

"I need to be audited," I insisted. "I own a business, and…"

"I'm sorry," she interrupted, and at last she was giving me her undivided attention. "That's impossible. You don't call us; we call you. Do you have an appointment?"

"No, but I've always heard that the I.R.S. audits people…"

"No, it's impossible. Now I suggest you leave immediately. Until you hear from us, I don't want to hear any more about this."

She was very authoritative, a woman who was used to being obeyed. I took the heavy box off the counter and walked out. Obviously I'd have to try another angle.

I found a pay phone in the lobby and called a local news station; maybe if I got the press involved, the I.R.S. would be forced to audit me. Nobody would listen. I went outside, put the cumbersome box down, and sat on the cold cement stairs. I was overwhelmed with hopelessness and began to cry. People walked by, all ignoring me just as the passersby had done in Mexico when I had sat outside while Aaron was in jail. It was as though I were a leper, someone it was best not to get involved with.

Finally, I got up and drove back to the store. I cleared my desk, filling several other boxes. I loaded them in the car. I went back into the store, knowing I would never set foot in it again. I looked around, remembering the day Bob and I rented the space and how hard we worked to build the business. For a moment I savored the memories, then "I turned the sign around to say "Closed" and locked the door for the last time.

I drove home and made trip after trip to carry all the records for the business into my tiny apartment. I got a bottle of champagne out of the refrigerator. The sun was almost down, and the surf was crashing under my deck. I dragged all the boxes out to the porch.

I smoked a joint and drank the champagne, waiting for just the right moment. It came when I saw a huge wave rolling towards me. As quickly as I could, I threw all the boxes over the deck. It gave me a quite a workout. It was hard to get each box up on the railing, just as it had been hard to lug the boxes upstairs. But I did it, and one by one they opened as they tumbled into their watery grave and papers scattered every which way. I laughed wildly as I heaved the last one over the railing and sank into a chair. The burden had rolled off my shoulders. Every business record and all the past due bills were gone. I'd never look back.

The sun sank and the stars came out. I fell into bed, drained. Everything in the apartment seemed to be swirling around. I couldn't focus; it was as if I'd dropped acid. "God? Are you there?" I didn't know how to pray. "There's nobody else to turn to. You're my only hope. See what a mess my life is? I'm putting it all in Your hands." When I finished my prayer, it really looked as if the moon smiled back at me.

In the morning I went to Rachel's shrink to get some pills to calm me down. I sat on the couch sober and straight, but everything seemed to be moving.

I talked to him for a while and he asked if I believed in witchcraft. He strongly suggested I admit myself to the mental hospital. "It's out of the question," I told him. "Who would look after Heather?" He finally gave me a couple of prescriptions.

Later, Rachel called me. "My shrink called and said he gave you a couple of prescriptions. And I wondered – have you read the book I left with you?"

"Oh dear," I answered. "I've read it, but I forgot to get it back to you. Do you need it right away?" She was always reading about psychology; she had her own battles with depression.

"No, it's not that," she murmured. "But I wondered if it helped you at all."

"Well, you were right," I replied. "A lot of the case histories in the book sounded like me. Maybe I'm manic-depressive. But what was the name of the drug they're using now? It's probably what I need. I was hoping your shrink would give me a prescription for it."

"It's lithium," she said, "but you don't just get a prescription. The drug is so strong that it's dangerous unless you take it under a doctor's supervision, with a lot of checkups and tests along the way. Actually, I did ask him about it, but he said it isn't what you need at all."

"Then what does he think I need?"

"He said you're a very sick girl," she said. "He said you really need to be in a hospital."

"No way," I said firmly. I could feel the net of my concerned friends closing around me. "I'm leaving town. I'm taking everything I can, whatever will fit in my car. You know where I always hide the spare key; feel free to let yourself in and take anything you want that I've left behind. And I'll make sure your book is on the kitchen table."

"Oh JoAnn," she sighed. "I hope it works out for you. You always have such incredible adventures, but lately I'm starting to think your real story has more to do with what's happening inside you than everything that's going on around you. I do wish you'd get the help you need. Please promise you'll be careful."

"I'll be careful, and I'll stay in touch" I promised. Where would I find another friend like Rachel? But I looked at my watch. If I left now, I'd have time to pick up Heather from the babysitter and drive to Santa Cruz before Ron and Marie got to bed. "But it's time to go," I said. "I've got a long drive ahead."

Twenty

SLEEPING WITH A SHOTGUN

I picked Heather up and headed for Santa Cruz. My mind was hazy as we made the long drive, but somehow I managed to get to my sister's house at 9 p.m. They'd lived with me briefly until they'd found their own home, and some of my things were stored at their house.

Ron helped me move back into my lonely little farmhouse the next day. It was cold, damp, and bleak. We were carrying a heavy dresser and suddenly I felt a pressure on my shoulders, as though I were carrying a cross. I looked around but nobody was there. And why a cross? I had never been religious. We went on moving things, but I would think about this incident for months to come, wondering what message was being sent to me and who was sending it.

Within a couple of weeks I enrolled Heather in a private school. I dropped her off on her first day, came back home, and lay in bed. I was overwhelmed with depression and hopelessness and began to cry. My despair seemed almost tangible, like a whirlpool, and I was sinking fast and didn't have the strength to resist its downward pull. With all my might I screamed at God: "God, please, if You're there, help me!" Wasn't that what God was for, someone to call upon as a last resort? I don't know what kind of answer I was expecting, but the silence was deafening.

So I tried again, screaming until I was hoarse, and then I collapsed in a heap of tears. I fell back into bed and thought about it. I had been screaming for several hours, pausing at times to catch my breath and then starting in again. Was there any special merit in an ear-piercing plea? If He was God, couldn't He hear me even if I whispered? I'd never thought about things like this before. Maybe my situation wasn't desperate enough, or maybe I wasn't the sort of person He would answer.

I got up, deciding it was time to do something practical. It was scary to be so isolated. The house made noises, and though my mind told me they were just the normal sounds of an old house settling, they still spooked me at times. Then the tall redwoods around us were beautiful by day, but they looked sinister as the sun sank over the horizon. I'd feel safer with a watchdog.

I still had some time before I'd need to pick Heather up from school, so I drove to the pound. The imprisoned animals were all vying for my attention, barking and jumping up in their cages. Their sad eyes broke my heart and I wished I could let them all go. A big Irish Setter with a sweet face caught my eye, and soon he was at my side, thankful to be released from jail.

For safety's sake, I also stopped and bought a shotgun. I had no idea how to use it, but how hard could it be? The man behind the counter showed me how it worked.

Heather was excited about the dog. "What should we name him?" I asked.

"Mac!" she said without hesitation. "I think he wants to go out in the yard and play now." She was right; we all had a good time.

I put Heather to bed and tried to feel safe with Mac. Every noise startled me, but Mac slept on, untroubled. Maybe he was such a good watchdog that he knew better than to react to normal sounds; maybe he was asleep on the job. To play it safe, I loaded the shotgun and lay down in bed. This became the pattern for the next few weeks: sleeping fitfully with my loaded shotgun under the covers, while Mac slept through the mysterious noises of the night, noises that always woke me up.

As winter approached it started getting cold. We had a fireplace and a propane space heater I didn't know how to light, so we got in the habit of wearing sweaters and coats indoors. I held back the tears one night as I looked at my sweet uncomplaining daughter. She was bundled up in her winter coat as she sat at the dinner table and ate a can of chicken noodle soup.

"Mommy, can we turn on the heater?" she asked innocently. To her it was simple.

"Honey, we don't have a heater," I said.

"Why, Mommy?"

"Because this house was built before they had heaters," I explained. "They used to build big fires in the fireplace to keep warm. I don't know how to make a fire," I said, anticipating her next question.

"Mommy, I know how to make a fire," she said brightly. "You get a match."

"Yes, Honey," I agreed.

"And Mommy, I'm not supposed to play with them, but you can."

"I'll try to get some wood tomorrow," I promised. I got a knit cap and put it on her head to warm her ears.

There was a propane stove in the kitchen. Maybe it could heat at least part of the rambling house. Heather's optimism had spilled over, and I decided to try to light it. I opened the oven, lit a match, positioned its flame it by a nozzle, and turned on the gas. Instantly I heard a hiss and a whoosh as a ball of fire jumped out at my upper body. "Mommy, Mommy, are you okay?" Heather cried out as I turned off the gas.

"Yes, Honey, don't worry," I said, trying to sound calm. But I could smell burning hair and my face and arms were in terrible pain. I ran to the bathroom.

I swatted the hair on top of my head until it stopped smoking and I took stock of the damage. My face and arms were an angry red, there was hardly any hair left on my arms, and my eyelashes were almost gone. I grabbed a pair of scissors and cut the singed part of my hair off so Heather wouldn't see it, and got her in bed as quickly as I could.

I needed help but there wasn't anybody. I had no telephone and I was in too much pain to drive. I would have to take care of myself. I filled two buckets with cold water and wrestled the ice cubes out of their trays and into the buckets. Somehow I made a way to lie down with my arms soaking in the ice water. I didn't get much sleep this way, shivering all night. Miraculously, my arms felt better by morning and my face had started going back to its normal color.

When I took Heather to school, I saw a lot of posters advertising Tai Chi classes, promising tranquility. I wrote down the address.

I picked up Heather after school and took her with me to the Tai Chi studio. She waited patiently in a small room off the kitchen while we went through our exercises. It was fascinating to watch the instructor move like a serene river, ever so slowly making contact with an unseen force. He was captivating. He seemed to have the answers to life as he taught us about Eastern religion and showed us some basic exercises. I felt clumsy as I tried to imitate his simplest motions.

He started talking to me after class and suddenly I noticed everyone had left. Heather was sound asleep on the sofa and we ended up spending the night.

I went home the next day and got very sick. I felt like evil was coming out of me. I knew something supernatural was happening, like what had happened when Rafael put the curse on me. I threw up violently and a vile odor filled the room. It went on for hours.

On Saturday I didn't have to take Heather to school so I decided to drop some acid after we got dressed. I sat at the typewriter to write in my diary:

> The acid is just starting to come on so I'll see what kind of thoughts fill my brain as it takes me away...away where I can be a bird on the wind rustling through the trees. Hush, I'm a leaf floating around. Hear me crackle as I fall to the ground. Oh no, don't step on me, crushing my delicate crunchy form. I am a moth fluttering about...I love the sound of the woodpecker.

I stopped because I was tripping too hard to type. I took Heather for a walk around the deserted farm. We checked out the ants and watched them travel from one spot to the next. We went back in the house where she fed me crackers while I lay on the kitchen floor. As soon as I chewed them up, I spit them out like a machine gun and made her laugh. "You're silly, Mommy," she said as she put more crackers in my mouth. She giggled as I made my voice sound like the machine gun was sticking.

She lay down for a nap and I went back to my typewriter.

> I'll let fate take me on a wild ride once again. There is no time to lose because there is no time to win ... Oh Strawberry Jan, I miss you. I thought perhaps you went away...

Heather woke up. By now the LSD began to wear off a bit and Heather and I went outside to collect scraps of wood for a fire. The air was crisp and the sun had begun to set. We hurried along, picking up anything that looked as if it might burn. Heather held two pieces of wood in her little arms and was proud of her catch. She tottered under the weight of her burden and we hurried back to drop our first load on the porch.

It's hard to gather firewood when you're coming down from an acid trip. Rainbows surrounded everything I looked at, making some things look too precious to burn. But the sun was sinking lower and the chilly wind made me less cautious. Soon we each added another armload to our pile on the porch.

I carelessly placed a few pieces of newspaper under a large log and set the match to it. The newspaper burned quickly and the outer edges of the wood caught fire, filling me with hope. Then the fire flickered out. I tried again with another twig-and-paper combination, but it too flared up then died out. I tried again and again.

"Mommy, it's okay," Heather said with sympathetic eyes. "I can get my warm coat."

"I'm going to try one more thing," I said. There was a can of barbecue starter under the house.

I got my flashlight and turned it on as I forced open the basement door and stepped in. A thick dusty spider web wrapped itself around my face and I recoiled, frightened of spiders and any other creepy thing I might find. I hated this dreary spot under the kitchen and hurried about my task as quickly as possible. Though the effects of the LSD lingered, there were no rainbows down here.

Triumphantly, I ran back to my challenge and piled up lots of papers, twigs, pine cones, and pine needles. I tossed two huge logs on top, adding a liberal dose of lighter fluid. Was this enough? I thought about it, and then I decided to saturate the logs. This time I wouldn't fail! I struck a match and tossed it into the fireplace.

Whoosh! The flames shot out suddenly and started burning the wooden mantel. I had to scurry for water, and by the time I had saved the mantel I had also put out the fire in the fireplace. There was nothing left but a waterlogged mess, a depressing smell, and a pall of smoke.

Heather timidly got her jacket and I grabbed my warmest sweater, and we went outside for one more walk in the final moments of daylight. I turned my attention to the beauty and tranquility of the rugged mountains and towering trees around us. Somehow I'd conquer the cold.

Days slipped by, lost in many LSD trips and love affairs. One of the guys, Eric, stayed with me for a few weeks. "This isn't Malibu," he warned me. "When winter gets here, you're going to be facing some serious cold. We've got to get you a supply of firewood. And you've got to learn how to heat this house. You've got everything you need, but you've got to learn how to use it."

So he added several loads of logs to the pile on my porch and gave me lesson after lesson about how to light the space heater and how to build a fire. The relationship lasted only a few weeks, but at least it got me ready for winter. Funny; I'd never looked for anything like this in a relationship before.

Heather was enjoying school. Every day when I picked her up, she excitedly chattered about all that had happened that day, and about anything that was coming up soon. I was glad she was happy.

Thanksgiving came. I decided to treat it like just another day. For Heather, it was just a day without school. I told myself she wasn't really missing anything. I fought off my memories by smoking a few joints and reading Heather's favorite stories. She particularly liked one about a goose named Petunia. "Mommy, read me Petunia one more time," she urged me after I'd read it twice.

"Honey, why don't we pick another story?" I asked, glancing hopefully at the stack of books on her shelf.

"Oh please, Mommy," she pleaded.

I heard a car pull up and I hurried to the door, peering out through the dark pane of glass to see who it was. Garrett, Monica, and her three children piled out. I opened the door, surprised to see them.

"We didn't want you to be alone on Thanksgiving," Garrett said, giving me a warm hug.

"So we brought you this duck from a Chinese restaurant in San Francisco," Monica added.

It really was good to see them and we had a lot of laughs around the kitchen table. We could hear squeals of laughter as the children played in Heather's room.

The day ended. We got the children to bed, I gave my room to Garrett and Monica, and I said goodnight and went into the spare bedroom. A while later I heard a light tap on my door.

"Yeah?" I said rubbing the sleep from my eyes.

"Can we come in?" Monica asked.

"Okay," I answered warily.

Monica was dressed in a skimpy black see-through negligee and Garrett stood behind her fully clothed. Garrett said "Monica and I would like to make love to you."

"Get out!" I roared. A threesome? I'd already crossed a lot of the boundaries I had grown up with, but this was too much. "Get out now!"

At first Garrett got angry, but I was in such a rage I could have killed them both. They meekly retreated and shut the door.

Garrett and I were the first ones up the next morning. I made coffee.

"Look, I can see now that we should have done this a different way," he apologized. "But I love both of you, and I want to take care of both of you. I've already talked it over with Monica, and she agrees that this is the only way."

"What does Monica really think about all this?" I asked. I felt sorry for her. I was sure she didn't like the idea, but Garrett had manipulated her into it.

"Oh, she's fine with it," Garrett said with a shrug. "She's good about keeping an open mind."

Soon Monica came into the kitchen. "The kids are awake," she said. Sure enough, they clattered in a few moments later. We ate breakfast and they all packed up and loaded the car. Then Garrett and Monica took me aside and assured me, "Any time you need it, you have a home with us – whenever you're ready." They left with waves and smiles and shouts of "See you soon."

How could I stay angry? Garrett had a big heart. He really did want to do his best for everyone.

I decided to surprise Heather and decorate her room, so I went to a fabric store and bought an assortment of fabrics printed in various designs, all in different shades of pink. It took one day to plan the design and another to get the pieces ready to glue. Then on the third day, while Heather was at school, I glued the fabric to the walls. When she came home that afternoon, she said, "I got new wallpaper, huh?" But I didn't expect her to be excited yet. The best was yet to come, and she wouldn't see it until she went to bed the next night.

The final touch was to paint a giant rag doll on the back of the door, with a big smile, a patchwork apron, and hair made of yarn. I surprised Heather when I tucked her into bed that night. She had never liked it when I shut her door at bedtime, but now I said, "Look at your new friend! You don't have to sleep alone!"

She took one look and squealed, "Oh, Mommy! I love it!" And from then on, closing the door at bedtime was not a problem.

But no amount of decorating could keep us warm. The nights were getting longer and the winds were getting colder, and even though I now knew how to get a fire roaring in the fireplace, it wasn't enough. By the middle of December I was ready to move. I made a few phone calls to see what my options were. A plan came together.

I went to Heather's room and announced, "We're moving. We're going to go somewhere warm."

She had her crayons out and was coloring. "Oh good," she said. She didn't look up from what she was drawing.

I had expected more of a reaction. "How do you feel about moving?" I asked, hoping to coax a response out of her. "Would you like to go somewhere warm?"

"Yes, I'd like to be warm," she said. But it didn't seem to make an impact; she was focused on her coloring.

In the next four hours I braved the cellar to toss all my possessions under the house, packed our bags, and loaded the car. I phoned Eric, and he said he'd take Max. But suddenly Heather was excited about something and didn't want to get in the car.

"Mommy, come look at the rag doll," she said.

"Heather, get in the car," I said. "I want to leave now."

"Please, Mommy," she pleaded. "You have to see the rag doll."

I reluctantly went with her and she pointed at the rag doll. A small drop of paint was running out of its eye, forming a tear.

"The dolly is sad because we are leaving, huh, Mommy?"

"Well I guess she is, Darling," I said, lifting her up in my arms while taking a last glance at the incredible sight. How had this happened? The tear hadn't been there before. It was unsettling; I hoped the doll didn't know something I didn't know.

But it was time to go. We drove to L.A. I left my Mercedes with a friend who had said he could get $5,000 for it, and left for Hawaii.

Twenty One

CONNING THE SHRINK IN HAWAII

We got to Hawaii. First we had to find a place to live and get our-selves set up. Then it took a few days just to figure out how to enroll Heather in school.

Heather seemed to want my attention continually. "Mommy, watch me swim – dance – swing." I loved her dearly, but it was hard to focus on anything. Everything seemed so complicated. Shopping and dinner were nearly impossible. How would we survive?

I felt like an empty shell searching for heaven but living in hell. Why were we so tortured in life? What was the point of our senseless and unending pain? What had I done to deserve this? Oh Lord, forgive me please. I was praying every day for Him to forgive my sins and enable me to be happy once again.

My apartment walls would close in on me like a prison, but then I would go outside and the world felt like a bigger one. Maui seemed to be one big insane asylum and I was just another patient. The days were get-ting emptier. Sometimes I wondered if my depression would crush me.

I forced myself to walk down to the Pioneer Inn for breakfast every morning, and on the way I would stop in a little Episcopalian Church and kneel to pray. We really needed somebody to help us.

I felt numb all the time. Nothing seemed real, as though I were in a dream and couldn't wake up. Meal times often crept up on me and took me by surprise; too often, I fed Heather a bowl of Jell-O or cereal in-stead of a real meal. Sometimes I forgot to watch her. Once in a while I realized I wasn't giving Heather what she needed, but then the fog would roll back in and I'd lose touch again.

We got through Christmas with a minimum of fuss, and a week later it was a new year. New? The only thing new about it is that I'd have to remember to write a new number when I dated a check. Things contin-ued to get worse and the depression got so heavy I was spending more and more time in bed.

I thought I had a bladder infection, so I found a doctor and made an appointment. After the examination, Dr. Kaplan sat down, looked me in the eye, and said, "JoAnn, what's wrong?"

Why on earth was she asking me? She looked professional enough, and had just given me a bunch of tests. "Just a bladder infection, I guess," I replied. "Isn't that what you found?"

"You were right about that," she assured me, "and we can take care of it. But that's not what I'm asking you. JoAnn, what's wrong?"

Until now I had seen nothing but her oversized glasses, her tiny frame, her dark fluffy hair parted on one side. But the second time she asked what was wrong I was startled to see deep compassion in her eyes. She cared; she really cared. Suddenly I couldn't help myself, and I broke down and cried.

Before I knew what was happening, she called the Department of Mental Health and a shrink came over to talk to me. "I'm Dr. Gifford," he said, reaching out to shake hands before he sat down. Tall and good-looking, he seemed young for a doctor. In a matter-of-fact voice he said, "I'm here to ask you a few questions."

It was more than a few, and they came fast, one after another. I felt confused at first, but then I saw a pattern and began to feel cornered.

When the questions finally slowed down he said I would have to put Heather in a foster home. I tried to argue but he insisted that if I wouldn't give her up voluntarily, he would see to it that papers would be filed immediately and the State of Hawaii would take her from me. He was kind but firm, informing me that it would be much more difficult for me to get her back if he had to proceed in that manner. I knew the drill; this is the kind of thing they'd told me at Mt. Sinai.

I asked him for a little time to think about it and he left the office. A few moments later Dr. Kaplan came in with a priest. "This is Paul Schaeffer," she said. "He's here to help you. I'm going to slip out and let you two talk."

"I'm Paul," he said, "and I'm here to find out how I can help you." He smiled broadly and though the situation was weird, he put me at ease.

"Father, I'm not sure where to begin."

"I am," he said with a laugh. "Start by calling me Paul. I'm an Episcopalian rector, not a Catholic priest. You don't have to call me Father." He sat back in his chair.

So I told him about Heather, about my visit to Dr. Kaplan, and about

Dr. Gifford's insistence that I place Heather in foster care. "Everything's happening so fast," I said miserably. "I came in to take care of a bladder infection, and now I have to think about putting Heather in foster care."

"And that's why I'm talking to you," said Paul. "I'd like to take Heather into my home. My wife, Karen, and I have three adopted children and three of our own."

"Where do you live?" I asked numbly. If this was going to be good for Heather, I hoped it wasn't too far away. "I have to be able to see Heather."

"Do you know the little church right on the beach near the Pioneer Inn?" he asked.

"Yes," I answered as my heart skipped a beat. Could it be that he was connected with that church I prayed in everyday asking for someone to help us?

"Well, I'm the rector and our family lives right behind the church," he said.

This was too good to be true. Maybe God had heard my prayer. "You're kidding!" I gasped. "I've been going in that church in the mornings to pray for somebody to help us." It had to be a sign, and I gratefully accepted his offer.

"Good," he said as he shook my hand. "We'll be expecting you and Heather this afternoon." He started out the door but turned back and added, "I think you should plan on staying for dinner to get her used to her new surroundings." Then he was gone.

Dr. Kaplan returned with Dr. Gifford, who wanted me to sign papers turning Heather over to the Schaeffers immediately.

I sat there clenching my fists, stunned by the rapid events. It was one thing to take Heather to stay with the Schaeffers; it was another to sign papers.

"It really will be the best thing for both of you until you are feeling better," Dr. Kaplan said in an assuring voice.

"You must come to see me tomorrow morning," the shrink said absently, scribbling his name on a prescription form.

I felt threatened by his tone of voice and wondered if he was going to lock me up in the nut house on the other side of the island. I sat there searching my soul. On one hand I knew I wasn't taking care of Heather, and I didn't mind her staying with the Schaeffers. On the other hand, what would it mean if I signed the papers?

I became frantic at the prospect.

"Mr. Schaeffer said Heather could stay with him and his wife. Why can't I just take her over there until I'm feeling better?" I asked. "Wouldn't that be enough?"

"No, but we are willing to let Heather go to the Schaeffers'," Dr. Gifford said. "They will make wonderful foster parents; they've done it before."

"And they have a lovely home for raising children," Dr. Kaplan added.

I realized I had been set up. I sank into my chair.

"Listen, you don't have a choice in the matter at this point," the shrink said firmly. "As I told you earlier, it will be easier for you to get Heather back if you sign these papers voluntarily. Now if you refuse, I will see to it that she is taken from you immediately. Believe me, it will be a lot easier for you if you give her up voluntarily, and it will look better on your record."

"But this isn't fair," I cried. "You're not asking me; you're telling me." I began crying uncontrollably. I had come over only because I thought I had an infection and now these strangers were threatening to take Heather away from me.

They left me alone again to think for a few minutes. Should I sign the papers? I was torn apart. How would Heather feel about it? Would it hurt her? How could I put her through any more pain? "Oh God, do I even have a choice?" I sighed.

I looked all around the office, desperately wondering if I could find a way to escape. Maybe a back door, but no – the only door was the one I had entered. Maybe a duct in the ceiling – no, nothing there. But even if I got away, what would I do? Run to the school to get Heather and catch a plane? Then what? Where would we go? And what if we got caught? The shrink said it would be worse for me.

There had to be another answer, but what could it be? Bob would know, but he was gone and I couldn't ask him. Maybe Shane, but he'd probably tell me to go along with what the doctors had said. The anguish was overwhelming and I knew I was trapped.

Dr. Kaplan knocked gently before she opened the door.

"JoAnn, we really are trying to help you and your daughter," she said sincerely. "Do you feel you are doing something wrong?"

"Yes, what kind of mother would turn her daughter over and make her a foster child?" I asked. The words sounded horrible as they came out of my mouth.

"A mother who really loves her daughter and wants to get well so she can take care of her properly," Dr. Kaplan said in a loving voice. Her kind eyes swept over me and somehow I realized I didn't have to feel ashamed.

I blinked back the tears. "You really do think this is best, don't you?" I asked, longing for the right advice.

"Yes child, I really do," she answered. Child? Yes, she might have a child close to my age. Somehow it was as though I were her little girl who had lost my way, and she was older and wiser and wanted only what was best for Heather and me. I felt I could trust her; and as far as that went, I really liked Paul Schaeffer.

"Is Karen nice?" I asked hopefully. Surely anyone who adopted three children after having three of her own had to be special.

"She is a woman I admire very much," said Dr. Kaplan, smiling serenely. "I don't think there's an unkind bone in her body. I'm sure Heather will be very happy living with their family. They go on outings and there will be children to play with and good hot meals every day."

The smell of home cooking filled my mind. How I longed for a nice meal made with loving hands. Perhaps this was the right thing to do. I wished they might adopt me too.

"She will be well supervised," Dr. Kaplan continued.

A kind family, children to play with, outings, good meals, good supervision... It would be selfish for me to keep Heather. The cloud of confusion seemed to clear for an instant as I realized the most loving thing I could do was to make this sacrifice for her. "Okay Dr. Kaplan, I'm ready to sign the papers."

"Fine, Dear," she said. She nudged them gently towards me and seemed to sense my struggle.

I tried to read them but they were complicated, and I changed my mind so many times my head began to pound.

"Would you like something to relax you?" Dr. Kaplan asked with a hint of concern in her voice. "But first I have to ask – did you drive here or walk?"

"I walked," I replied. "And yes, I think I do need something to help me relax."

A few minutes later she returned with a glass of water and a green and black pill, which I took gratefully. She added, "But don't take this if you need to drive anywhere later today."

"It's okay," I said. "I live a block away and everything I need is within walking distance."

"Then I'm going to see a few patients and I'll be back in a while," Dr. Kaplan said, leaving me alone with the papers and a pen.

What kind of pill was this, anyway? I was becoming very relaxed very fast, and now it was hard not to fall asleep. It was a good thing the shrink didn't come back in right now. Dr. Kaplan was kind and knew this was difficult for me. I tried once again to find another solution, but there wasn't one. My heart broke as I signed the papers. I'd lost Bob, and now I was losing Heather.

I gave them to Dr. Kaplan when she got back. As I got up to leave she said, "Don't forget your appointment with Dr. Gifford tomorrow."

"What If I do?" I asked.

"It will go down on your record and they will pick you up," she said. "Dear, can't you see you need help?"

"I don't know," I answered numbly, "but it seems things are out of my control." Instinctively, I looked around the room just once more. Maybe there was a way to escape, and I had overlooked it? But no, I was trapped.

"They are, but you will be grateful someday," she said. "You are too sick to realize that you need someone to take over for you."

I walked home and packed Heather's suitcase, wondering how I would tell her. I went to school and waited until class was over.

The bell rang and a swarm of shrieking children poured out of the doors and scrambled to go home. I waited, but Heather didn't come down the stairs. So I peeked in her classroom, and there she stood, talking to her teacher.

"Hi Mommy, I drew you a picture," she said proudly as she held up her artwork.

I took her hand and we walked towards the Schaeffers'. How was I going to tell her?

"Do you think it would be wonderful to have brothers and sisters?" I asked.

"Oh yes, Mommy," she said.

"What if you could live in a house right on the beach with a mommy and a daddy and lots of toys and kids? Do you think that would be great?" I asked.

"Mommy, where would you get lots of kids and a daddy?" she giggled. "You're silly, Mommy."

"Well, I'm going to take you to a place like that. There is a mommy and daddy and they have six children," I said cheerfully. "You are going to stay with them for a while."

"You mean a baby sitter that is a mommy?" Heather asked innocently.

"Yes, like a baby sitter," I said. I decided not to say any more about it unless it became necessary.

The Schaeffers had a lovely oceanfront home. The waves were lapping at the long stretch of beach. Karen and Paul were waiting for us at the door, and they looked good together. He was almost as big as Garrett, good-looking with dark hair and a laugh in his eyes. She was tall and pretty. Her straight blond hair was pulled back in a ponytail and her blue eyes sparkled with kindness. It took only a few moments to see how gentle she was with children.

Her kids were excited. "Heather, come see the room where you'll be staying!" In no time at all she was running through the house, playing as if she'd been there for months. If anything, I wished I could have lived there myself.

The meal was scrumptious, and soon there was hot chocolate and it was bedtime. I marveled as the children went off to bed in an amazingly orderly fashion, and followed Heather to her room to kiss her goodnight. "Do you like it here?" I whispered in her ear as she snuggled with her favorite teddy bear.

"Yes Mommy. Will you come get me tomorrow?" she asked.

"We'll go for a walk tomorrow after you get out of school," I said.

That seemed to satisfy her and she smiled and closed her eyes as I turned out the light.

The next day, I went for my appointment with the shrink. I drove up in my old beat up green Volkswagen and shuddered when I saw the hospital. The top floor had bars on the windows, and I could hear screams from somewhere inside. I knew it would be nothing like Mt. Sinai in Beverly Hills if they threw me in there, and I knew I'd better come up with a good story to tell the psychiatrist before I went into his office.

I remembered Rachel's book. I'd been a little irritated when she'd said, "You need to read this. The people in this book sound just like you. But there's a new drug that's helping them." The book looked really boring, but Rachel was such a good friend that I was ashamed not to try to wade through it. The people really did sound like me, and lithium was working wonders.

Would it work for me? I thought about Rachel's shrink. He had said I didn't need lithium; but I needed to be in a hospital. These guys all thought mental hospitals were the answer to everything. But at least I would have a story for Dr. Gifford. And if lithium really wouldn't help, maybe he'd think of something else. I walked into his office.

"My psychiatrist in California diagnosed me as a manic-depressive," I lied. "He wanted to put me on a drug called...let me see…" I paused, pretending I didn't know the name. "lidamo or limone, something like that." I didn't want him to realize how much I knew about the drug. I wanted him to think I was doing my best to remember what the doctor had told me.

"Dr. Ashton said it was important that I find a competent psychiatrist when I arrived in Hawaii because this drug is very powerful and the patient must be monitored carefully," I said stroking his ego. Of course there was no Dr. Ashton, but I knew my story would sound better if I gave him a name. I hoped I wouldn't have to remember it later.

Dr. Gifford looked thoughtful as he listened. Really I was just giving him a review of Rachel's book, but with a few embellishments I thought I could pass it off as a Beverly Hills psychiatrist's diagnosis. I watched his face carefully to see if he was falling for it.

He paused before he spoke. "We do have a lithium program here," he said finally. "I suppose I could put you on that and see how you do before considering other alternatives.

"Yes, lithium! That was the name!" I tried to sound delighted that he'd helped me recall the name of the drug, but then I asked my next question warily: "What do you mean by other alternatives?"

"Hospitalization," he said firmly. The word sent a chill through me. "Now I must tell you that lithium is an extremely strong drug and I'm going to have to check your blood twice a week to begin with. You won't feel any effects for the first two weeks or so. I'll have to keep a very close watch on you. Do you have your own transportation?"

"Yes, I can come as often as you want," I said. I was determined to cooperate. I wanted nothing to do with the hospital.

"I'll take you over to the clinic now and introduce you to the nurses," Dr. Gifford said confidently, as though he had solved my problem.

I expected to drive somewhere, but instead he led me deeper and deeper into the hospital. It was badly run down, and it got creepier with every step. Eventually we arrived in a large waiting room where people were roaming around like zombies. Dr. Gifford turned around, smiled proudly, and with a wave of his hand announced, "Here it is!"

"Here's what?" I asked. Had I been tricked? This looked like a mental ward in a horror film.

"This is the Lithium Clinic," he said enthusiastically, as though this was going to be great fun. "Let me introduce you to the nurses."

I looked around, and the people looked scary. A tall Hawaiian man was shuffling about aimlessly. Others sat, nodding in agreement with people the rest of us couldn't see. Some of the patients looked like people I'd known who had taken too much heroin. Was this what I'd be like after taking lithium? Or maybe these people were the hopeless cases, the ones who were much worse off than me. I was horrified, but I told myself it was better than being locked up.

Dr. Gifford introduced me to the nurses. "They'll run a blood test and check your vitals, then they'll bring you back to my office so I can write your prescription." With that, he left, walking briskly. It was hard not to panic as his footsteps grew softer on his way down the hall, but I knew I'd better not look too nervous.

The nurses looked as dispassionate as the patients I had seen in the waiting room. Robotically, they got me through the tests, jotting things down on a clipboard. It took just a few minutes. To my relief, one of the nurses waved the clipboard proudly and announced, "That's all we need, Dearie. Time to go back to Dr. Gifford's office." I felt lighter and freer with every step.

I had never been so glad to see a shrink's office. I sat down, the nurse left, and he riffled through the papers on the clipboard for a few minutes. Finally he spoke. "I'm going to put you on 1450 milligrams a day to normalize your system. But I have to warn you," and now he gazed intently into my eyes. "1450 milligrams is very close to a toxic dose, so if you have any side effects, you need to call in immediately."

"What kind of effects?" I asked.

"Your speech becoming slurred, or impaired vision," he said as he wrote the prescription. "Anything questionable, just give me a call."

"O.K." I said. He seemed to know what he was talking about, and I wasn't quite sure what he would consider questionable. But he went on.

"Come in once a week to have your blood checked. That is extremely important, so we know if you are getting the proper dose. We may have to change your prescription periodically."

I left, relieved that I had to return only once a week. It was half hour away from home and I didn't like the long and tiresome drive to that part of the island.

On my way home, I met Heather as she got out of school and took her for a walk on the beach. Heather had settled in with the Schaeffers. The transition seemed easy for her, but she was so sensitive and precious I wondered if she was trying to do what was best for me.

I moved into a funky place a few days after Heather was gone. It used to be an old Philippine Camp in a section of Lahaina everyone called the "Ghetto." It was full of cockroaches and bugs; the six units shared one shower, located outside. It was no place for a child, but it would do for me. It helped that the rent was cheap.

Then I found a battered old bike for $10, and now I looked like I belonged in my new neighborhood. Nobody would ever know I had owned a business or driven a Mercedes. I looked like another hippie from the mainland, just getting by. I loved it.

Two other people lived in this dump with me; we each rented a room and I was low man on the totem pole because it went by seniority. So I had to sleep on a wooden bench with no mattress in a cubbyhole near the front door. The two other rooms had doors and real beds. The bedroom I wanted was in the back. It had a built-in table – if that's the right name for the piece of scrap wood and two angle brackets screwed into the wall below the window. It seemed elegant compared to my cubbyhole, and I pictured myself sitting there and finishing *Strawberry Jan*. The weeks dragged by, and by early March, nobody had moved out yet.

I began making friends in the neighborhood. My best friend was gay, a kid named Ryan, and he had an old bicycle built for two. We called it our Cadillac, and we would go out riding almost every day. Every night we went out dancing; he wasn't looking for a woman and I wasn't looking for a man, so we were both covered.

The lithium was working. The depression had always been a pressure coming from outside, but now it was an internal dull ache. I would try to explain it to people and I could tell it didn't make sense to them, but I really could feel a difference. I felt so heavy it was hard to move, and at the same time I was so numb that nothing bothered me – so I wasn't depressed in the way I used to be. After making up the story about my fictional shrink in California and his supposed diagnosis that I needed lithium, wouldn't it be funny if lithium really was what I'd needed all along?

In the middle of March one of my roommates moved out, and I got to have a bedroom with a door. It felt good to move up in the world! I was so excited about the door that I didn't care that the room was stuffy. If it was hard to sleep at night, I could always go down to the beach and take a nap by day. Then before I had gotten used to my room, the other roommate left too. Now I had the room with a table, the room I'd wanted for months. I had the added perk of being top dog, though nobody else was here.

A few days later I met a new roommate. I was lying on the beach in front of Lahaina Shores, where Heather and I used to live, and I saw a big dog lift his leg and pee all over a woman who was sunbathing next to me. She jumped up and shouted: "Oh, if my friends in Santa Maria could see me now!"

"Santa Maria, California?" I asked. "That's where my family lives."

"Yes, that's it!" she exclaimed. "Small world!" Her daughter Valerie, who looked about my age, joined the conversation, and we hit it off right away. She was an artist and carved scrimshaw. Soon I learned she needed a place to live.

"Come stay with me!" I said. "I was sharing a house with two room-mates and they both moved out this week." She came to look around and agreed to move in.

"But the rent's so cheap, I'm wondering if we really have to have an-other roommate," she said. "What if we both paid a little more and had the whole house to ourselves?"

So that's what we decided to do. It would be good to live normally with each of us having a bedroom with a door, and without a third person sleeping in the cubbyhole across from the kitchen sink. And I had never quite connected with my other roommates, but Valerie was fun. "Just think," I said with a laugh. "I never would have met you if a dog hadn't peed on your mother."

"Who knows?" she giggled. "Maybe the landlord pays the dog a finder's fee whenever he needs a new tenant."

Twenty Two

OVERDOSE

Maybe it was a side effect of the lithium, but I'd lost interest in writing and art ever since I'd come to Hawaii. I'd always surrounded myself with artists of one kind or another, though I never thought I was an artist myself. Yet now that Valerie was staying with me and I saw her working on her art every day, I realized that writing and drawing had started to become part of me.

Nevertheless, I couldn't seem to get back into the flow of writing. From time to time I would thumb through *Strawberry Jan.* I knew I needed to finish it, but the ideas just wouldn't come.

Then one day I came home and found a giant picture of Strawberry Jan airbrushed on a sheet hanging on my bedroom door.

"Valerie," I called out suspiciously.

She bounced out of her room with a sheepish grin on her face. "Yes, Strawberry, what do you want?"

"How did you know about this fairy tale?" I asked. She'd been snooping; otherwise she couldn't have known about the book, for I was sure I'd never mentioned it to her.

"Today while you were at the beach I was looking through your things and found it," she explained without apology, and then she shifted to a pleading tone. She sounded as innocent as a little child, and my irritation melted. "JoAnn, it's great. I just love it. Please write more."

"Well, it doesn't work that way," I said. "I have to be inspired, and it just hasn't been happening since I got here."

"Well it will," she said confidently. "I just know it." She left the room to carve scrimshaw – her current project involved a huge elephant tusk.

Every day I came home to various sketches of the fairy tale, which Valerie was skillfully bringing to life. Soon I was inspired. I started giving up my days at the beach so I could sit at the old Smith-Corona in my stuffy little room. It felt good to be writing again.

I had left California behind, but somehow my past due bills started catching up with me. How did they even know where I was? It didn't matter. I would take the bills to my room, scratch out my address, and scribble "moved – please forward to 64 Hyde Park, London W1, England." Then I would walk to the post office and mail them with a laugh. It was fun to try to imagine who was receiving the bills and what they did with them.

I liked living in a neighborhood where everything I needed was within walking distance. Often I walked to Heather's school or to the Schaeffers'. Whenever I saw Heather, I could tell she was happy. Dr, Kaplan had been right – the foster home was working out well for her.

Garrett sent a telegram saying to call him right away because he was coming to Maui for a visit. He arrived, took one look at where I lived, and blew up. "How can you live in this dump? No way I'm coming inside!" His outbursts usually blew over quickly if I didn't argue, and this time I took it in stride. Was it the lithium? There were no ups and no downs – just a steady, monotonous straight line.

He calmed down right away. "Let's get a room at the Sheraton," he announced, and off we went. At a resort where everyone else was dressed for the beach, Garrett looked out of place. Nobody else wore heavy black leather in the hot sun; nobody else carried a huge Anaconda bag. He was too big to overlook, but he always enjoyed making an impression.

It was nice to hide in his arms for a week, and he took me with him to Oahu for a few days before he left. "Why don't you come back with me?" he asked, and I was tempted. But I didn't go. My mind felt two beats away from whatever was happening. As Garrett left I felt a wave of loneliness, but somehow I felt detached even from that.

I was putting on weight. As I walked around in my little neighborhood I would fill a shopping bag with chocolate bars, éclairs, creampuffs, or napoleons. But I was too ashamed to buy everything at one store. I would visit two bakeries and two stores that sold candy. I would take my goodies home, sneak them into my room, lock the door, and dump it all in a pile in the center of my bed so I could gorge myself. This started happening every day.

Then one night I was in the local hangout sipping an exotic tropical drink, and Carolyn walked in. It was good to see her. She had run off with some guy and left James. They rented a great house on the beach in Kihei. I went over there frequently. She cooked dinner every night; I don't know how many times I found her baking a turkey. More important, it was a home, and I loved visiting. It was as close to normal life as I could get.

Once in a while Valerie would come on to me, telling me she was bisexual. It made me uncomfortable, but I told myself it really wasn't a big deal. A lot of men had come on to me, and it was always up to me either to resist or to go along with it. With Valerie I always said no and stood my ground, but she was a good friend and I liked her a lot.

Ryan never got physical, but I still had to guard my space at times. One day I went for a walk and Ryan rode up on his bike. Valerie had just airbrushed it the day before, and it was bright and garish and pink. "Shall we go for a ride, darling?" he asked. The warm breeze played with his long black straggly hair. I hopped on the back and we pedaled along through the heavy tourist traffic.

"I thought you might need a chauffeur, my dear," he said coyly. "I wish I had a magic wand." He turned to me with one eyebrow raised. "And do you know what I'd do with the magic wand? I'd..."

"Stop the bike!" I interrupted. "I need to get off!" I really didn't want to hear any more; I was feeling nauseated. Ryan skidded to a halt and I got off.

"What about tonight?" he asked, but this time there was no pretending in his voice. "Are we going out dancing tonight?"

"I don't know yet," I shrugged. I walked home, glad for the fresh air and wondering if I was turning into a prude.

When I got home, I found notes in various sizes, shapes, and colors, all over the house. They all said, "I'M DEAD." Artists could be strange. I wondered if I was going to become strange too, now that I was becoming an artist.

I peeked into Valerie's room and said, "You're a nut." She was sprawled in her bed with a green gooey facemask smeared all over her skin.

"I'm bummed out," she said with a grin.

"Why?"

"Cause I'm fat."

"You are not," I said firmly. I wasn't sure why she had this preoccupation, but lately we had been having this conversation several times a day. I closed the door and went back to my room to write.

I heard her leave a few minutes later. I went out to walk by myself, stopping for chocolate and pastries. It wasn't Valerie; I was the one who was putting on weight. I came back home and Valerie hadn't returned yet. But still, I took no chances. I locked my door, emptied the bag on my bed and wolfed all my goodies down. Then I did a bit more writing and went to bed early.

I woke up in the middle of the night with something crawling on me; it felt like a cane spider, which I knew to be as big as a baseball. I screamed, jumped out of bed, and turned on the light. It was the fringe on my bedspread. I went back to bed but couldn't get back to sleep.

I lay there thinking. How'd things ever get so crazy anyway? People shared their lovers as though they were passing around a dish of chocolate covered peanuts. Some men wanted men, girls wanted each other, couples wanted to add one more. Everybody was chasing around, trying to find somebody and trying to be found, and we all felt bored, lonely, and empty.

Was it the devil? Were we all in hell? If God even existed, He sure did set up the system with a lot of loopholes. Why were there so many loopholes, anyway? Why were there so many ways the devil could block up everything like some incredible chess game? Yes that was it: God and the devil were playing chess, and people were the pieces. "Who's winning?" I asked aloud. Nobody answered.

I got up. My mind was racing, and I took a sleeping pill. I woke up the next day to the sound of Joni Mitchell playing loudly in the next room and Valerie standing over me with a carbohydrate book.

"I'm fat, huh?" she asked pointing to her stomach. "I gotta lose weight, huh? I'm fat, huh?" She was thumbing through the book like a mad professor.

I groaned. "Valerie, you've asked me that question about ten times a day since you moved in here." I rolled over, sat up, and rubbed the sleep from my eyes. "How many times do I have to tell you that you're not fat?"

"Well, I am fat," she said, getting in the last word. Then she pouted defiantly like a two-year-old.

"Valerie, I had an outrageous dream last night." I wanted to change the subject.

Her eyes lit up. "What was it?"

"There were broken hearts, ripped to shreds and laid out on a long white driveway which led to an emerald green castle," I recounted.

"The castle was surrounded by very tall dark trees. I stood in the middle of the stark white driveway, dressed in a white dress and the red torn hearts laughed at me. I was very pale and my eyes were bright, bright green and I wore green lipstick which shimmered like the castle. My fingernail polish was also green and I had on a white wide-brim hat with emerald green flowers. I asked the hearts what they were laughing at and they told me."

I paused.

"What'd they say?" Valerie prodded.

"They said they were laughing at the reality and absurdity of love," I continued. When they said 'absurdity' it echoed like a million tiny voices and then Joni Mitchell came on and woke me up."

"Oh, too bad," Valerie said. "Gosh, that sounds like a good painting. I'll try to draw it today."

One morning I woke up feeling strange. I tried to read, but the words made no sense; they seemed to be running all over the page and I had a hard time focusing. My speech was really slurred and sometimes I couldn't put sentences together.

The pharmacist at the drug store said I was reacting to the lithium. "You've had an overdose. How many pills have you been taking every day?"

"I don't know." I was too spaced out to remember.

"Well, you'd better not take any more until you can see a doctor, because you've had an overdose." But it was Saturday and the clinic wouldn't be open until Monday. There was nothing else to do but to walk home.

My friend Kelly was there and she was feeling a bit lost and depressed. I had about 100 hits of L.S.D I'd brought from California and I asked her if she wanted to drop some with me.

"Sounds great," she said enthusiastically. "Let's do it!"

I got it out of my special hiding place and showed it to her, but it didn't look right. "It's shrunk or something," I said. "Seems to be melted together."

"What do you think happened to it?" she asked.

"Well, maybe it's the humidity," I surmised. "It is windowpane acid, and shortly after I got here it started to change. But I've taken it a few times since it's turned weird, and nothing unusual happened – as if an acid trip can be usual," I laughed.

"Well, I'm game," she said.

I handed her one of the withered panes and popped another in my mouth, and we both went outside. We decided to go for a ride on the big pink open-air bus that takes tourists back and forth through town. The warm ocean breeze felt luxurious as I drank in the sights. Foolish looking tourists were bustling around everywhere, taking pictures or handing their cameras to strangers so they could all pose together for a photograph.

We started laughing at a very heavy couple in Bermuda shorts and Hawaiian shirts. As they walked, great rolls of fat jiggled like Jell-O with every step, but they didn't care about that. They were frantically lapping at their triple-scoop cones before the sun could melt the ice cream, but they weren't quick enough. A thick pale liquid was starting to drip down their hands and onto their stomachs or legs. They were getting madder and madder. It was fun to watch, but suddenly I realized something wasn't right. I'd taken that same batch of LSD about thirty times, but it had never felt like this before.

"Kelly, something's wrong," I said, almost choking on my words.

"Oh JoAnn, don't be silly; just enjoy the trip." she said brightly. "It's wonderful."

"No you don't understand – I've taken this stuff lots of times and this is different," I said, pleading with her to listen.

Kelly turned away and ignored me.

"Kelly," I said loudly. "I'm telling you: something is really wrong. This stuff is too strong."

"JoAnn, don't bum out my trip," she whined. "If something was wrong with the acid, then my trip would be going wrong too."

She was making sense, but Kelly didn't have an overdose of...

"Oh my God," I said out loud. "The lithium – it's the combination. Kelly I've got to get off this bus."

"Fine," Kelly said nonchalantly. "Get off the bus."

"But you gotta help me," I pleaded.

The bus stopped in front of Lahaina Shores where I used to live with Heather and I got off as quickly as I could, with Kelly reluctantly following me.

"Listen, JoAnn, I'll get your friends that live here, but then I'm taking off. You're bumming out my trip."

Heather in the tall grasses
by the sea in Hawaii.

I didn't answer as I looked down and fell to my knees in the dirt. Immediately I was sucked into a dark tunnel that was huge at my end but was narrowing further ahead. I knew I was dying and that little tiny speck of acid I'd so carelessly taken just a short while ago was going to do me in.

Heather's sweet face passed through my mind and I thought about the fact that she was better off where she was than with me. I also thought of Garrett and how angry he'd be because he hated my taking acid; he used to yell at me for it. Then I saw how foolish it was to worry about trivial things like dirty laundry and beds that weren't made, bank accounts, unanswered letters...

This had to be another dimension. As I zoomed further into the dark tunnel, I saw shafts of bright light and heard carousel music beckoning me. I quickly reached the tunnel's end.

The next thing I knew, I was riding the most beautiful carousel I'd ever seen, and was more peaceful and content than I'd ever felt in my whole life. The colors around me were vivid, unlike any I'd ever seen before. Everything seemed alive.

Suddenly, a being of light asked me if I knew why different events had happened to me in my life as they had. I wasn't afraid in the least. I felt immediate trust and never wanted to leave his presence. Large television screens in beautiful gold frames appeared around the carousel. There were many of these elegantly bordered screens, like those you would see in the finest art galleries, showing motion pictures of various scenes in my life.

The carousel moved towards the first scene and I looked at it carefully. There I was doing something. I was asked why I thought things had happened that way and what I'd learned from the experience. If I was right, the carousel continued to move slowly towards the next sequence of pictures. But if I couldn't figure it out, I was given an instant replay until I gave the right answer.

The being of light was patient and gentle, no matter how long it took me to figure things out. The answers were in me, however deeply buried, and I felt safe as the being of light watched over my process of discovery. It was as if fear had been removed from that realm, and I felt serene and content.

I remember in one set of pictures that it seemed the good things in life were happening to everyone but me. Then I suddenly realized that I had had my share of joys also. However, I was unbalanced because I always recalled the negative experiences and quickly forgot about the pleasant ones.

I also saw a succession of tragedies – earthquakes, wars, floods and many natural disasters, with tearful faces looking at me. I felt grateful that the tragedies hadn't affected me, or my family. I relived feelings I'd had when I'd seen newscasts of these same events, relieved that nobody I knew was involved.

As I searched through the pictures, I really wanted an explanation of the purpose of my life. All I saw was that I was an example. I certainly didn't understand what that could mean.

I felt like the biggest fool in the world when I saw my life in its entirety. The being of light didn't tell me I was a fool, though certainly he knew I was. He was kind and understanding and let me come to the conclusion myself. I didn't feel condemned – just loved and accepted in all my foolishness.

The pictures were turned off, as if someone pulled a plug, and he asked me sweetly: "If you could have anything in the world that you wanted, what would it be?"

I just knew it was going to be something wonderful and felt like a little girl, sitting there on that lovely carousel and trying to guess. He seemed to enjoy the excitement I felt as I let my imagination run wild and was urged on by his tender manner.

"No, something more wonderful than that," he would say after each guess.

"Oh, I just can't guess anymore," I said, feeling as if I would burst if I didn't find out soon.

"If you could have anything in the world, what would you want?" he asked again joyfully, letting the words sink in and echo through me. "Why, your husband, Bob, of course."

"But that's impossible," I said.

Suddenly, Bob was there holding me, and it seemed a million explosions went off around me and I realized I was dead. I had never experienced a better feeling in my entire life.

I heard voices desperately calling my name at the other end of the dark tunnel and wished they would stop. Certainly I had no desire to go back there, yet the voices got stronger, and suddenly I was lying on a bed with my friends shaking me and calling my name. "My God," John shrieked. "Are you okay?" What was John doing here? Suddenly I remembered that Kelly had said she would find my friends in the neighborhood.

I felt stunned and had a tremendous pain under my tongue. I knew what had happened to me, but also realized they would just think it was part of my acid trip so I lay there quietly drinking in what I had just experienced. I knew God had sent me back for a purpose, and that He was real. I also knew I would have to answer for my life when I died, which was a sobering thought.

Later, the people who were with me said they had found me fallen in a heap and had carried me up from there as quickly as they could so the police would not find me, and that I had had several severe seizures. They had tried to stop me from biting my tongue but didn't know how. That was why it now had a deep bloody gash.

"I called the hospital and told them what was going on," John said softly, slumping down on the couch. "What a trip. Do you know what they told me?"

"What?" I asked, sipping a cool lemonade.

"They said there was no use sending an ambulance because it was an hour round trip, and you'd either be dead in half an hour or would pull through."

In the days that followed, I pondered what had happened in the tunnel with the being of light. I started searching for God. I found a book at Carolyn's called *Stay Alive All Of Your Life* by Norman Vincent Peale, and read through it. My mind was clouded from so many drugs that it was difficult to understand most of what it said, but I treasured the small fragments I did comprehend.

I threw away all my LSD and stopped taking Lithium. I never told the doctor. I figured so many people were trudging in and out of the clinic, nobody would ever notice. This turned out to be the case; I was never contacted.

It was time to build a life. The only thing I was doing that seemed to have any sense of purpose to it was writing, so I finished *Strawberry Jan*. As I talked to friends in person or on the phone day by day, I realized I needed to go back to New York to try to sell it. Rachel kept telling me I needed to go, and if it hadn't been for her, I might not have gone.

I told her I'd been there before, and New York was a scary place. She laughed it off. "I don't know what you're worried about. Whatever comes up, you always manage to maneuver your way through it. Remember the rental car in Louisiana?"

I laughed too. "Yeah, but we were together. New York isn't the kind of city where I'd want to be alone."

"Then why don't I meet you there? I'm about due for a break." So we worked out the plans.

I still didn't really want to go. Maui felt warm and safe, like being in a mother's arms; New York seemed cold and menacing. I hated to think of being away from Heather, with her sweet voice and soft, shining hair. I couldn't take her with me; the counselor said she still needed to stay with the Schaeffers. At least she was being well cared for, and I knew she was happy there.

But the day came when I had to visit Heather to say goodbye. It tore me up to see her, because a premonition was telling me I'd be in New York longer than I expected. But what else could I do? I packed my things and called ahead to make arrangements. And I prayed for God to help us.

Twenty Three

ALL THINGS ARE POSSIBLE

I got to New York, and Rachel arrived the next day. We went out to see the sights, but all I saw was the people. It was the crazy woman scrabbling frantically through the garbage cans. It was the elevator operator calling out the floors dispassionately. It was the wealthy woman with a manicured dog in its diamond-studded collar, passing a blind beggar and his cup.

My imagination created stories for each of these people: their backgrounds, what they would go home to at the end of the day, and what they had to look forward to – if anything.

We took the subway down to Greenwich Village. We got off the train, climbed the steps lazily, and stepped out into a group of people as outlandishly dressed as the crowds at Mardi Gras. It was as if we were at a Halloween party and had forgotten to wear costumes ourselves.

"I've seen enough," I said. "I told you this city could be scary."

"You're right," she replied. "I guess we chose the wrong time. But we can come back and see Greenwich Village another day," Rachel said. "Let's go get a hotdog at Nathan's."

Nathan's wouldn't have been my first choice because I was trying to change my eating habits; I wanted to shed the pounds I had gained in Hawaii. But at least it would get us out of here. We got back on the subway. I saw crowds everywhere.

Thank God I didn't have to live here! I'm not cut out for cities. Crowds make me nervous, even when the people are normally dressed.

The train stopped and we went up the stairs and on to Nathan's. It was packed, but what did I expect? While Rachel stood in line I waited for an empty table and pounced. Once I was seated, I looked around and saw a pretty woman about my age stuffing herself with food that had been left behind. At first I assumed she was just finishing what her friends had left, but then she grabbed a cup full of ketchup and sucked it clean. Her eyes were wild as she looked around, searching for more food but watching to make sure she didn't get caught and kicked out.

She saw a half-eaten hotdog across the room and rushed over. She devoured it, looked around again, and darted to another dish of leftovers.

Rachel arrived with her food and sat down to eat. I pointed, trying not to be too obvious. "Watch that girl over there with the gray cap pulled over her ears."

Rachel's eyes wandered around the room until she spotted her. As soon as she realized what was happening, she stopped eating, made eye contact with the girl, and nudged her box to a vacant place at our table. The girl rushed over and gorged herself with the remains of Rachel's meal. I tried to hand her some money but she thrust it back in my face. Like a wild animal, she would take food, but money seemed to mean nothing to her.

As Rachel and I walked back to our hotel, I thought about the degradation in the world. It took an effort to hold back my tears.

Rachel stayed for a few more days and helped me get settled in the Barbizon Hotel for Women. I was told that in the past, young women seeking fame and fortune stayed here. Not too many years ago, I would have had to supply references to become a guest, including a letter from my minister.

After Rachel left, it was time to start selling my fairy tale. I didn't know where to begin. How could I even get anyone to take a look? I decided to call my friends in Rhode Island; if nothing else, they had connections in New York. Soon I got into a whirlwind of traveling back and forth.

My Rhode Island friends gave me plenty of leads and I called one office after another, but nothing was connecting. Everything was frustrating. If I called an agent, he was out of the office for the rest of the day. If I called a publisher, he was on vacation until next week. I wanted to work hard at what I was doing but couldn't develop any momentum. Then for a few days I couldn't do anything because it was the 4th of July and offices were closed. I was trying to focus, but at every turn I had to wait for a day or a few days before I could take the next step.

So with time on my hands, my mind drifted. I had a scare; I tried calling Heather and the Schaeffers didn't pick up the phone. I called everyone I could think of in Hawaii, and nobody knew anything. What could be wrong? I finally reached them on the 7th; they had gone on vacation.

My feelings for men were on the wane again. Paul was with me in

Rhode Island for a few days and Garrett called to ask if he could come for a visit. I told him that this wasn't a good time and we got into an argument. I thought about Stephen every day but felt indifferent towards him.

I had time to ponder many things, and there was no rhyme or reason to it. My grandfather used to say, "You're the girl with a thousand questions." If only he could see me now! What made the birds sing? If the sky is blue sometimes, why isn't it blue all the time? Why do we work the way we do? Why did life seem to be such a dreary chore? Why were there disasters that nobody can control?

I spent hours thinking about these things. Why was there jealousy and hate, and how could I get it out of my life? Why do we get such pleasure in talking about other people and ripping them to shreds with our poisonous tongues? Who made depression and what was it for? It certainly had no value to me.

Why are some people blessed with wealth and fame and others left crippled from a high school football game? God must control all of this. Sometimes it angered me, but then I would look at a star twinkling in the sky and ask myself who I was to question God. I was so insignificant. Did it even matter what I thought?

I wondered if it had been a mistake even to come here at all. It had seemed so right to come, but now I wasn't finding a publisher for *Strawberry Jan* and I was thousands of miles away from Heather.

But what if *Strawberry Jan* was just an excuse to get me here, and the real purpose in my trip was something else? What if I was going to meet someone, and would not return to Maui alone?

No matter how I looked at it, it didn't make sense. I would lie awake at night, unable to sleep because of the battle in my mind. I told myself it was a good thing people couldn't see the war raging in my thoughts; they'd think I was nuts. Then another thought struck me: what if everyone had this kind of battle going on inside? Life was bad enough now, but think what it would be like if we all could see everything going on in one another's minds.

Brooks was the person I most wanted to see, and he had moved to South Carolina. We were all like nomads; I wasn't surprised that he had moved to Myrtle Beach. "You've finished *Strawberry Jan*?" he asked. "Can you come down here and let me read it?" So I planned the trip, but at the last minute I went to Montreal.

It was a once-in-a-lifetime invitation. Carl Frederick had written *est: Playing The Game The New Way* and it had just become a best seller. He rented an apartment in Montreal and threw a party to celebrate. And he invited Julie and me.

It was quite a party. People were drinking and dancing in the streets. I went to one Olympic game to watch the gymnasts and it was really boring, so I never went back. But aside from the games themselves, there was always something to do. We all played and refused to rest.

In the midst of the non-stop party, I found time to pray. Somehow I was looking past my needs and I found myself asking to be put in tune with God's purpose for my life, whatever it was. I had never heard of praying anything like this, but it felt right.

I got back from Montreal at the end of the month and was feeling restless and disgusted. What was I doing here? I had been sending Heather a postcard at least once a day and phoning whenever I could, but I missed her terribly. I called her one night when I was back in New York and she said, "When can I live with you again, Mommy?"

I didn't know how to answer. All I knew was that, in spite of everything, I wasn't supposed to go back yet.

I went to South Carolina to stay with Brooks. The heat was appalling. "Why on earth did you leave the cool breezes of Rhode Island to come here?" I asked.

"Off-season rates," he said with a smile. His mane of red hair flared around his high forehead and his green eyes flashed with the delight of someone who had beaten the system. "It isn't bad here in the summer if you stay in the air conditioning or in the water. Then I go back to Narragansett off-season. But who cares about that? What matters is that you've finished *Strawberry Jan*. When do I get to read it?"

My hopes soared, but days passed and though Brooks came up with one good idea after another and he made a lot of calls, nothing seemed to move forward. It was the summertime blues: key people were on vacation, or too busy to look at it until next week, or out of town on another project. I felt stuck in the mud.

I was battling depression again. I was lonely; I missed Heather; I wanted to settle down and give her a home. I had tried to start eating right, but I was stuffing myself with chocolate again. Booze and grass would help me throw off depression for a few hours, but it always came back.

Brooks could take care of things in South Carolina without me, so I returned to the Breslows' house in Rhode Island. I constantly had to fight the urge to forget about my book, get on the plane, and go back to Heather. I had to keep forcing myself to stick with it and resolve things here, one way or another.

Still, I loved it in Rhode Island. In the morning I would watch dawn break across the gray sky. Fingers of fog reached over the distant green hills as darkness gave way to light and yesterday became another memory. Prisms of color burned through the mist as the world lay slumbering, and the silent dawn stirred the birds to hail the new day.

Larry offered me $80,000 cash for the rights to *Strawberry Jan* but I turned it down. He said he'd talk to his attorney to get his advice.

Heather's sixth birthday arrived, and again I wouldn't be with her. Last year I had been in the hospital; that's when I'd started writing the fairy tale. The first words I had written were, "For Heather's Birthday."

So I called to say happy birthday and nobody answered. I kept calling until 3:00 a.m. which was 11:00 pm in Hawaii; still no answer. Worry went through me like a knife. What could be happening?

Finally I reached Heather the next day. They'd gone camping; that's why they hadn't answered the phone.

It was a rainy day and I watched raindrops scatter on the windowpane. I wished I could spill out my tears just as the summer sky spills out showers. I wanted to take a million sleeping pills and fade away. I was tired of talking to the walls; I felt like I was shrinking.

Meanwhile, Larry kept making offers for S*trawberry Jan*. He said he wanted Brooks out of the picture, but I didn't feel right about it. Where would I be if he hadn't encouraged me? Larry persisted. Would I take $300,000 plus 30 percent to sell him the rights to *Strawberry Jan*? He wanted me to go to New York and take care of the copyright.

I called Brooks and told him the offer. "Go ahead without me," he replied. "Don't miss this opportunity just because you want to be loyal. I'd jump in myself, but I'm tied up in other projects right now."

Even with his permission, I still didn't feel right about making a deal that would cut him out.

The next few weeks were a time of wild ups and downs as I tried to market *Strawberry Jan*. I went back to New York, where Paul's attorney, who usually charges $150 an hour, said he'd charge me the minimum as a favor to Paul until I got started.

The fourth anniversary of Bob's death came. I started the day with chocolate cake and a stale beer left over from the night before. I walked the streets for hours, until my feet were blistered. I drank several martinis and passed out. It wasn't much, but at least I got through the day.

I went back to marketing my book and prayed that God's perfect will be done. Everybody seemed to know everybody, so I wasn't surprised to run into Carl Frederick. He needed to go to Rhode Island, and offered to drive me there. Brooks had offered to negotiate the deal, and Carl had a private conference with Larry. I don't know what happened, but after they talked Larry refused to call Brooks. We had a big fight and he went berserk, yelling at me and telling me to get away from him.

I had to assume that was the way that God wanted it, because I had prayed and asked the Lord to make this fair to everyone. The story wasn't mine; it was a gift from God. I decided to continue in prayer for the right answer.

The next day I met with Mark, a writer for *Variety Magazine*. His credits included a stint with Associated Press, and he had covered the Paris Peace Talks. He said he would be happy to edit the fairy tale for me. I left the manuscript with him and he said he'd call back.

It could be exciting to work on the book, but inevitably I'd have to slow down, and then I would realize how much I missed Heather. Whenever I would call her, it might make the ache better or it might make it worse. But I could tell my life was changing. One day I got up at 7:00 a.m., the earliest I'd gotten up in years, and completely organized my bills and paperwork. I wouldn't have been able to do it even a few weeks earlier, but maybe my mind was clearing now that I wasn't dropping acid.

Mark called. "You ruined my football game," he teased. "I always sit down with a manuscript and read the beginning, the middle, and the end during commercials. But I was so captivated by the story that I couldn't put it down. The game was happening right in front of me, and I missed the whole thing." He went on to say that although he'd written a novel, he didn't feel qualified to try to edit *Strawberry Jan*. "I wouldn't know where to begin. But I can recommend an agent – Scott Meredith. You're just a few blocks away from his office."

I went back to New York. I tried staying with a couple of friends, but it was too chaotic. People were coming and going all the time and I couldn't get anything done. I noticed the same thing here I had seen in Rhode Island: everyone was seeking fame and identity. Did they realize what they were reaching for? I remembered when Rebecca was dating Elvis and he had to hide among a bunch of guys in the back of the limousine so he wouldn't be spotted. Fame and fortune could be a prison.

I moved back to the Barbizon. I was putting ten to eighteen hours a day into the fairy tale and working out in the gym. For the first time in years, I was sleeping well. But in spite of it all, I was crying a lot, sometimes because I missed Heather and sometimes for reasons I couldn't understand. I tried reading a book about God, but the tears didn't stop.

Someone told me Amelia lived near New York, and I tracked down her number and called her. I was surprised to learn she had gotten married. "We'll have to get together," she said. "I come into town every few days. I'll call you next time I'm coming."

The next day I woke up crying, and I realized that even my crying was changing: I wasn't sad about anything. The tears seemed somehow to be cleansing me. I noticed that my tears didn't always have anything to do with me. I would listen to the news or see poverty in the streets; I would look into the eyes of bewildered children, dirty and dressed in rags; I would see a man with his arms and legs amputated, using his stumps to propel himself around the neighborhood on his wooden platform with roller skate wheels. Why? Why? Why? Why so much misery and lonely suffering? I went home and prayed for all these people.

Sometimes I didn't feel very brave. I wanted to tear up *Strawberry Jan*, run to the airport, fly back to Hawaii, and hold onto Heather. But instead I made myself go to the Scott Meredith Agency and drop off the manuscript. It was out of my hands now.

The next morning, I woke up again in tears. I got up and reread a few chapters of *Stay Alive All Of Your Life*, sang "Somewhere Over The Rainbow" to myself, and tried to feel as positive as I could – and then once again, an invisible cloud seemed to surround me and I broke down and cried. I felt bad for all the wrong that I had done, and especially that I hadn't been a good mother.

I prayed for guidance and forgiveness. I cried because I wanted to go home but didn't have one. This tiny, lonely cubicle in this hotel was all

I had. I cried and wanted a cig-arette. It seemed to be my re-placement for everything else.

Then I took a deep breath and said aloud: "I believe God is helping me. I believe I will be leaving here soon to be with Heather. I believe God is guid-ing me. I believe God loves me. I believe I will be reward-ed with love and a home for Heather when I've done what He wants me to do."

When I said those things, the sorrow lifted off like a heavy lead garment. Suddenly I could believe God was allow-ing these things for a purpose,

A happy time with Heather.

perhaps to test my strength or faith, because I had turned my back on him for so long. I never thought I'd really believe in God or pray again. After Bob died, I didn't think there could possibly be a God – or if He did exist, He certainly must be terribly cruel.

I went to the Marble Collegiate Church where Norman Vincent Peale was the pastor and found their bookstore. I bought the last two hard-cover copies of Peale's *Stay Alive All Of Your Life*. After I paid for the books, I went inside the Church. I could feel something magic there, but a few people came in, started carrying on a loud conversation, and disrupted the peace.

So I left and found "The Little Church Around The Corner", an Epis-copalian Church that really was around the corner. I walked inside and serenity enveloped me like a warm loving friend. I sat still for a while and enjoyed the peace.

I left the Episcopalian Church and decided to see if there was a 740 Madison Avenue. That is the address I had written in the fairy tale. I had no idea if the address really existed or why I'd chosen it, but I had to see what was there, if anything.

The bus creaked through the crowded city streets until we reached 74th and Madison. I got off eagerly. The first thing I saw was a big sign across the street, and it said "Birthday Book." That's impossible I thought – the first words of the fairy tale are the dedication, "For Heather's Birthday."

But was Birthday Book at 740 Madison Avenue? I crossed the street to see, and it was; and I looked at the display in the window and found they had set out only one thing: a red T-shirt with dark blue letters saying, "All Things Are Possible." It felt like a dream as I stepped inside.

I didn't stay long. As I went back outside I stared at the window once again. Suddenly something clicked.

It hit me that the fairy tale was for Heather's birthday, and there was the T-Shirt announcing "All Things Are Possible" while I stood at an address I'd written while I was in the mental ward at Mt. Sinai.

"Wow," I said aloud as I went back inside to buy the T-Shirt for Heather. They didn't carry children's sizes, so I got one for me.

As soon as I got to my hotel room, I put it on and looked at myself in the mirror. I turned sideways and noticed there was something written on the back. I couldn't read it in the mirror, so I pulled off the T-Shirt and now I could see that it said, "Pass The Word."

Twenty Four

THE MERCIFUL JUDGE

I was changing. One part of me seemed to be fading away while something new was coming alive. Whenever I prayed, cleansing tears would fall. I wept and wept, and it felt right. I didn't understand it, but it felt so good I didn't fight it. Could it be that poison locked up inside was spilling out in my tears?

I still was myself, but little things would make me know I wasn't what I used to be. For instance, I had never felt prudish about magazines like *Penthouse* or *Playboy*; some of my friends had been featured in those magazines. But now I couldn't even walk past them on a magazine stand without feeling revulsion and having to turn away. What was happening to me?

I was up until 4 a.m. one night, reading the Bible and *The Power Of Positive Thinking*. I prayed for rest and awoke to a beautiful sunny day. Amelia called about two minutes after I opened my eyes and told me she was coming to the city.

We went out to lunch and had so much fun chattering that I didn't even notice what I ate. We decided to go and have a professional makeup done by Trudy; she'd done several of the girls for the Miss America contests. I hardly recognized myself when she finished.

Amelia asked me if I wanted to come home with her and spend the night. I was happy to be with my old friend and thrilled to leave the city. After a few days in New York, it was easy to forget that there was more to the world than tall skyscrapers and hordes of pushy people.

As she was driving home, Amelia asked me if I would mind if she stopped at confession.

"Amelia, I didn't know you were a Catholic," I said. I was shocked.

"Well, I guess we never talked about things like that before," she said with a sweet smile. "I started going back to church when I was thrown in jail. It gave me some comfort."

She told me her story. Amelia, beautiful Amelia, had left her fabulous apartment and sophisticated lifestyle with Norman and had run off with

Ryan. We had met him in Hawaii, and I never understood what she saw in him. Yes, he was young and flamboyant, but to me he seemed too sure of himself. Was it his sense of style that made him wear red patent-leather platform shoes, or was he just trying to look taller than he really was? He always had money, but never had to work. He seemed glamorous to Amelia, but I thought he was a con man.

So Amelia had given up her modeling career to live with Ryan. He followed her to L.A., assuring her he could afford to relocate. It turned out he robbed houses, but he told Amelia it wasn't just for money – it was for adventure. Soon he got her to start going with him, and eventually they were caught. She did hard time.

I wouldn't have guessed Amelia would have turned into a churchgoer, but I figured I could at least go in and hang out with her while she stood in line.

As a child, I couldn't wait to be 18 so I wouldn't have to go to Mass every Sunday. That one dreary hour in the dark church felt like eternity. The priests droned on in Latin until the reprieve came at the end of the hour. Grim looking ushers were stationed at the doors and would open them mournfully, as though it were a tragedy that Mass had ended so soon and now they had to release us into the wicked world. Then like a prisoner who had paid her debt to society at last, I'd rush through the nearest door, glad to reunite with the light and fresh air outside.

"I haven't been to church since high school – do you think it will cave in if I go?" I joked.

"No, God's always happy to see us," she said.

"Gosh Amelia, this will be a different trip for us," I said. "I dropped my first acid with you. Now we're off on another adventure."

Amelia stopped by her apartment, a dingy row house in Yonkers. Right after we walked in the door, her husband Lou and his brother came in. They were both obviously very drunk. Amelia spoke sharply to Lou and it quickly escalated into a huge fight about his drinking. I wished I could sink through the floor.

"Let's get out of here," Amelia said, grabbing her purse. I was glad to go. I kept looking at her beautiful face as we drove along though the narrow streets of the little town about an hour and a half north of New York City. I recalled her days as a model, when she had lived in style in Bel Air. How had she ended up married to a drunk and living in a small town in the middle of nowhere?

"There's a Mass going on. I hope you don't mind," Amelia said as she pulled into the church parking lot.

We sat down and I was amazed. I'd never been to a Mass like that before. People were playing guitars and singing and the priest spoke in English and faced us during Mass. Nearly everybody wore blue jeans and everyday clothes.

A pretty little girl sat in the pew in front of us. She reminded me of Heather, and I began to cry. I wanted to reach out and pick up the little girl and give her a long hug for a moment's comfort to soothe the ache in my heart for my daughter.

When Mass was over, I stood in line with Amelia while she waited to go to confession. She was in front of me and I wasn't planning to go, but suddenly I went into the confessional and was on my knees reciting what I had learned in catechism: "Bless me Father, for I have sinned. My last confession was..." – and now I had to pause to figure out how many years it had been – "...14 years ago," I said meekly.

"What, praise God, made you come?" the priest asked exuberantly from the other side of the dark screen.

I had expected stern disapproval; instead, I found joy and unconditional love. What was this about? Priests didn't get excited about anything, yet this one seemed genuinely happy that I was there.

"I don't know why I came in here," I admitted, and suddenly I felt out of place and wanted to leave. "Maybe this isn't the time."

"Of course it's the time. You're here," he said gently. I felt reassured.

I told him what had driven me away from God and about my years as an atheist. Then it came time to confess my sins.

"Father, I honestly have forgotten what a sin is," I said. "Can you help me?"

Patiently he went through the Ten Commandments, and when he got to the one about premarital sex I corrected him. "That isn't a sin," I told him.

"Yes it is," he said sweetly.

I argued with him about it for a while and suddenly realized I was arguing with God's commandments, and then I felt ashamed. I had to admit it was going to be really hard for me to follow that one.

"Well," I said, "I've committed all those sins except for 'Thou Shall Not Kill.'" I figured I was going to get so much penance I'd need a wheelbarrow full of rosary beads and would be on my knees for hours.

"I would like you to say three 'Hail Mary's' and three 'Our Fathers',," he said mildly, pronouncing the blessing.

That was all the penance I was given? The priests I remembered from my childhood were as unyielding and harsh as a bear trap. This is what I had expected, but now I left feeling pretty good.

On the way home I told Amelia about my confession.

"I just told him I'd done everything but kill someone," I said.

"But you have killed, JoAnn," Amelia said gently.

"What on earth do you mean?"

"You've had two abortions, JoAnn."

"Oh Amelia, how can you be so archaic?" I asked. "My gosh, it's legal now. I went right to the hospital to have it done. No, Amelia I just can't believe that was wrong."

"It's murder," she insisted.

"Well, I'm going to ask God about that," I said. I was sure of myself as I said it. It couldn't possibly be wrong.

But Amelia was satisfied. "He'll tell you," she assured me.

We went back to Amelia's house and Lou and his brother were gone, so we sat up talking. Amelia didn't say anything about her marriage. We talked about old times.

When Lou got home, there was a lot of tension in the house. I excused myself and said I needed to go to bed. Amelia pulled the hide-a-bed out of the couch in the tiny living room and disappeared into the only bedroom with Lou. I got out my diary and read a part from a few years ago. I was surprised that I was now disgusted with the filth that had been in my mind. I wondered if I would become a Catholic again. I was surprised that it seemed so appealing, but I had to admit there had been something beautiful in church.

I could hear Amelia and Lou arguing in the other room. I prayed for guidance and for Heather, and for God to help Amelia and Lou. Then I asked God to let me know if it was wrong to have the abortions.

The answer came faster than I expected. That night I dreamed that I was given a baby to take care of, and I squashed it by accident. I went to the police station with my friends to explain the situation. The policemen must have been thirty feet tall and stood behind a very high podium. I had to look up a long way to see them. They were very imposing looking in their dark blue uniforms and high rounded hats with chin straps. They didn't look stern or mean, but neither did they look merciful or compassionate. They looked impassive, just, and resolute.

My friends had carefully wrapped the baby in a blanket and waited with me to hear the verdict. The police conferred with one another and I strained to hear them but couldn't. They had so much authority and were so big, I knew they could reach down and squash any of us in an instant.

The biggest policeman was in the middle, and finally he stood up straight and looked down at me. His unyielding face became tender. "It was an accident; you are free to leave."

When I woke up I knew it was God's way of showing me that abortion was wrong and that I had killed my children, but I was pardoned.

Amelia drove me back to the city. We worked out in the hotel gym and then went for a wonderful dinner at Serendipity. After she left, I felt lonely and decided to go to a movie. I'd never gone alone before and it felt weird sitting by myself in the huge theatre, but it was a double feature: *Lenny* and *One Flew Over the Cuckoo's Nest*.

It wasn't the relaxing evening I had expected. I was depressed when I walked out of the theater, and I freaked out when I got back to my room, pounding my head on the floor and screaming. What was wrong with our society? Was everybody sick? I had listened to people laughing at the mentally ill in *One Flew Over The Cuckoo's Nest* and wondered if they would laugh at cancer on the screen. The movies had pushed me into depression and despair. What effect were they having on others?

I got up early the next morning to go to confession; I had my first Communion in 14 years.

I still felt a little depressed and prayed as I made my way through the hellish city streets. Every day I would see men or women screaming crazy things at the top of their lungs, and those around them laughing. Today it was an unshaven man in tattered dull brown clothes; he'd probably slept in them for many nights. He screamed curses at anybody and everybody, and people just walked by, laughing at him as though he were an entertainer.

It was like the laughter in the movie the night before and anger welled up inside me. I felt like shaking them and saying: "Can't you see this is a human being and he's sick? He needs help!"

I had to see my attorney, and once that errand was done I decided to go back to the serenity of St. Patrick's where I'd gone to Mass in the morning. On the way, I passed a sign that read "Gypsy Tea." I went up a dingy staircase to the tearoom. About ten women, dressed like gypsies, sat at tables along the wall and did readings while other customers waiting their turn drank tea in the large restaurant.

I asked the bored looking woman at the register how much it would cost to have my fortune told. "Three dollars," she replied limply. I handed her the money and she took me to a table, placing the number 38 in front of me.

I sipped my tea and looked at the variety of people waiting. Some were obviously uptown, with their designer clothes and expensive jewelry. Others looked like they could hardly afford a cup of tea.

My number was called and I was led to a woman in her late 40's who shuffled her tarot cards as I sat down. Her large dark eyes never quite looked at me: they looked down inside me and they darted all around me, apparently tuned in to visions the rest of us couldn't see. She spread the cards in front of me, and a voice that seemed to come from another world poured through her painted red lips.

"You will be signing a contract shortly, but there is some opposition," she said. "However, it will turn out okay. Soon you will be going to another state and your life and ideas are going to change drastically between now and February."

She looked up from her cards but still didn't quite look me in the eye. Her dark hair fell carelessly across her tiny shoulders and her face looked tired.

"May I ask a question?" I said.

"Yes, what is it?"

"I want to know about Stephen."

She looked intently at the cards and lifted her face slowly, looking at something behind my left shoulder. "He's irresponsible, and don't do too much for him," she said.

I left and headed back to the church. My spirits were lifted. Going to another state soon? That was good; soon I'd be reunited with Heather. My ideas about life? They really were changing rapidly. Contract? This was probably something about *Strawberry Jan*.

I got to the church and asked if I could speak with a priest because I had questions. I was told it would be about an hour, so I waited in the small reception area and absently thumbed through magazines.

Father Thurman came in and introduced himself, and he led me into his study. I sat across from him and wondered why he'd become a priest. He was handsome enough to be a model, with his dark brown hair and perfect features.

"What can I do for you?" he asked kindly.

"Well, I have some questions because I'm thinking about becoming a Catholic, but I want to know some things first," I said hoping he'd give me the answers I was looking for. "What do you think of premarital sex?"

"It's a changing world and you have to listen to your own heart," he said.

What a relief! It made a lot more sense than what the priest had told me in the confessional. Apparently some priests were more old-fashioned than others.

"What about psychics and fortune tellers?"

"There's nothing wrong with that," he said.

"Gosh, I guess the Church has changed," I said. "What do you think about Jesus? Is he real?"

"If he isn't, then the Church would be in a lot of trouble," he said, but he looked as puzzled as I felt.

"What do you mean?" I asked. I hadn't expected to agree with everything he said, but it rattled me that he didn't seem sure of anything. "Why would the church be in trouble if Jesus isn't real?"

"All of Christianity is based on Jesus Christ rising from the dead," said the priest. "If He didn't, then it all would be meaningless."

"Oh," I said as distant memories of Him hanging on the cross filled my dormant brain and jarred something loose. I suddenly realized I had forgotten that Jesus had anything to do with the Catholic church.

We talked for a while but eventually it was time to go. "You might like the prayer meeting that meets tomorrow in the church basement," he said as I rose to leave. I thanked him and left, wondering about Jesus. It didn't seem to me that Father Thurman was sure about him either.

As I left St. Patrick's, I bought two antique crosses, one for Heather and one for me. For the first time in my life I realized what the cross means.

This was my prayer when I went to bed that night: "God, I had a nice day and I want to dedicate my life to You. I hope that I will be a better person tomorrow and help as many people as I can. I believe in you,

God, but I don't know about this Jesus trip. Will you let me know if Jesus is really Your Son?"

Then I fell sound asleep.

What could be simpler than wanting to go to a prayer meeting at noon? But I woke up the next morning with a battle going on in my mind, and I lost count of how many times I changed my mind about going. Finally I decided I had nothing to lose, and I went.

Even as I walked I was tempted to turn back. Part of me absolutely didn't want to go and was determined to stay out. As I walked down the stairs of the church I heard singing, and I turned around twice with the irrational thought that something terrible was in the basement and I had to get away while I could. I told myself I was being ridiculous, and quickly descended the stairs.

I felt uncomfortable and hoped nobody would speak to me. Fortunately a lot of people had arrived and I would be able to get lost in the crowd. The chairs were arranged in a circle with several rows, and nobody paid any attention to me as I squirmed into my seat. There was a lot of singing and people spoke whenever they wanted to. It reminded me of group therapy.

At the end, a man read something out of a book and it was just for me. After the meeting I approached him and asked for the name of the book. "The book is *God Calling*," he said kindly. "Here, let me get a piece of scrap paper and I'll write it down and tell you where you can get a copy."

I hurried to the bookstore and bought my book, and then I returned to my room to search for what the man had read. This is what it said:

"The work of righteousness shall be peace and the effect of righteousness quietness and assurance forever. (Isa. 32:17) My peace it is which gives quietness and assurance forever. My peace which flows as some calm river through the dry land of life, that causes the trees and flowers of life to spring forth and yield abundantly. Success is the result of work done in peace. Let there be no hurry in your plans. You live not in time but in eternity. It is in the unseen that your life future is being planned. Abide in me and I in you so shall you bring forth much fruit. Be calm, assured, at rest. Love, not rush. Peace, not unrest. Nothing fitful. All effectual. Sown in prayer, watered by Trust, bearing flower and fruit in Joy. I love you."

I knew God was speaking to me – I couldn't have explained to anyone how I knew – but I knew. It answered my question about the fairy tale, and much more.

Then I opened to the front of the book and read that *God Calling* had been written by two women who had lived together and had shared a prayer adventure, seeking to hear from God day by day. Their lives were fraught with hardship; at least one of them battled insomnia; one of them was in so much pain, death would have been a relief. But day by day the messages came, and they had shared them in this book. The preface ended with these words:

"It is published, after much prayer, to prove that A LIVING CHRIST SPEAKS TODAY, plans and guides the humblest, that no detail is too insignificant for His attention, that He reveals Himself now as ever as Humble Servant and Majestic Creator."

I stopped to absorb the words "SPEAKS TODAY" and realized I had asked God just last night if Jesus was his Son. This book, *God Calling*, made me see that Jesus is real. I prayed and asked Him to come into my heart.

Two things happened immediately. My nose had been so burned out by coke I could hardly breathe through it anymore; it was completely healed. More important, I was instantly filled with deep peace and tranquility.

It struck me forcefully that Jesus came to do good and to suffer as all men suffer, to show the world that no matter how much we suffer we can be at peace with God in our hearts.

I knew I didn't need anything but God, and I wanted to help people who are lost. What a magic world this is, I told myself. I no longer have the slightest doubt that God is leading me where I'm going.

I stayed up all night reading *God Calling*. I finally fell asleep at 8 a.m. and woke up three hours later.

It was raining when I left the hotel and the city looked dreary, cloaked in gray. I was on my way to the bookstore when I got an urge to go to Mass at St. Patrick's.

During Mass, everything became very mystical. The pillars, candles and arches appeared 40 dimensional as they stretched out towards me. It was indescribably beautiful, awakening many of the same feelings I had experienced when I was dying and I felt very small and insignificant.

The priest's voice rang with rich deep tones and melted hardness out of my heart. After Mass, I read about the saints and knelt in front of St. Ann. For a moment it felt as if someone had just draped a cloak over me, but nothing was there. I continued to pray and it happened several times. It almost seemed as if I was wearing a nun's habit. Was God calling me to be a nun?

I went into the little gift shop attached to the church and bought prayer cards and a rosary and had them blessed. I left feeling as if I were floating.

Everything looked dreamy, like illustrations in a book of fairy tales. The sun had broken through and the clouds were too perfect, too white, and too fluffy to look real. For a few moments the sky seemed to radiate a special glow, and it made the otherwise drab town shimmer with loveliness. An odd side effect came with this light: I could tell if hair had been dyed. The phony color was garish; the slight blue rinse in one lady's hair was illuminated like a neon sign.

It was as if my vision was supernatural for a few minutes. Was this how things always looked to God?

I was higher than I had ever gone on drugs, and yet it wasn't a drug that had taken me there. It was clear and clean and there was no fear – only peace and love and indescribable joy. I had never felt so happy. Could it be that drugs were a counterfeit of this experience?

The next day, I sent all my jewelry and fancy clothes to my friends; it felt good to simplify. I cut off my long nails and removed the bright purple polish and decided not to wear makeup. It didn't seem right to be flashy and draw attention to myself.

A few days ago I had seen elegant clothes in store windows and coveted them, but now they seemed insignificant. Now I wanted to cover my ears when people used the same language I had used myself a few days earlier. My world was changing.

I went to mass and Father Thurman was the celebrant. His message was that the Church is going through changes. After Mass, I went out of my way to greet Father Thurman. What's going on with me? I asked myself. I used to be the first person out the door when church ended. Now I'm hanging around to chat with the priest. I couldn't get over how much I was changing.

Neither could Father Thurman. "You certainly do look different," he exclaimed. "The last time I saw you, you were wearing a blue turquoise snake necklace and a lot of other exotic jewelry."

"I don't know what's happening with the church," I told him, "but I sure know I'm changing. Have you seen this book?" I handed him a copy of *God Calling* and added, "I've been reading it lately."

"Oh yes," he said as he glanced at the title and returned the book to me. "I've read it myself."

"I feel like I need to make a retreat," I continued. "I'm not sure why, and I'm not even quite sure what a retreat is; but something deep inside says to go on a retreat."

"Let me get you a number," he said. I waited as he went to his office and returned with a scrap of paper. "Call this number and say you want to make a retreat."

When I got back to my room I dialed the number of the convent Father Thurman had given me.

"Bethany House, Sister Mary Kathryn speaking," the soft voice said on the other end of the line.

I was staring at the copy of *God Calling* sitting in front of me on my desk. "Hello, my name is JoAnn Dejoria and..." Suddenly I stopped; I didn't know what to say.

"God is calling you," she answered sweetly finishing my sentence.

Looking more intently at the cover, her words echoed in my heart. "Yes, yes, I think He really is."

"Come right away," she said without hesitation.

Twenty Five

THE SEAGRAMS 7 CROWN MISSION

I had a rough night. I had been trying to call Heather for a couple of days and nobody answered. It was probably nothing to worry about; this had happened before, and it had always turned out that the Schaeffers had taken a vacation. But tonight I missed her so much I couldn't sleep.

Then something weird happened: twice it felt like I was dying. What was happening to me? I told God that if I had one last request in the world it would be to hold Heather one more time. I'd tell her to search for God always, that He is more important than anything the material world has to offer, and to remember that she lives in eternity, not in time.

I gave up trying to sleep and went downstairs for coffee. I heard a voice in the crowded elevator begging, "Somebody help me. Please, somebody!" I struggled to catch a glimpse of who it was, as the elevator stopped on other floors and more people got on. Everyone ignored her; nobody even hinted where this desperate person pleading for attention might be. Everyone stared at the doors as if they couldn't hear her. Maybe I was losing my mind; maybe I was imagining the whole thing. But when the elevator reached the lobby and everyone quickly got off, I saw a pathetic woman slumped on the dirty floor. She looked up at me through red watery eyes.

"How can I help you?" I asked touching her head gently.

She grabbed her cane and stood to her feet, trembling all over.

"I fell in the shower and need a drink to calm my nerves," she said. Her voice was shaking as badly as her body was.

I had no idea what was wrong. She was about 60 years old and looked very poor.

"What can I get you?"

"Rye," she said handing me a plastic change purse as people began to spill into the elevator once again.

I touched her gently and shoved the little purse back into her shaky hand. She looked at me with pleading eyes.

"Let me take you back to your room," I offered. "Don't worry, I'll take care of you."

Her name was Ruth. I helped her into bed, went back downstairs, and walked to the nearest liquor store. "What is rye?" I asked. I'd never been a heavy drinker, so I'd never had rye.

The man behind the counter showed me the display. I'd have never guessed there are so many kinds of rye. "Which is the very best you have?" I asked, still scanning the shelves.

"Seagram's 7 Crown," he said.

I remembered my Grandfather drinking that brand. "I want the biggest bottle you have," I said.

A few moments later I tapped on Ruth's door.

"Come in," she said shyly.

I had thought my room was small, but hers was even smaller: barely enough space for a single bed, a tiny desk, and a rickety chair. She was sitting on her bed as I handed her the Seagram's. She was shaking so hard she could barely hold the big bottle up to her lips. Much of it missed her mouth and dribbled down her face. She guzzled it quickly and dabbed at the mess on her chin, but didn't get it all.

"I'm sorry my room is so dirty," Ruth said. "It makes me feel ashamed. I'm not used to having guests." A mountain of disordered papers was on the desk and a few rumpled clothes hung over the back of the chair.

"Oh, please don't feel ashamed," I said, carefully laying the clothes on the foot of her bed and turning the desk chair so I could sit facing her.

"I have a drinking problem," she admitted after she'd had a few more belts.

"Do you want help?" I asked.

"Yes, I want to stop drinking," she said.

I used her phone to call Father Thurman and found out about a place called "Catholic Worker". I got the address and made arrangements to bring Ruth in.

"Shall we go?" I asked.

"I'd like to take a bath and put on something clean, but my clothes are all dirty," she said.

"I have some things you can wear," I offered and headed for my room.

By the time I got back her shaking had almost entirely subsided.

"I took 50 aspirins last night because I wanted to kill myself," she said. "Today I was going to get some sleeping pills because the aspirins just made me sick. I would have done it if I hadn't met you."

"Well Ruth, I'm glad we met," I said.

"So am I."

"Listen, I am going to check out of my room because I'm going on a retreat later today," I explained. "Also, I'm going to call my friend Terry and ask her to go with us. She knows the subway system and we've got a ways to go."

I left my things in Ruth's room and we waited for Terry in the lobby.

We took the subway down to the Bowery district and Terry said we still had a long walk ahead of us. I hired a taxi; Ruth had a bad hip and had to walk with a cane, and I didn't want her to have to walk far. The neighborhood was really run down and when we found the building, it too was in disrepair. What have I gotten myself into? I wondered. Like its exterior, the interior of the building needed work. But it was squeaky clean.

A sister met us at the door. She was sweet but wary. She showed Ruth around and offered her a bed, but now Ruth too was edgy. "I can't stay here," she protested. "I'm not feeling well. I need to get back to my room."

I was bewildered. "Are you sure? Father Thurman said they have everything you need here…"

Ruth was sure. "I want to get back to my room," she insisted, snapping at me.

We descended the steps. I hadn't counted on this delay, and realized that now I would miss my retreat. Disappointment swept over me, and I was irritated. I didn't feel like shelling out for another cab. I was more in the mood to punish Ruth, so I asked Terry for directions to the subway and we started to walk.

The stroll seemed to do Ruth some good. We had to pass a cluster of drunks lying in the street. Some lay in their own vomit, and a pungent odor filled the air. Others sat with heads lolling and eyes half-open. They all wore filthy clothes, and each clutched a wine bottle while gesturing with a free hand and shouting obscene comments at us.

I could see in Ruth's face that the drunks made quite an impression on her. They made one on me too; I was grouchier than ever when we got on the subway. We sat down and I scowled at Ruth, who seemed to be in her own private world.

I wondered why I was even doing this. Face it; people could be a lot of trouble. Oh God, how in the world would I ever become a nun if I don't like people? How could I ever sacrifice myself the way they do? I'm much too selfish. I must be losing my mind. We got off the subway and I chatted with Terry as we walked back to the hotel, allowing Ruth to hobble along behind us. She fell about a half a block behind. I didn't care.

"Do you want to wait for her?" Terry asked, turning around and noticing she wasn't with us.

"No, she knows the way."

I couldn't wait to get my things out of Ruth's room, so as soon as we got back I told her goodbye and went downstairs, leaving my suitcases with the bell captain.

Terry and I went out for a very late lunch and suddenly it hit me that I was too tired to leave. I would have to start my retreat at least a day late. I went back to the Barbizon and checked in at 4 p.m. Fortunately, my room was still available. I looked at the clock as I fell on the bed and dozed off to sleep. It was 4:10 p.m.

I woke up feeling rested and happy. The clock said 6:30. I went to the window and tried to get a sense of what the weather was going to be like for the day. However, it was still pitch black outside. "It's always darkest before the dawn," I thought, overjoyed that I had slept for more than 14 hours. It was the best night's sleep I'd had in a long time.

I lay down again, waiting for the sun to rise, and began to plan my day. It was so early I could attend Mass and then go to see Dr. Peale before I left for the retreat. Suddenly I became depressed, and uneasy about the convent. Was I really called to become a nun and never get married again? I didn't think I could do it, and yet with my Catholic background, I could think of no other reason that God was going to so much trouble with me. He had to be calling me into the religious life.

Then I began to think about the many times when someone promised to help me and left me hanging. Memories of feeling abandoned filled my head and I thought of Ruth and felt sorry for her. When I became concerned about Ruth rather than myself, the depression lifted and I looked at the clock.

I was shocked that it said 8:00.

"Where has an hour and a half gone?" I asked aloud, looking out the window. It was still pitch black outside. This meant either that the sun wasn't coming up today, which at this point, wouldn't have surprised me, or that I'd only slept 2 1/2 hours. Or of course I might have slept through an entire day. Maybe that was it; I felt so rested that it was hard to believe I might have slept only a few hours.

I called the desk and asked for the time. "8 p.m.," she said.

"And what day is it?" As the words came out of my mouth, I knew the words sounded strange.

"Saturday, September 18," she said with the weary voice of someone who'd had to answer this kind of question too many times before.

Amazed that I'd only slept a few hours, I called Ruth to see if she needed anything.

"I would love a pack of cigarettes," she said meekly. I rushed out and got her a carton. She accepted it gratefully and I noticed she looked a lot better. I sat in her room and as we talked, there were several times when she peered into my eyes, as if to search out a hidden mystery. "Why are you helping me?" she would ask. "I just can't believe it."

I watched her try to light a cigarette. She was shaking so badly she had trouble lighting a match; and then, it was a struggle to hold the flame to the cigarette long enough to light it. So throughout our conversation, I would light her cigarettes for her.

She poured out her story. She'd been an alcoholic for ten years and had been through detox several times. She'd tried A.A. "But I'm a private person," she said; "do you know what I mean? Sometimes in an A.A. meeting I had the feeling some of the people were there to get their kicks out of listening to all the drunks share their miserable lives. Not everybody, of course. Some of the people were there for the right reasons. But I don't like sharing all my secrets with strangers in a meeting open to the general public."

I could understand.

"As long as I'm here, is there anything I can do for you?" I asked.

"Well, I don't know if this is asking too much, but could you help me straighten up my desk?"

I recalled how difficult it had been for me to handle the simplest paperwork when I was confused. "I'll be glad to," I said.

The first thing was a letter to an insurance company. She had tried to type it, on the bottom of the note dated September 6 she had scribbled, "I'm sorry this has taken me so long." Oh, if they could only know how sorry she really was. Because she couldn't stop shaking she had made a lot of typing mistakes, and she had too much pride to send it out messy.

When I typed it I made a few errors myself. "Maybe we can try again tomorrow," she said. I could tell she was worried that she was asking too much of me.

"No, let's try again," I said. As I put a fresh sheet of paper into the typewriter I breathed a silent prayer for help. I typed the next two letters perfectly. Now we had a new problem: she was shaking too badly to sign the letters. I signed them for her. I folded the letters neatly and put them in the envelopes, remembering how satisfied I had felt whenever I managed to mail anything. "I'll take this to the post office for you tomorrow morning," I promised.

Ruth rubbed her eyes.

"JoAnn, you've been so good to me. Can I ask one more thing of you?"

"Sure".

"Would you mind going up to the T.V. room to see if anyone has any Visine I can borrow?"

Rather than going there, I decided to go over to the market. They didn't carry any and told me there was an open pharmacy, but it was quite a ways down on 49th Street. I enjoyed the brisk walk in the cool evening and found the little pharmacy. A teenager ahead of me was being very cruel to the pharmacist. "Gimme a cup of coffee," he said. "I know you have a coffeepot in the back room." The pharmacist ignored him and looked over at me.

"Then gimme a quarter," the kid demanded loudly.

I paid for the Visine and added some cough medicine; maybe it would help Ruth's persistent cough. Then I handed the disturbed kid 40 cents so he'd leave the weary druggist alone. I just smiled and nodded at him, telling myself it was for the Lord and watching the kid's angry features turn soft as he smiled back at me, jammed the change into his pocket, and ran out of the store.

I counted the blocks from 49th to 63rd and realized I felt worn out. I wondered if I could get something that would taste good to Ruth. Her stomach had been in turmoil for several days and she wasn't able to keep anything down. The Baskin-Robbins sign seemed to be calling out to me so I went in to find something for her. "What can I getcha?" the kid behind the counter asked.

I scanned the flavors, and found one that might work. "I want an Apricot Brandy Sherbet Malt." I'd never heard of such a thing, but it seemed like something Ruth might like.

"That sounds awful," the kid said, turning up his nose.

"Maybe so, but it's what I want."

I watched as he reluctantly put the ingredients together. "I hope it's okay," he said.

"Well, I'll try it and let you know," I said. I stuck the spoon in hopefully. I was surprised at how wonderful it tasted. "It's great!"

"I'm glad," he said. "I've been having a bad night. I just made two shakes for a couple that were in here a few minutes ago and they guzzled 'em down before they paid, and then they told me it wasn't fit for human consumption and left."

I walked back to the hotel. Ruth was trying to boil water when I got back to her room but she was too shaky to hold the pan under the faucet.

"Here, I'll do that," I said, quickly taking over. "You just sit down."

The water boiled and she insisted she could pour it herself. She poured too much into the bowl and the instant oatmeal floated over the top and sloshed onto the table.

Disappointment welled up in her face and her eyes filled with tears.

I handed her the milkshake and her eyes brightened. Her shaky hands grasped it and she took a big sip.

"What is this?" she asked. "It's really good."

"Something new," I said as I cleaned up the oatmeal.

She finished every drop and I pulled her covers back so she could crawl into bed.

"Would you like to go to church with me tomorrow morning to hear Dr. Norman Vincent Peale?" I asked. I was sure she'd decline.

"I would love to go. What time?" she asked anxiously. I told her and went to the door to leave. She called out to me.

"JoAnn?"

"Yes, Ruth."

Her eyes filled with tears once again as she glanced at the bottle of Seagram's on top of the dresser.

"I never thought I'd give away booze, but I don't think I'm going to be needing that anymore," she said, pointing towards it. "Would you leave it for the maids? They've got a secret corner where they go and take a snort. You know the door right next to mine? It's just a closet. Put it in there. Hide it in the towels, and they'll get it."

I took the bottle, noticing it was still almost full, and kissed her on the head.

"Good night, Ruth. I'll call you when I wake up."

"Boy, if only I had a sister like you," she said wistfully.

"You do," I said. First, I found the closet door next to Ruth's and left the bottle behind a pile of towels. Then I returned to my room, picked up my diary, and wrote God a note:

"I finally have a beginning, now that I've given up the material world and all of the sinning. I've given you my life, and you will make my plans and I pray that I will serve you with all my heart. I hope that I'll not question what happens to me, because I'm only the twig and you are the tree."

I didn't get to sleep till 7 a.m. I was up all night talking to God and reading. I woke up at 9:30 a.m. feeling fantastic, and I waited until 10 a.m. to call Ruth.

Her first question was, "What time are we going to church?"

I went down to her room and was shocked when she opened the door. She was neatly dressed with her hair shining; it was washed and carefully combed. She'd meticulously put on light makeup and looked so nice I hardly recognized her. But there was another surprise. I looked around in amazement. "Ruth, what has happened to your room?"

"Oh, I slept for a few hours after you left and woke up about 3 a.m. feeling better than I have in years. I wasn't shaking a bit and that's a miracle. I can hardly believe it. I decided to clean my room and get myself ready."

I handed her a copy of *God Calling*, overwhelmed by what the Lord was doing in our lives.

We were greeted by a beautiful sunny day as we left the hotel. Ruth strode ahead of me, almost running.

"We don't want to be late!" she called out excitedly. In spite of her cane and her damaged hip, she was hard to keep up with. I enjoyed chasing her, watching her race towards the bus stop, feeling such joy in my heart. God, You're great! I thought as we hurried along.

We went in the church and found a place to sit. I looked around; people looked so happy they seemed to glow. The service began, and Dr. Peale spoke. It ended too quickly, but as we filed out we were caught in the stream of people that poured into the fellowship hall. I watched Ruth chatting with the man who had been sitting next to her in the service; he'd been sure to invite us for coffee. I saw a glimmer of sophistication in Ruth's mannerisms and I wished I knew more of her story. I knew she'd never been married and had lost many years in a bottle, but that was about it.

I felt like walking when we left, but it was several miles back to the hotel. "Do you mind taking the bus by yourself?" I asked.

"Of course not," she said sweetly. "Do what pleases you." She gave me a hug.

"I'm leaving for the convent late this afternoon; I'll keep in touch," I said, waving goodbye.

I started my walk back to the hotel and realized I was radically happier than I had ever dreamed a human being could possibly be.

I decided to stop by St. Patrick's and pray. It had become like a good friend to me and I loved being there. I arrived during Mass, so I got to take communion.

When I left, I was asking for God's guidance and I started to feel as if I was floating down the street like a puppet on invisible strings. I knew I could choose to do whatever I wanted; consequently, I chose to let the invisible strings guide me, and I abandoned myself. Maybe it was a drill from heaven to let me know that God really was guiding me, because I kept crossing the same street over and over again. I'd heard people tell about similar training in boot camp, when someone would be ordered to dig a hole and then to fill it up again, without knowing why.

After I had crossed the street a few times, I was led further. Now it felt more like the tug of an invisible magnet rather than strings, because the sensation got stronger as I yielded to it. I crossed that same street once again and my eyes lit on a paper on the sidewalk. The magnet pulled me towards it and I picked it up. It was a small flyer that said "Jews For Jesus." Until now, I hadn't realized there were any Jews who believed in Jesus.

The magnet pulled me again about half a block down the street. It stopped me and I looked down at the ground. There was another pamphlet lying there; this one too had the words "Jews For Jesus" inside.

The magnet then turned me around and I noticed a streetlight that was still turned on. I looked around and no other streetlights were burning. A poster on the lamppost said "Different Drummer" and I chuckled to myself. God really must have a sense of humor I thought as the words to the song ran through my head. Different Drummer? It's the story of my life.

The magnet lifted and I walked back to the hotel to pack for my retreat.

Twenty Six

"*TURN, TURN, TURN*"

I arrived at Bethany House for my retreat and resolved to spend most of my time alone with the Lord, reading, meditating, and talking to Him.

I looked at my quarters and wondered if I would be able to sleep. The convent was huge and I was alone in the wing reserved for retreats; the nuns all slept in another part of the building. Ordinarily I would have been terrified to be so alone in such an isolated place. But just before I went to sleep, Sister Mary Kathryn came in to say goodnight. She placed her hand gently on my forehead and blessed me. A blanket of peace settled over me and I fell asleep.

The next day I went out to explore the woods surrounding the convent. I was still wrapped in the blanket of peace, so when I came upon a cemetery I was not afraid. It was a burial place for priests and nuns. I sat down, leaned my head against a gravestone, and read my Bible for a few minutes. Then I looked around again, savoring the colors of a New York autumn and the smell of wildflowers and of freshly mown grass. I gazed at a large cross that was in front of me, and fell asleep.

After lunch, I went for another walk and found a beautiful spot that overlooked a large lake on the convent's property. Wherever I went, the scenes were as perfect as the pictures on postcards. But the woodsy smells were another part of the beauty. A postcard could have shown the still waters reflecting the deep blue of the sky and the tall trees surrounding the lake, but it would have missed the smell of pine needles underfoot.

Whenever I was in the building, I kept running into a little nun, Sister Rose Alice, who bugged me every time I saw her. With a bounce in her step she would come up to me, smiling brightly as light reflected off her hopelessly old-fashioned glasses. "Are you having a good time?" she would ask, and I'd tell her about something I'd seen on the grounds. Then she would answer excitedly, "Oh, that's nice, dear. But you'll have to go to Mass with me at the House Of Prayer, and you can meet Father McGrath." Apparently it was a few miles away.

But they had Mass here at Bethany House, and I got up at 5 a.m. the next morning to be there with the sisters. I didn't get much out of it; maybe it was too early in the morning. I battled depression for the rest of the morning, missing Heather and facing a sudden onslaught of second thoughts about the changes that were happening in my life. Was I becoming someone who couldn't fit into the world anymore? I was starting to feel like a misfit.

After breakfast, Sister Rose Alice kept inviting me to go with her for the rest of the morning. She followed me to the library and I told her I'd think about it. Then I escaped to the lobby, but here she came again with her smile, her enthusiasm, and her invitation. I decided I might as well go; maybe if I got it over with she would leave me alone.

On the way to Mass she stopped at something called an Aglow meeting. A large room in someone's home was filled with pudgy women dressed up in heels and suits, and they all were waving their hands. A lady with a guitar led the singing. I wanted to run out the door. Sister Rose Alice was bouncing up and down in time with the music. I felt weird and uncomfortable and couldn't wait to leave. But eventually we did. It was time to go to Mass.

We got back in the car. What have I gotten myself into? I wondered. We drove for about five minutes and Sister Rose Alice cheerfully announced, "Here we are at last!" I realized it wouldn't have bothered me if we'd had to drive for an hour. But here we were. At this point, there was nothing else to do but to go inside.

The Mass was in a large Victorian house, with the parlor converted into a chapel. Father McGrath looked traditional in his white robe with a huge gold cross. He was tall and grey-haired, with large round eyeglasses. This was as traditional as things would get.

It was a Charismatic Catholic Mass, again using guitars instead of the organ. It was like the Aglow meeting because people everywhere were enthusiastically praising Jesus aloud. Again I was extremely anxious for it to end, and it seemed to last longer than the usual one hour set aside for church. After Mass, Father McGrath invited everyone to stay for lunch. He was surprisingly kind and gentle, and I felt comfortable conversing with him. But when it was time to go back to the convent, I said goodbye and he replied, "Feel free to come by any time you need to talk."

So we went back to the convent. After supper, one of the Sisters said, "We can't be spiritual all the time, you know. A few of us are going to have a game of cards tonight. Would you care to join us?"

What, nuns play cards? What a trip! "I wouldn't miss it for anything," I told her. So I joined them for the most innocent party I had seen in years: no booze, no drugs, no looking for a lover. Yet I saw something I had never seen in all the parties I had gone to: they were happy. They were giggling like little girls at a slumber party, and I sat there trying to figure it out. Maybe if you start off happy, it doesn't take much to have a good time, I told myself. But if you start off miserable, even if you do any wild thing that comes into your head nothing breaks through the depression. Their joy was contagious, and I realized I was having more fun than I'd had in years.

I woke up the next morning feeling the Lord wanted me to go to the Charismatic Mass again, even though my insides shuddered every time I heard someone praise Jesus out loud. So I asked Sister Rose Alice if she would take me, and she was surprised and excited that I wanted to go. I was surprised myself.

Why was I supposed to go? I never did find out. I went and nothing unusual happened. But I was learning that each day seemed to bring its lesson to trust Him.

I tried to call Heather and found out the Schaeffers were in Michigan and the children were staying with neighbors, so I had no way to get in touch with her. My heart ached to be with her.

I couldn't understand what was going on inside. One moment I would overflow with love and peace, and then for no reason a dark despair would suddenly engulf me and I would feel as if it were going to strangle me. The feeling would be so strong it seemed to have its own life.

Of course, it could just be mood swings. And this wasn't the first time my moods didn't reflect what I was going through. For instance, I might have anxiety when I couldn't reach Heather, but almost immediately God's peace would pour into me, assuring me that everything was alright. Likewise, in a Charismatic Mass I would hear someone saintly, praising Jesus, and something dark would rise up inside with pure hatred. Was this a mood swing, or another personality?

I went to the Charismatic Mass again for the third time and Father McGrath spoke on Ecclesiastes 3:11, "A time to be born, a time to die." Wow! I never knew this was in the Bible; I thought it was a song The

Byrds had written. I decided to write to Ricky and Laura to let them know.

I finally reached Heather. She sounded so tiny and far away, and she asked resignedly, "Mommy, are you ever coming back?" It broke my heart.

So I was crying off and on all day, sometimes because of the strange thing that was going on inside, sometimes because I was separated from Heather, and sometimes because the retreat was about to end and I wasn't sure what to do next. "Jesus, I'm standing at the door and you have the key," I prayed.

When the retreat ended, I made my last trip to the Charismatic Mass. Father McGrath asked if I'd like to stay in the House of Prayer for a while. He said another man and a nun also lived here. This was an example of what can happen when you trust God day by day – exactly when I needed to know what to do next, this door opened! I moved in.

By the next day, I wondered if I had made a mistake. Father McGrath said something during Mass that really upset me, and I left in the middle of the service. I felt like packing everything up and getting out of here. "Oh God," I prayed. "If this is the devil, then cast it out."

I ran to the cemetery up the street. It was a place where I could get away and think; nobody would bother me there, even if I started crying. I pondered a few philosophical questions. Why was there evil? Why was there suffering? Suddenly a more mundane issue gripped me: why was the cemetery filled with spiders? I didn't linger to wait for an answer. I left and went for a walk.

I wandered until I saw the Ananda Ashram Yoga Society, and went in. A meeting was in progress, so I sat down and listened to the Yogi for a while. His words made sense, but I suddenly became confused. It was becoming clear that God wasn't calling me to be a nun, but what else could I be called to? Nothing made sense. I slipped out and walked back to the House Of Prayer, wondering what God wanted to do with my life. Did this happen to other people?

I got back to Father McGrath's by dinnertime. "Where have you been?" he asked. Something in the tone of his voice made me feel like a child being reprimanded.

"I went to the ashram to listen to a Yogi," I said smartly.

I could tell by the look in his eyes that he was upset, but he didn't say anything. For some reason, it gave me pleasure to hurt him. I wasn't sure why, but sometimes I almost hated him and Sister Pauline and Vince, the other two people living here.

But it was only sometimes. I deeply respected their faith and commitment. Every day a bell rang at 7:00 a.m., calling us downstairs to prayer. Most of the time, I didn't want to get up, but I read this little saying I saw at the convent: "We must die to self in order to feel nothing but Gratitude and Wonder." With that in mind, I would go to the prayer meeting. Whenever I could rest my life in the Lord, I began to feel like a smooth pond with no ripples. But whenever my mind would try to figure out what was happening in my life, waves would rise up and start to overwhelm me. I was living with people who had learned to live without waves.

After prayer and breakfast the next morning, I came up to my room and asked the Lord when I would get to go home to Heather. As had happened a few times before, my Bible fell open to a passage that directly answered my question: "And everyone who has left houses or brothers or sisters or fathers or mothers or CHILDREN or fields for My sake will receive a hundred times as much and will inherit eternal life."

I would simply have to trust that He knew what He was doing, because obviously I wasn't the first one who'd been asked to give up someone they love for a time.

One good thing about being here: I had gone a week without a cigarette. It had been a three-pack-a-day habit, and I was tempted sometimes. But if I reached for a cigarette, I would see a picture of the devil on the box, and that helped me not to take one out. It wasn't that they had printed a devil on the carton; it must have been a vision of some sort or just my imagination. Whatever it was, it helped me quit smoking.

I woke up the next morning feeling very depressed. I expected the depression to break at the prayer meeting, but it only got worse. I began to feel as if I would suffocate if I didn't get out, so I told Father McGrath I was on my way to the ashram. Clearly he disapproved, but what could he do about it?

The ashram had beautiful grounds and I went for a long walk around their lake after dinner. There were a lot of ducks quacking at each other like friends catching up on old times. I slowly followed behind them, and they never even noticed me. I moved only when they did, collecting big red autumn leaves and savoring the smells of early fall.

The sun dipped lower and lower into the sky. The mountains were ablaze with color as autumn was painting them in a palette of reds, oranges, and gold. I returned to the ashram for meditation in the holy room. Afterwards, I attended a group meeting as we sat silently for about an hour in peaceful meditation. The fragrances of incense tickled my imagination. I spent the night there.

I awoke at 4 a.m. and read the Bible for an hour and a half, and then did yoga and meditated with the group as someone softly played a flute. I chose the name "Jesus" for my mantra, and meditated on Him. The sun slowly crept over the horizon as we sat in front of a huge plate glass window. The birds began to sing and the new day unfolded before our eyes. The trees, clothed in their warm shades of gold, red, and brown, glistened over the lake.

Tears ran down my face. I was overwhelmed by the beauty of nature mingled with the serenity of the flute.

I decided to return to Father McGrath's. I walked back quickly; the chilly morning reminded me that winter was on the way and I was not in a warm climate. I had given my coat to Terry, and the rest of my things were still in New York.

Father McGrath, Pauline, and Vince were sitting at the kitchen table finishing breakfast when I arrived. "Good morning, JoAnn," they said cheerfully.

"Hi," I said, quickening my pace so I could escape to my room without being questioned.

I called the Scott Meredith Agency later and spoke with Mr. Chitchat. He said the fairy tale had created quite a stir and that's why it had taken them so long to give me an answer. Because the agency was divided on the decision, the matter went to Scott Meredith himself for the last word. He decided against it and would send me a letter to explain his decision.

My mood started to nosedive, and then suddenly it reversed and soared. Hadn't I committed the fairy tale to God? It happened when I heard a television preacher in Santa Cruz saying that if you dedicate anything to God, it will succeed. So I dedicated the fairy tale to God, expecting it to make a lot of money. That was the only success I could imagine. But somehow, my trying to market the book had led me not to money but to the Lord Himself. I realized that I had found true riches.

The next day I didn't hear the prayer bell and I overslept. I lay in bed for a moment. How would I face the day, now that my time of waiting for an answer from the agency has passed? I prayed and thanked God for my lesson yesterday with *Strawberry Jan* and told Him I was disappointed to have my dream shattered, but I trusted Him.

I was surprisingly happy when I went down to breakfast. Joy seemed to bubble out of me. It certainly had nothing to do with my circumstances.

It was a wonderful day of prayer and in the late afternoon I made homemade chicken noodle soup, cornbread, squash with cheese, and a banana concoction for dessert. I was happy because now I could plan to go back to Hawaii to be with Heather, and soon we could find a home.

The day ended with a call from Brooks, letting me know he was in New York. I agreed to go back to wind things up. I went to bed.

After Mass the next morning, Father McGrath invited everyone to stay for lunch. My heart sank because I'd heated up only the leftover chicken soup, and about twenty people piled into the kitchen, sniffing and making comments about how good it smelled.

I was certain we'd run out of food and was irritated that Father McGrath had been so generous.

I began filling the soup dishes after the blessing, figuring it was his problem when it was gone. Before I knew it, everyone had a full bowl of piping hot soup and I stared at the pot in disbelief. It was still full! It didn't look like I'd taken out even one dishful. How had it happened? I couldn't imagine. I was blown away, but Father McGrath took it all in stride. "God is faithful," he said with a smile. That was the way he always did things; if a toaster broke, he, Pauline, and Vince would pray and God would fix it.

After lunch, Father McGrath said, "I know you need to find a way to get to New York City, so why don't I take you?" It was a generous offer; it would take him at least three hours round trip. Pauline rode along with us and Father McGrath began to praise Jesus out loud, which still bugged me.

"JoAnn, it's important that you begin to praise Jesus audibly," he said kindly.

I didn't want to, but I felt obligated because he was going out of his way to drive me back to New York. I opened my mouth forced myself to say, "Praise You, Jesus." My insides began to churn. I felt uncomfortable, and was happy he and Pauline continued to say, "Praise the Lord," without me. Why did it bother me so much to hear anyone say that?

I checked back into the Barbizon, and soon got a call from Julie. "I just got to New York," she said. "I bought a Porsche; I needed a car so I can drive back to California. And I ran into Brooks, and he said you were coming. So I thought I'd call."

We hadn't seen each other for a while and we chattered excitedly; there was a lot to catch up on. "Where are you staying?" I asked.

"I'm at Sir Robert's – you know, the hairdresser? I was planning to leave for California right away, but a really famous photographer is staying here. He does a lot of work for Penthouse and Playboy, and we're hoping he'll do a shoot of shoot me together with my cousin Marilyn. So whatever happens, I'm going to be here at least a few days – why don't you come visit?"

I met Julie at Sir Robert's flat. His style was minimalist, with a lot of black, white, and chrome and everything kept in such perfect order that it appeared nobody even lived there. The apartment was spacious and people mingled together in little clusters. Julie was sniffing coke like there was no tomorrow. She had just had a nose operation because she'd burned it out from too much snorting. My first reaction was to breathe a silent prayer that God would save her from herself.

I wasn't worried about myself. I had been so surprised at the changes happening in my life that I was sure that the things that used to tempt me wouldn't have any power over me anymore. But one thing led to another. Brooks was there, and I met the photographer along with a lot of other people who'd come for the nonstop party. Then one of the guys announced that his parents would be out of town for the weekend, and we could go to their estate in Oyster Bay to party.

Julie, Brooks, the photographer, and I piled into Julie's Porsche and headed for Oyster Bay. I looked at the rolling lawns with pools and fountains and knew the inside of the house would be even more elegant. It was. But with Mom and Dad out of town for the weekend, there was nothing to inhibit the party. I ended up drinking, smoking and getting stoned over the weekend.

Even though I was determined not to, I just fell into it. I was disappointed with myself. The plush estate, the abundance of drugs, and the wonderful bar – it was just too tempting, and now I felt lost. How was I supposed to relate to my old friends? I didn't see how I could be around them without getting sucked back into my old lifestyle.

We got back to New York, Julie did her shoot, and I ended up checking out of the Barbizon and staying at Sir Robert's.

One night I sat alone in my room and wrote this prayer in my diary:

Jesus, please help me, I've fallen down and am a pitiful wretched filthy human being. I am so dreadfully lonely I can't stand it. I want to die a zillion times, and I beg for the strength to go on. Where are You, God? I miss You. I miss Your warm love.

Certainly You have not forgotten me, I hope.

Have I been cast out with the hogs? I give You my worthless life, feeling clad in blank stares, and screaming silently behind my foggy brain. Someone please love me, hold me, and make me feel alive…Oh God I am

L
o
S
T

Twenty Seven

RAGING BATTLE IN MY MIND

We returned to Sir Robert's and I started having acid flashbacks. I would glance at the old brick wall of an apartment building and see its mortar oozing out like a living thing while the bricks were breathing; bricks and mortar both would come towards me then shrink back. I would wonder if my head was turning blue and disappearing into the sky, if flowers screamed, if doors that were never there were tearing down the unrealistic dreams of barbers who wanted to become superstars. And what of the photographer who spends so much time looking into his lenses that he never really sees anything?

It was all slightly connected to reality. I really was seeing brick walls and blue skies and flowers, and I was among hairstylists who had become superstars. And the photographer staying at Sir Robert's apartment told me he'd talk to Brooks about using part of *Strawberry Jan* in his spread for *Penthouse*.

"It's the chance of a lifetime," Brooks told me. He had taken me out to dinner to share the good news with me. "I showed it to the photographer – he'll be here any minute, by the way, and he saw the potential right away."

"But all his work is for *Penthouse* and *Playboy*, isn't it?" I didn't feel right about this.

"Well, sure; so we'd have to find something in the story that would interest their readers. But you've got a great story; all you need to do is find a way to get people interested in it."

"I really don't know," I said nervously. "I need a moment – I need to make a phone call." I went to the pay phone and called Father McGrath.

"It's JoAnn," I said, and as quickly as I could I told him the situation. "My promoter says it's the chance of a lifetime, but I don't feel right about it. What do you think I should do?"

"I think it's obvious," he replied. "You obviously know it's wrong – this is why you don't feel good about it. It doesn't matter how good the opportunity is; if you know it's wrong, stay away from it. And sometimes you run into something and don't know whether it's wrong or not, but if you don't feel good about it, this can be God's way of warning you to stay away from a bad situation."

I wasn't surprised at his answer, for it matched his character. But it was foreign to the way I had always done things before and it didn't match my character at all. Or did it? It suddenly hit me that I was changing so much that it shouldn't surprise me if I needed to make choices I had never made before. This was going to take some getting used to. I asked once more to make sure. "So you don't think I should sign the contract?"

"Absolutely not," he said, "and I don't believe you think you should, either."

"Thanks," I said. He was right, and he was confirming what I knew in my heart, however strange it seemed to me. "I've got to go for now, but I'll talk to you again." I hung up and went back to my table.

Brooks smiled up at me; he was fidgeting with the nervous energy of someone who is betting on a sure thing.

I took my seat. This wasn't going to be easy. "I'm sorry Brooks, but I can't get involved in smut," I said.

His smile instantly became a look of pure fury. "Are you crazy?" he erupted, as though he were a father reading the riot act to an outrageously wayward daughter. "Have you lost every marble in your head? You can't pay for this kind of exposure, and that's what you need if you expect to get ahead. You've got to get your name out there!"

Then his voice changed; now he sounded like a teacher going over a lesson once again with an especially slow student. "I've told you before that we have to get everyone talking about *Strawberry Jan*. That's how this business works. It's all hype, kid. I was the vice-president of Faberge, Christian Dior, and Raynette. I know what I'm talking about."

I stood my ground. "Brooks, I know you're disappointed, but I don't feel in my heart it's right to go about it this way. It violates my conscience and I'd rather never make a penny than hurt the Lord any more than I have during my life."

As I was speaking, the photographer walked in and sat down next to me. Brooks turned to him and boiled over again. "She's crazy," Brooks shouted. "She says – Miss Innocent here says – that she doesn't want *Strawberry Jan* getting dirty by putting her in *Penthouse*."

The photographer turned to me. "Listen kid, the Catholic Church ruined my sex life. I got even with them though. It took a lot of discipline, but I did it."

Brooks perked up. "Yeah, what did you do?" he asked interestedly. I could tell this was something he had never heard before.

"I became an altar boy and told the priest I wanted to become a priest. Eventually, I went to seminary and got a free education. I never intended on becoming a priest. I used them," he said gleefully.

"I don't want to hear any more about this," I said standing to my feet.

"You're crazy – get out of here!" Brooks screamed. "I don't want anything to do with you if this is how you're going to act." People sitting around us had begun to stare.

I left the restaurant, leaving my dinner uneaten. I felt like a child being sent to bed without any supper. How was it that I was trying to do what was right, yet somehow I'd been made to feel I was doing something wrong? I redoubled my resolve to find God, even if it meant I would have to be peculiar for a while. Nothing and nobody else was important. I was not going to do anything intentionally that would keep me from Him.

I packed my bags and left the apartment early the next morning, taking the train to Rhode Island. I boarded and wandered through the crowded cars to find a seat.

I found a bunch of kids playing the guitar and singing songs to the Lord. Everyone in the car joined in and sang and clapped with them; it was as though we were all old friends. The time went by so quickly I didn't want to get off. As I neared my station, I walked back through the train and felt sorry for the people in the other compartments. The atmosphere in their cars felt lonely and oppressed.

I went to stay at Julie's, looking forward to a few days that would feel normal. It would be good to be with a family again, and I really needed to get away from Brooks and the photographer and the pressure to turn *Strawberry Jan* into smut.

There was only one thing abnormal about the house in Rhode Island: it was haunted. The first time I'd visited, someone at dinner had told about the ghost, and, like everyone else, I was skeptical. So it gave us all something to joke about before bed that night.

Later that night, I woke up and saw a disjointed figure floating through the air. At breakfast the next morning, it came out that we all had seen the same thing. Nobody joked about it, but soon everything and everybody was back to normal.

Still, ghosts can be a lot of fun. One of the locals took us to the place where the druids had conducted their rituals deep in the forest, but one visit wasn't enough. We started piling in the car every day to revisit the site, and we realized somebody was using it every night. We found something different there every day: a pile of stones, fresh ashes from a bonfire, or an arrangement of twigs and leaves on a tree stump that seemed to serve as an altar.

We always joked about it, but inevitably someone thought we should go back at night and see who would be there and what they'd be doing. So we chose a night, got stoned, and went just before midnight. It was so dark we got lost in the forest, but we were laughing at everything until we heard something thrashing through the undergrowth. What could it be? We didn't wait to see. We ran away as fast as we could, scattering in three directions as we tried to find the car. But our courage found us again when we finally got back to the house. "It was probably just a deer," someone suggested, "or maybe a wild turkey." We laughed about it for days.

Somehow the ghost had always been a lot of fun, something to joke about. We had enjoyed being spooky and giving each other the creeps. Once in a while at breakfast we would learn that many of us had seen something, but more often nobody had seen anything at all.

So as I went back now, I remembered the ghost. Should I stay somewhere else? It hadn't bothered me before, but it bothered me now. I asked myself why, and couldn't come up with an answer. Eventually, I decided it was silly to worry about it. It didn't occur to me that an encounter with a ghost might go beyond just seeing something.

This time I was physically assaulted. I woke up in the middle of the night with a sharp pain in my back, and I felt claws slowly penetrating my spinal column. I was paralyzed; I realized it as I tried to move but found it impossible. What's going on? I screamed on the inside. Am I going to be like this for the rest of my life? In a panic, I began to call out to Jesus, unable to cry out audibly but calling upon Him only in my mind. Doesn't God see the heart? I hoped He could hear my silent cry, but the claws seemed to plunge in deeper. I kept screaming in my mind, "Jesus, Jesus, Jesus!" Then the claws began to loosen and the horrible pain lessened a bit, and I squeezed out a whisper, "Jesus." It was a battle just to speak his name into the atmosphere. Finally, I sensed the battle was turning in my favor, and each time I spoke the name "Jesus" I could feel the claws backing out. Movement returned to my body.

I lay in bed wide-awake, my heart pounding. I didn't sleep much that night.

I got up earlier than usual and called Father McGrath as soon as I thought I could. Surely he'd think I'd lost my mind, but who else could I talk to? I told him what happened.

He seemed to believe my story, and didn't suggest that I had just dreamed the whole thing or that I was losing my

What was going on in here?

mind. "Child, you need to get out of that house right away," he said firmly, and a wave of reassurance swept over me as he spoke the words. "Don't spend another night in that house. How soon can you leave?"

"I'm sure I could get out of here today," I replied. "I just need to decide where to go."

"No you don't," he said. "You should come here."

I certainly didn't need to be coaxed. I was on my way within an hour after hanging up the phone.

It was good to get back into the peaceful atmosphere at the House Of Prayer, but my mind was foggy and I couldn't seem to get a sense of purpose. I felt more alone than ever; I was finding it harder and harder to relate to any of my old friends. I called Rachel and when I told her about Jesus, she was horrified. "Oh JoAnn, please," she said. "Don't marry him – he's got enough wives."

A sense of direction came the next night. I dreamed that someone told me to be baptized in the Spirit. It woke me up in the middle of the night, but pen and paper were by my bedside so I wrote it down before I went back to sleep.

Then in the morning someone called my name and woke me up. Who could be in my room? I heard Father McGrath ringing the bell for prayer and I looked around, but nobody was there. I was puzzled and at breakfast, I asked who called me. Nobody had. "Maybe it was an angel," someone said.

So I asked Father McGrath my next question. "What is 'being baptized in the Spirit'?"

I watched everyone glance at one another and realized I had struck a nerve.

Father McGrath spoke up. "How did you hear about that?"

"In my dream last night someone told me to be baptized in the Spirit," I said.

"Well, I think it's time to prepare you then," Father said with a sweet smile.

"How do I get prepared?" I asked.

"I have some things I want you to read. One is a book called The Healing Of Memories written by my two friends, the Linn Brothers. There are some assignments in the book I want you to do."

I read the book and prayed until I met with Father McGrath after lunch. I confessed my sins of sorcery and hate and many things. He had me go into details and renounce my connection with all sorts of things: witchcraft, Tarot cards, astrology, and Ouija boards. He seemed very sure of himself, but I had questions. "Renounce Ouija boards? You've got to be kidding," I protested. "It's only a game. It almost never works."

"The point is that it's an act of your will to open yourself to the psychic realm," he answered. "It opens a door to allow demonic activity in your life. It takes only a moment to speak the words of renunciation that will shut that door." So I let him lead me in prayer and repeated the words after him. He was right; it took only a moment. In spite of his explanation, I felt silly renouncing Ouija boards and astrology. I'd never taken either of them seriously, but I said the prayers. Better safe than sorry, I told myself. Too many things had been too weird in my life for too long. It couldn't hurt to be thorough.

We also prayed for the children I had aborted. I felt God's love protecting me because if I fully realized the extent of my sins, I would feel too unclean and unworthy to ask the Lord to touch my heart and forgive me. But then, how can anyone be worthy of that?

I went through an exercise where I was supposed to have the Lord show me a time that was very painful for me in my life.

I sat still before Him and He gave me a mental picture. I was about five years old; I was standing on a chair and drying the dishes because I was too short to reach the sink.

I knew my Daddy didn't love me and I asked my Mom why. She went in the other room and asked him. I heard Dad say it was because I always went to my grandfather and not to him. The ache in my heart was too painful for a child to bear and whenever that memory would try to creep into my mind I'd turn off the scene, though it was always there bubbling under the surface.

As I kept my eyes closed, I thought for sure that Jesus would come into the kitchen and give me a big hug. Instead, He walked out of the kitchen and gave my Dad a hug! The Lord showed me that my Dad had pain in his life too. I'd never thought of how He felt; I'd thought only of myself. Daddy had died a long time ago and I couldn't talk to him about it now. But there was something healing about seeing my father in the light of Jesus' love.

The next morning I taught Father McGrath how to cook pancakes. It was fun to reverse roles and be the teacher instead of the pupil. He seemed to enjoy it as much as I did. "Child, does cooking always make such a mess?" he asked. He looked sadly at the egg that had broken on the counter and dripped on the floor, the flour all over the counters, and the batter that had managed to splash on all the spices and canisters. "And don't people usually need a recipe?"

"I never use recipes," I laughed. "I have a hard time following directions. And usually I make a mess. Besides, nobody needs a recipe for bacon." It was sizzling in the pan, and it was almost done. "But part of what I always do isn't in the cookbooks: I never saw a recipe that said to melt the butter and syrup together in a pan, but the cookbooks don't know what they're missing."

"You mean you do things that aren't even in the cookbooks?" He asked, looking around once more and surveying the mess with dismay. "I'd better be writing this down." He pulled a little notebook out of his pocket and started asking questions, writing briskly as I answered.

"How many eggs?" He nodded as he wrote. "Is there an accepted way to break an egg?" I couldn't give him anything to write down this time. "And how do I know when to turn the pancakes over on the griddle?" This time he spoke the words as he wrote: "Ahh, watch for bubbles."

Meanwhile I had set the bacon out to drain, had poured the butter and syrup mixture into a pitcher, and was gathering the golden pancakes from the griddle and stacking them on a plate. "I have to admit it smells scrumptious. I can't decide which smells better: the bacon, the pancakes, or the syrup."

Then he looked through the doorway into the dining room and said to Vince and Pauline, "I've just witnessed something like what happened in Genesis 1. The creation began with chaos, and day by day God made something good with it. I've just seen JoAnn do the same thing in the kitchen."

Everyone made quite a celebration out of it, as though it were a miracle. "It's just pancakes," I protested, but I had to admit the butter and syrup came out better than usual.

"That's because of the offerings given to our ministry," said Father McGrath. "One of our ladies has family in Vermont, and whenever she visits them she brings us a bottle of fresh maple syrup. And another family has a farm, and they bring us fresh butter."

They insisted that since I had done the cooking, they'd clean up the kitchen. I didn't argue. My stomach was upset. I knew it wasn't the breakfast; it seemed to be coming from something in my heart. I felt a revulsion against my sins; especially about my unborn children and the many ways I had failed Heather.

It found it hard to believe what was happening to me. I had thought est was the answer and when I had found out it wasn't, I was sure I would have to go to India and study yoga for many years and find a guru in order to obtain enlightenment. But now, how was it happening that I, the rebellious nonconformist, was turning to God, let alone Jesus?

I thought of all the times I'd heard people mock. I'd done it myself. We used to eat at an open-air restaurant in Santa Cruz, and three people in tattered Salvation Army uniforms would stand nearby and sing. They seemed hopelessly out of touch, like someone who might wear a Halloween costume to a wedding. So we would laugh at them and puff on our joints, wishing they'd go away. And now, suddenly I could see that I'd been mocking people, even if God had sent them to tell me something.

But now I was becoming a Jesus freak, and I didn't care if people mocked me. I had come out of the tunnel knowing I must find God, and I didn't care who God was as long as He wasn't Jesus. It was cool to believe in anything but Jesus. But in spite of everything, Jesus began making Himself known to me and changing my life as nothing else could.

It wasn't easy. My friends thought I was crazy, and a battle was raging in my mind. I was caught in the middle between two opposing forces trying to gain control.

I spoke with Father McGrath again and we prayed for Stephen. He gave me a book called *Come and See*, and it told about speaking in tongues. I didn't quite understand tongues, but if God wanted me to have it as a present when I was baptized in the Spirit, then I wanted it.

I called Heather and she sounded so happy. "Will you go to church with me on Thanksgiving?" she asked. At first I wondered why she was asking me to go to church with her, then it clicked: she had been going with the Schaeffers.

"Of course I will, Sweetie." The whole story came back to me: my desperate prayers in the little Episcopalian church by the beach; the doctor's insisting that I sign the papers releasing Heather into foster care; learning that her foster parents would be the rector and his wife.

"And what about Easter? Will you go to church with me on Easter too?"

I remembered what a drag it had always been to sit through church on Easter morning, and now I wanted to go. "Yes," I replied. "We'll go on Easter too."

That night I began a Novena to the Holy Spirit. I was starting to think demons were in me. It almost seemed as if they were trying to get out and couldn't. My head would buzz and get hot; I would feel a pressure in my throat; I would feel like I was about to throw up, and it reminded me of the time in Santa Cruz when I had gotten so violently sick. As the Novena began, I silently asked Jesus, "If there are any demons there, please cast them out."

I didn't say anything aloud. I was sure everyone would think I was crazy if I did.

But I had been getting worse and worse ever since I had gotten here. My stomach would roll in a weak nausea. My ears would pound at intervals and get very sensitive. My muscles quivered, my jaw got tingling pains, and my vision was impaired. It was really acting up during prayer or Mass. Sometimes my head felt as if it was burning up, but a cold chill would run up and down from the center of my forehead to my mouth, like an ice cube in a burning elevator shaft.

While I was reading the Bible, a scripture jumped out at me that said: "This kind comes out only by prayer and fasting." I prayed for guidance on how to do that.

I said the Novena to the Holy Spirit and felt compelled to dedicate my life totally to the Lord. I vowed not to have any sex with anybody unless I got married. Temporary relationships had always left me empty anyway.

Now the Lord wanted me to give up smoking, which I had started again in Oyster Bay. "Oh, Jesus, help me! It was easier to give up men!"

As I went to bed that night, I opened the window. An autumn chill rushed in with the smell of wood-burning fireplace. I didn't mind the cold; I had plenty of covers and would stay warm. But I wanted a view of the stars. The night sky was blacker than usual because we were far from the lights of the city, and I could see more stars than ever. As a child, I had enjoyed watching them twinkle at night. They were my friends, winking at me.

I gave my love for Stephen to the Lord and asked Him to do what He wanted with it. I stretched my hands up towards heaven and felt a tremendous pulling sensation, which started in my knees and came up through my entire body. It popped out through my outstretched hands and now I felt very peaceful.

I woke up the next morning and irrationally was very, very angry with Father McGrath. I wanted to find a knife and kill everybody in the house. Why? It made no sense to me, but the desire remained. I purposely ignored the bell for prayer. I made sure I was late for breakfast, and looking across the table I felt such hatred I wanted to spit on him. Suddenly I felt violently sick again.

"How are you today?" he asked. His voice was gentle and affirming but his eyes seemed to look right through me.

"I feel like I hate you today and I'm filled with anger," I said matter-of-factly. Was this any way to talk to a priest? I knew it would be out of bounds ordinarily, but somehow I sensed that this was an unusual situation and it was appropriate to be totally honest. I couldn't explain the fresh surge of hostility and rage that was boiling up, but I knew I needed to tell him about it.

"Oh," said Father McGrath. He seemed to be pondering what I told him but he didn't look surprised at all. He calmly sipped his orange juice.

Had I hurt him? I told myself I was really out of control. Maybe I had a demon – the kind that comes out only with fasting and prayer. Then I told myself, Get real. There are no demons. This is just a fantasy from a Hollywood movie. And another part of my mind said, How can I hate this godly man? How can I hate him, when he has been so kind and generous to me? I was ashamed of myself.

"Father," I said meekly.

"Yes," he said, and he looked me straight in the eye.

"I know this probably sounds crazy but..." I paused not wanting to admit my thoughts.

"But?" he asked

"I think I might have an evil spirit in me," I said, forcing the words between my clenched teeth.

I was shocked when he answered. "Well, praise God! I've been praying the Lord would show you that."

"You're kidding," I gasped. "You believe that stuff is real?"

"Certainly it's real," he said. "I've cast out demons before."

"Oh my gosh," I said. "Tell me about it." I was hungry for information.

"I think the less you know the better," he said.

"But Father McGrath, I've never even seen the movie *The Exorcist*. Can't I read a book about this or something, so I'll know what's going on?"

"No, my child. I don't want you to have any preconceived ideas about what the Lord is going to do or how it will come about. Now that the truth is exposed, it's important for you stay here on the property. I especially must ask that you don't go to the Ashram Yogi Society," he said.

"I won't," I said. He really thought I had a demon? Now I was afraid to do anything he didn't think I should do. I went back to my room to pray and get ready for Mass at noon.

It was hard for me to believe this was really happening. But at Mass

I saw a pinpoint of light above Father McGrath's head during communion.

After Mass a few people prayed for me, and I felt drunk when they were done. Father McGrath took me to the store with him and I felt like a little child. I was bubbling over with so much happiness that I danced in the parking lot, feeling about three years old. The euphoria was indescribable.

Something odd happened the next morning. I was still feeling good when I woke up. After breakfast I spoke with Father McGrath about the past and became depressed, so I went for a walk and had a cigarette. The moment I lit it, my symptoms came back again: blurred vision, shooting pains, and the tingling sensations.

I threw down the cigarette and called upon the Lord, and immediately the symptoms flowed out of me. Curiosity took over and I wondered if it was just my imagination, or was there really a connection? I lit another cigarette, and the symptoms flowed right back in again.

I found it hard to believe, even though it was happening to me. I asked Father McGrath what he thought of the incident. "You're in a special time of grace," he replied. "The Lord is so close to you that He is gently showing you how much he cares about every aspect of your life – even the little things."

Twenty Nine

Am I POSSESSED?

Father McGrath had to be out of town for a day, and I set it aside for silent prayer and fasting. I promised God that I wouldn't open my mouth and that I'd only listen to Him, so I didn't leave my room. It would mean a day without cigarettes, but I'd quit smoking before and then returned to the habit at Sir Robert's. Now I felt I should quit smoking again, to prepare to receive the baptism in the Holy Spirit, and I felt I should cover the mirrors on my dresser and in the bathroom. It wasn't time to look at my appearance; it was time to look to Jesus.

I wrote down many of my prayers in my diary, and if I thought God was speaking anything to me I wrote that down too. As the day progressed, I jotted down a few things from my background that I hadn't yet told Father McGrath. I reasoned that if I wrote them down now, I could show them to him later when he returned. Out of all I wrote that day, two would later catch Father McGrath's attention as I moved forward with the process of being set free from evil spirits.

The first was my est training. I had paid $250 for the two-weekend course, and as the first weekend ended they said we were all little gods who were totally responsible for everything. For example, I was responsible for my husband's death, what I looked like, what illnesses I'd had – every aspect of my life was what I had created. This teaching infuriated me, and I stood up to leave the auditorium. They tried to block my path several times but I walked out while the trainer was calling me back over the microphone in front of hundreds of people. They wouldn't give even a prorated refund for the classes I hadn't attended. So the only way to get my money's worth was to go back for the next session. But later I talked to friends who had also gone through the training, and their experience always matched mine. We would be euphoric when we left the sessions, but then we would hit bottom with a crash a few days later. By the time we went to the follow-up session six weeks later, most of the people looked downcast. I saw that, and decided the whole thing was a rip-off. They'd seen the last of me.

The second was Rafael's spell. It had caused me to speak with another voice, a masculine growl with a Spanish accent. I had learned a few things about Rafael from my sister-in-law. She had gotten to know him well enough that he had taken her to the room where he kept his witchcraft paraphernalia, mostly dolls and books. He'd also told her he had grown up in the Puerto Rican section somewhere, surrounded by witches who taught him the black arts from his earliest childhood.

But I didn't just write about my past. I spent the day reading the Bible, praying, and reading the sequel to *God Calling*. I came to a section that called us to listen to God for ourselves. I lay down, closed my eyes, and asked the Lord Jesus to let me hear Him.

He immediately said, "Relax, My child. I love you.";

I replied, "I love You too, Lord."

I lay still and felt a strange pressure, which was very heavy on my brain. My face muscles suddenly went out of control. A voice kept telling me to relax and surrender myself completely.

I fought the desire to open my eyes and run. I kept saying, "I love You, Jesus."

Suddenly, my jaw felt as if it was in a vise and started moving in impossible contortions. My lower lip pursed up towards my nose and quivered uncontrollably. Though my face was twisted abnormally, a voice kept telling me to relax. I tried, and I felt something even stranger was about to happen when my nostrils began to contract and spread apart widely. Then suddenly they were tightened and pulled upward rapidly and so tightly I thought my nose would be pulled off my face. A horrible odor filled the room, an unearthly stench as if I had I tumbled into a pit filled with dead things that had been left to decay. I cried out to Jesus, and almost immediately the smell faded away and the air smelled sweet.

I thought it was over but my mouth began to move in more spasms and my feet and legs felt half asleep, as if they were floating. My mouth quivered in a muscular spasm and my bottom lip pursed together in a V and began throbbing in the middle.

As soon as I was able to sit up, I started writing down what had just happened. I had gotten out a hand mirror to see if my face was still contorted. It was. As I sat and wrote, I kept glancing at my face in the mirror. I wondered if the Lord was letting things happen this way so I could verify that my experience was not just in my imagination, but was real.

The throbbing in my lip suddenly felt like a heartbeat and I felt a tremendous shot of power. I wasn't sure whether it came in or went out. I closed my eyes and felt like a lump of clay being molded and remolded.

I continued to look in the mirror and noticed that I looked as ridiculous as a child making silly faces.

I tried to read what I had written and couldn't. It was strange, but I couldn't understand the words. I could decipher the handwriting, but couldn't puzzle out the words and sentences. Yet I could open the Bible and comprehend anything I chose to read there. What was this all about? I couldn't understand myself.

By evening, I had managed to go several hours without any more contortions. I'm glad it ended, I told myself, but how do I know it won't start up again? Am I losing my mind again? I didn't have a grid for any of this. My Bible reading had taken me to an alarming verse that said, "This kind comes out only by prayer and fasting." Was I experiencing what happens when demons take over?

I woke up in the middle of the night and things were worse than ever. I could feel pressure all over my body, as if something was trying to break me open. My mouth was pulled so far off my face I expected to hear flesh tearing away from the bone at any second; I could feel horns trying to sprout on my head. I felt like the main character in a horror movie.

This time I wasn't hearing a reassuring voice saying, "Trust Me." I was terrified. I ran downstairs screaming, "Father McGrath! Father McGrath!" I got to his door and started beating it. "Father McGrath! Help!"

He opened his door a crack and peeked out at me. "Yes, JoAnn," he said patiently. "What do you need?"

"Help!" I screamed. "I think there really might be a demon in me!"

He nodded at me sleepily. "Calm down, child. Wait here while I get dressed, then we'll go to the chapel and pray. Meanwhile, may the peace of the Lord be with you."

His door closed, but two other doors opened. "Are you okay?" said Pauline. "I heard the racket and thought I'd better see if I'm needed."

Before I could answer, my face jerked again. I pounded the door and cried, "Father McGrath? Hurry!" Pauline was giving me a dubious look.

"What's going on?" said Vince.

His hair was sticking up every which way and he was yawning and rubbing his eyes. He glanced at me suspiciously, then turned and looked at Pauline meaningly.

"I don't know what's happening to me!" I cried. It still felt like my head was in a vise, and it was hard not to wince, but somehow I got the words out: "Father's taking me to the chapel for prayer." Then my mouth jerked violently to the side. "Hurry!" I screamed as I pounded Father McGrath's door again.

Pauline quickly sized me up, and then turned to Vince. "I'll go too, in case he'd like me to join in. I'll be there as soon as I can get dressed."

"And I'll throw something on too," said Vince. "Be right with you." Both of their doors closed, but a moment later Father McGrath's opened.

"Was that Vince and Pauline I heard?" he asked.

"Yeah, they said they're coming too," I whined. Something in the way they had looked at me and at each other made me unsure whether they would know what to do about what I was experiencing.

"Good," he replied. "There's strength in numbers, and it'll be good to have them in there." We walked to the chapel.

Prayer was simple and quick. He sprinkled me with holy water and said a few words. Suddenly the pressure lifted and my face relaxed. Vince and Pauline just sat and watched.

"Now go to sleep, child," he said. We all walked back to our rooms. Somehow the prayer in the chapel felt like an anticlimax. After all I'd been going through, all it took was a few simple words of prayer and a splash of holy water? I went back to bed, and fell into a welcome sleep.

But I was sarcastic and angry again when I woke up in the morning. I questioned Sister Pauline and Father McGrath about what was going on. I wasn't at all satisfied with their answers, so I stormed out and tromped up to my room on the third floor. As I reached the top of the long stairway and looked down, I had an incredible urge to jump. Voices in my head kept screaming, "Jump, and it will be over!"

I stood there looking down, and Pauline came up the stairs and handed me instructions on how to be baptized in the Spirit. Irrationally, I felt like tearing them up in front of her, but instead I simply threw them up in the air. Papers went everywhere, some landing on the stairs and others fluttering down to the first floor.

I heard people arriving for Mass. It occurred to me that I could get even with Father McGrath if I skipped Mass and went to the ashram. So while others were coming in, I went down the stairs, passing Pauline, who was collecting the papers I had tossed in the air. I was a little unnerved; she was so patient, tidying the mess I had made like a spoiled brat. But I kept going and headed out the door and down the street towards the ashram. I never got there. Why am I doing this? I asked myself. This won't hurt Father McGrath; I'm just hurting myself. I didn't understand the spiritual things that were happening to me, but none of it seemed to surprise Father McGrath. What was wrong with me? Why did I want to hurt him?

I swallowed my pride and went sheepishly to Mass, telling myself I could slip in unnoticed. But the large front door got away from me and slammed shut with a loud bang, and several people turned to see who was making the commotion. I eased myself into a back seat. My ears throbbed and pounded. My head started burning and a horrible icy feeling went up and down my face. It was a struggle to sit there

I was the first to leave when it ended, and Pauline followed me up the stairs. She was very gentle. "You're about to be baptized in the Holy Spirit," she told me, "and the enemy doesn't like it. He's doing everything he can to be disruptive." Could that be how spiritual things work? It made me wonder.

Suddenly, I realized the devil was the reason for the mental problems I had had. He was the one who had made me want to kill myself. I decided to fight him. I went to my room, read the Bible, and prayed.

Nothing unusual happened for the rest of the day, but when I tried to go to sleep the contortions began again. It was getting more intense each time it happened: my nose being wrenched upwards, the putrid smell, the feeling that my head was in a vise, my lips being pulled aside as though the skin was about to be tugged from my face.

Again it felt that my body was being torn in two and another person was trying to emerge from the center. How long could this go on? And how could it be a work of God? I was so confused that I began to wonder if Jesus was another of the devil's deceptions.

Then the fog lifted and I prayed. "Jesus, forgive me," I prayed, "but why is this happening? Help me, Jesus."

If God was God, couldn't He just snap his fingers, and the whole problem would stop? I lay there thinking about His power, still breathing prayers for His help. Slowly the pains and pressures subsided; the odor disappeared. I was able to get back to sleep.

The next day was very special because I was baptized in the Spirit and spoke in tongues. I felt self-conscious about it at this point, but otherwise was filled with peace and joy.

Later, during evening prayer, my face began to quiver again and I asked Jesus to bind any evil that might still be lurking in me. The spirits got stronger and I called out to Father McGrath. He came over and I lost control of my face, but he knew what was happening and he held a crucifix in front of me and said in a very authoritative voice, "In the name of Jesus Christ, come out."

I was frightened and suddenly felt like another pair of eyes popped out from my own, as if my eyes were looking through supernatural glasses. My body shook uncontrollably and something took over from within me. By now, Pauline and Vince had rushed over to join Father McGrath in the prayer. One spirit after another began speaking and my feet thrashed about as my face made ugly and defiant sneers.

Schizophrenia was one spirit that came out; est was another. My body kept having spasms; at one point I jerked so violently I was thrown out of my chair. My thrashings were moving me further and further back from the front row where I had sat. Eerie sounds were coming out of me and my face kept contorting.

It was a living nightmare, yet in a way I felt detached from it all, as though I were watching it happen to someone else in a movie. How much control did this other thing have? My body was doing things I couldn't understand, yet deep down I could still choose to keep repeating in my mind, "I love you, Jesus. I trust you, Jesus."

When Father McGrath addressed the curse Rafael had put on me, a new set of shrieks and sounds came out of me, and they seemed more horrid than the rest. Father McGrath instructed me to forgive Rafael. He held his cross up to me and I kissed it and said, "I forgive you Rafael, and I pray for you in the name of Jesus." The tremor subsided – my body was still having spasms, but now they were dying down as I lay there and forgave everyone I could think of. My legs would kick and my face would sneer as hatred towards someone would flare up, then I would say that I forgave them and my body would start to relax. After several rounds of that, I said, "I forgive myself." The last of the spasms stopped.

"It's done," Father McGrath said.

What? It was over now? I couldn't believe my ears. First a whole lot of stuff was happening that I couldn't control, and then Father McGrath was acting like it was normal somehow, and now he said it was done? What was going on? Was "It's done" just another burst of lunacy? Maybe I was losing my mind again, but worse than ever this time. I got up and walked a few steps but felt so weak I had to lie down on the floor in the big entry hall.

I finally got up to bed and lay down. Suddenly I felt motion around my face. I ran downstairs and found Vince, Pauline, and Father McGrath in the chapel. "Now what's going on?" I demanded. "I thought you said it was done!"

"Now calm down, JoAnn" said Father McGrath, patting me on the shoulder and looking at me wisely through his glasses. They prayed for me and Father anointed me with oil, addressing the spirit. However, nothing happened. Then Father McGrath said, "I don't think this is anything we need to worry about. I think this is nothing but fear and confusion. Let's face it: you've been through a lot today. It's time to trust Jesus completely, and now we all need to go to sleep."

You'd think that after a few hours of having demons come out violently, I would wake up the next morning with peace and a sense of God's presence. But the opposite happened; I woke up confused, angry, and depressed. I noticed that today would have been Bob's thirty-second birthday.

I went to morning prayer and my mood began to improve. But then I took my mail up to my room, and it was nothing but problems: Xerox was suing me and I had to be in court in California; my tenants in Santa Cruz hadn't paid rent for months and now were refusing to move out; my landlord in Maui was raising my rent; Credit Swiss was notifying me that they'd misplaced my account with $15,000 in it.

"What is going on here, did the postman save all the bad news for today?" I screamed as I threw it all on the bed.

I went back downstairs. There wasn't much I could do about the mail just yet because offices in California wouldn't be open until it was almost lunchtime in New York. There was nothing to do but wait.

But Father McGrath had an idea. "It might be nice to visit Sister Rose Alice at the convent," he suggested. "She'll be excited to hear what's been going on in your life."

We got in the car to go. On the way over I really got furious at him. "Are you sure you did the right thing, getting all the spirits out of me?"

"What do you mean?" he said. My question obviously startled him.

"I feel so desolate," I said. "I don't even feel like myself." We bickered all the way to the convent, and by the time we arrived I refused to go in, pouting like a child. "Fine, then; you can wait in the car while I go in," he said patiently. He went inside. Before long Sister Rose Alice came out on the porch and gave me a sweet little wave, melting my heart. She gestured for me to come inside, and I did.

I sat down next to her and told her how I was feeling. "That's all to be expected," she reassured me. "The spirits have controlled so many areas of your life for so long that, now that they're gone, it's left holes in your life and you don't feel like yourself."

"But don't worry," she reassured, squeezing my hand. "He'll fill the holes. Just be patient with yourself and with Him, and give Him time to work."

"I do feel like I've had an operation, and now I feel empty," I admitted.

We went to a prayer meeting and then she drove me back to Father Mc-Grath's. Now it was time to get on the phone and take care of the emergencies that had come in the mail. One by one I made my calls and did what I could. When I didn't appear in court, they decided in favor of Xerox and now I had a $7500 debt.

Suddenly I felt very sorry for myself, remembering that it was Bob's birthday. I opened the Bible for some comfort and my eyes fell to something about burying the dead. I closed the book and knew the Lord was telling me that I must bury Bob and go on with my life now.

I wasn't quite ready to yield to that. Out of habit, I reached for a cigarette and lit it. Suddenly I felt very strange.

I looked at a picture of Mary holding Jesus after the crucifixion, and put out the cigarette. If He died for me, I could stop smoking for Him. I knew that cigarettes were a symbol of my old ways. I was at a crossroads; I could choose God or sin. I crushed the whole pack of cigarettes and went downstairs to ask for prayer.

My irrational cruelty towards Father McGrath continued. I knew my attitude towards him reflected a sense of rebellion against all the changes that were happening in my life, but even at that my attitudes were hard to understand. I was ashamed of the way I was treating him, but somehow he seemed to take it all in stride.

Meanwhile, God was continuing to help me by leading me to scriptures.

I became troubled with a premonition that Heather was about to die and prayed that Jesus would replace that ugly thought with faith. I opened the Bible and it fell to Heb. 11:17: "By faith Abraham, when God tested him, offered Isaac as a sacrifice. He who had received the promises was about to sacrifice his one and only son." Too much! If I had tried to search for the proper passage for comfort, it might have taken me hours, but the Lord always showed me something immediately.

I felt it was time to go back to New York City. "A lot has happened to you, JoAnn," Father McGrath said. "A whole new chapter in your life is ready to begin."

"I hope you're right," I said. "I didn't do very well the last time I tried to go out on my own."

"Well, maybe not," he said. That was an understatement, but his tone was gracious. "But look at what's happened. Here you were, full of demons. You got into a crowd that is engaged in all sorts of ungodliness, and ended up staying in a haunted house. Is it any wonder you had so many problems?"

So before I left, he, Vince, and Sister Pauline gave me a crash course in how to live in the real world on my own. "Stay in prayer...stay in the Bible...avoid ungodliness...as much as possible, stay in a godly environment."

I went back to the city and checked back into the Barbizon. As soon as I got settled, I called Ruth's room and there was no answer. She'd probably gone out. I tried again several times; still no answer. Eventually I called the desk clerk. "Can you tell me where Ruth is?" I asked. Everyone in the hotel knew her; she'd lived there for ten years.

"Are you a member of the family?" she asked guardedly.

"No, this is JoAnn Dejoria. I'm just a friend," I said. I sensed something was wrong.

The clerk hesitated for a moment, and then she spoke. "Ruth passed away yesterday."

I was dazed and didn't get much accomplished as the afternoon dragged on. How could she be dead? I had known her for only a short time, and had begun to feel as close to her as if she were a member of my own family. I thought about the compassion I had felt towards her. How had this happened? It wasn't that I was a nice person. Somehow I had been able to pour out love that was not my own.

A chill went through me. Was it possible that God had known she was about to die, and had used me to bring His love and mercy to her in the last days of her life?

I was thankful for my brief friendship with Ruth, and it was hard to believe she was gone. It was even harder to believe that God had used me to help her. God could find a way to use someone like me? Incredible!

In just a brief few days, I had experienced two things that were way out of my grid: having God use me to bless Ruth, then all the stuff I'd been through as Father McGrath had cast the evil spirits out of me. One thing was clear: not all spirits are alike. The Holy Spirit wanted to pour His love through me; the other spirits wanted to destroy me and everyone around me. It was all supernatural, but the contrast between light and darkness was stunning.

I called Father McGrath and he prayed with me for Ruth.

Twenty Nine

EXORCISM

I was praying as I got ready for bed, and a crazy thought flashed through my mind. It seemed like a voice, commanding me to praise the devil. I resisted and lay down. Suddenly, the vise clamped down on my head again and my teeth started grinding together. I turned on the light and my vision was blurred. A voice in my brain was screaming profanities and telling me I was stupid and ugly. You think what you went through at Father McGrath's was real? It wasn't, you stupid fool! It was all a lie! Satan is ruler of the universe, and you'll never get away from him! You'd better jump out the window and end it all. Once again, I was filled with hatred towards Father McGrath, Sister Pauline, and Vince, and wanted to kill them.

I panicked and tried to call a church, but I had no dial tone; I couldn't even reach the hotel operator. I threw on some clothes and rushed down to the lobby, screaming at the people at the desk that I was going to sue the hotel. And I ran over to the switchboard operator and called her a terrible name.

I stayed in the lobby for a while because I was too scared to go back to my room. But my face continued to contort uncontrollably, and what if somebody noticed? Frightened or not, I decided I'd better go back to my room. I kept my head down so nobody would see what was happening.

I looked in the mirror. My pupils were dilated. Whenever I closed my eyes, I saw flames with white light overhead. My face would look normal for a few moments and then it would twist out of shape. My teeth kept grinding and there was terrible pressure around my mouth. My lips were puckered; they felt as if they were on fire. Sometimes my jaw clamped shut and I couldn't get it open. Once again, I felt as if my body was being torn in two. I was feeling more and more hatred towards Father McGrath; I wanted to beat him to a pulp, cursing him with every blow, until I could watch his life slip out of him. Was I flipping out again? Here I was, going through torment; meanwhile, another part of me was silently whispering, "I trust You, Jesus." Which was the real me?

Who would believe this? I thought. Though it was hard to concentrate, it seemed important to write down everything as it was happening. Meanwhile, a voice kept telling me to curse the Lord, using the tune of a song we sang in Mass.

I felt completely divided. My thoughts were repeating themselves, taunting me as a bully taunts a victim on the playground. This is useless. I can't be saved. The only way to end it all is to end it all. Just die! Join the devil and dance in the fires of hell. It'll be fun! This is useless. But I kept repeating a silent prayer: "Jesus, help me." I felt divided between heaven and hell. My ears were pounding. My whole head felt like a big throbbing toothache.

Had I really been delivered? "It's done," Father McGrath had said; but he had to be wrong. How did I know these guys knew what they were doing? It was easy for him to say "It's done," but he wasn't the one in the living hell I was going through. I felt another surge of violent anger towards Father McGrath, Pauline, and Vince. I needed another opinion.

My anger was uncontrollable. Why not just jump fourteen floors and end all of this? I had no answer, but something kept pulling me back. Oh Lord, help me please.

I finally got a dial tone at 4 a.m. and called Father McGrath's, waking Sister Pauline. She said he was out of town; I asked if she could pray with me. "I guess so," she said, and she said a prayer. But to me, she sounded reluctant and halfhearted. "Do you trust Jesus?" she asked. I assured her I did. "No, JoAnn; do you really trust Jesus?" She kept coming back to this question, and I suspected she was trying to say that if I really trusted Jesus I didn't need anyone to pray with me.

We hung up and I went back to bed. It was hard to get to sleep; the last time I noticed the clock it said 5:30. My sleep was fitful with visions of hell and horrible demons. I woke up at 9 a.m. and called St. Ignatius. I asked to speak with a Jesuit priest – Father McGrath was a Jesuit, so maybe another Jesuit could help me.

I told the priest what was going on. "You don't need a priest;" he replied. "You need a psychiatrist." I hung up, feeling more desolate than ever. Maybe Father Thurman could help. I called, but he was out. I tried Father McGrath again, and Sister Pauline said he wouldn't be back until late in the day. I panicked. How much longer could I fight this by myself? I recalled how strong the urge had been to kill myself the night before.

"Please help me, Jesus," I said. Then it occurred to me that I might find help at St. Patrick's. It should have been easy, but I had to make myself go. I put on a lightweight white suit I had bought when I was visiting publishers. It had been like my first date with David: it was time to stop looking like a hippie.

I stepped out onto the sidewalk and the cold hit me. This is crazy, I said to myself. I don't even have my winter clothes here, and New York is worse in October than Santa Cruz was in the winter. And what am I doing here, anyway? I wasn't planning to be here so long. I was wearing a light summer dress, but I noticed that everyone else was bundled up, and I could see everyone's breath.

I made myself keep going. Something kept telling me to run away and forget the church, because it couldn't help me. "Look at you now, more insane than ever," the voice mocked. The people in their coats were all wrapping their arms around themselves to try to stay warm, but I was burning up. I was starting to think I should sue the Catholic Church for stirring up the demons. My eyes felt as if they were on fire by the time I climbed the stairs to St. Patrick's. I forced myself inside the door and went right into a confessional.

I told the priest about Father McGrath, the deliverance, and what had transpired since I left the House Of Prayer. I asked if I could speak with him face to face because he was behind the dark screen.

"You don't have to be anxious, my child," he replied. "It's only your imagination, not the devil. There's no demon possession in America. I'm not saying it's not real; I've seen it in South America. But it's not in this country. I think this Father McGrath was misled and has given you a lot of wrong ideas. Your best bet would be to visit a psychiatrist."

It sounded convincing, but I wasn't sure, so I went to the rectory. I hadn't found two priests yet who were telling me the same thing. Did any of them know what they were doing? I expected a priest to be in the rectory, but none were available. I didn't know anywhere else to go, so I went for a walk. I was completely baffled. I started getting really sick. I saw a phone booth out on the sidewalk and had to prop myself up as I dialed Father McGrath. Maybe by now he had gotten back.

"Is Father McGrath there?" I asked when Sister Pauline picked up the phone.

"No," she said.

My heart sank and I felt I couldn't bear another moment of this torment. Perhaps I should just kill myself, I thought as I looked at the traffic racing by. A voice screamed inside my brain "Jump…jump."

"Wait, JoAnn; he just walked in the door," she said, interrupting my thoughts.

I told him what had been going on. "I know a priest in Long Island who might be able to help," he offered.

"Father McGrath, I'm really sick and can't wait long." I said, weakly slumping over in the phone booth. "I don't know if I can make that trip."

"I'll call you right back. Give me your number," he said.

I waited and waited. The phone rang and he gave me a name and address. I scribbled it on a piece of paper and waved for a taxi as I clutched my rosary beads. I got in the cab and gave the driver the street number. He turned around abruptly and asked in a heavy Brooklyn accent, "Are you sure?"

I read the address again and watched him look at me as he caught a glimpse of my rosary beads.

"I usually don't go down there, lady. It's dangerous, right in the center of Harlem, you know."

"No, I've never been there before," I admitted, fearing that I would break down and cry if he wouldn't take me.

"You really gotta go there, huh?" he asked.

"Yes," I said.

"Okay, I'll take you," he said. "I don't get asked to drive down there often. When I do, I usually take people to the border and then I have them switch cabs."

"That's fine; just tell me what to do."

"I'll take you all the way. I don't think a nice girl like you should be standing out on the street in Harlem. Now, don't worry."

He said not to worry, but Harlem looked as if it had been bombed and nobody had ever tried to rebuild. I felt very white and very blond, and the taxi seemed too clean and too new for the neighborhood we were in.

He stopped the cab in front of the address. "I'm not going to leave until I see you go in the door," he said. He gave two toots on the horn and waited until a nun answered the door. I rushed in and turned to wave. He waved back and drove on.

The nun was Sister Irene, and after she introduced herself she introduced me to Sisters Alicia and Joy. Soon they were praying over me, and I felt anesthetized: my ears were plugged, and it was as if I were seeing through someone else's eyes, not my own. Time stood still. Things were happening, but I felt detached.

Nevertheless, it was much more violent than when Father McGrath had prayed for me. The spirits groaned, spat and kicked. I hit things and was hurt as my body thrashed about on the ice-cold linoleum floor. I tried to choke myself several times and ripped the cross off my neck. I bit and clawed at the nuns. Unearthly masculine-sounding noises burst out of my mouth intermittently.

Part of me couldn't believe it was happening, but another part of me knew it was and I continually begged Jesus to help. I heard someone tell me not to be afraid, but who wouldn't be scared going through what I was going through? In my heart I prayed for Jesus to keep me strong.

Sister Irene turned to Sister Alicia. "It's time to get the prayer of exorcism," she said. At that my body went crazy. I felt as if I were in the battle of my life. I would later notice black and blue marks from the beating all over my aching body, and even bruises where I bit my wrists. It was a knock-down-drag-out fight with evil spirits, but in my heart I knew that Jesus would win, and that kept me brave.

Sister Alicia returned with the prayer book, and Sister Irene read the Prayer Of Exorcism; she held me in her lap like a child and Sister Alicia held my arms down while Sister Joy kept my feet from thrashing about. Soon we decided I should lie on the floor. As they worked their way through the prayer the spirits kept manifesting themselves, but seemed to be getting weaker.

Other nuns heard the commotion and wanted to come in, but Sister Irene went to the door and insisted they stay out.

"Most of the other nuns don't understand about deliverance or exorcism," she explained. "It's best to keep them out. What's happening today would only frighten them."

I tried to lie flat, but painful contortions wracked my body. Repeatedly I could feel my mouth being pulled away from the bone; I knew I was making awful faces.

Sister Irene addressed many spirits. When she tried to cast out the one that had come in with Rafael's curse, it said, "I'm not leaving. I love her."

"I rebuke you in Jesus' name," she replied firmly. "You're a liar. Satan can't love. You don't love anybody."

After several hours of prayer, there was a lull. They were worn out. "It's time to call in reinforcements," she said.

She went to the phone and Sister Alicia explained, "She's calling the elders at a Holiness church nearby. They have a lot of experience with deliverance."

Sister Irene strode back. "I got them," she said. "They offered to come here, but I think that would upset the other nuns." The sisters exchanged glances and seemed to agree. "So I told them we'd come over there. Let's hurry; they're at the church waiting for us right now."

So we walked to Refuge Temple to see Elder Kenneth L. Varner. It was only a few blocks, but the nuns walked in formation: one to my left, one to my right, and one behind me. Once again I felt very white and very blonde, but I was glad I looked conservative.

It was like the neighborhood where Ruth and I had walked, with men lounging on the front steps of every dilapidated tenement and staring at us as we walked by. Normally, I would have been afraid of them, but they were the least of my worries. Today I was more afraid of what was in me.

None of the men spoke to us, and we didn't speak to them. We marched straight ahead, not turning to the left or the right. I carried a rosary and kept my eyes lifted towards heaven, still wishing I weren't so white with such blond hair.

I was afraid that they might pray in front of the congregation and make a spectacle out of me, but we were escorted to a small study in the back of the church. Elder Varner had me stand up and I clasped my hands. As they began to pray, my body contorted as if I were trying to get free from a strait jacket. I could hear myself praying aloud and the spirits moaning inside me. Elder Varner put some oil on my forehead as he said in a very loud voice, "The blood of Jesus Christ." The oil touched my forehead and I felt as if an electric shock went through my body and unplugged my ears. Kicking frantically, I fell to the floor.

I was weak but forced myself to my knees. I was trying to get control.

It took a few tries but I finally made it up. I looked Elder Varner in the eyes and he had me say with him, "The Blood of Jesus."

We repeated it over and over again. I could hear the nuns in the background singing, "Hallalujah, thank You Jesus. Thank You for the Blood of Jesus."

With a depth of desperation I had never known before, I cried again and again, "The Blood Of Jesus!" At first I could hear bitterness in my voice. It was a demonic bitterness; I could tell the demons were starting to realize they were losing the battle. Hope surged in my heart. I kept saying "The Blood Of Jesus," and slowly the phrase became a happy song welling up inside me. I fell to the floor and cried with relief.

I crawled over to a couch and lay down, looking around the room. I blinked my eyes and said, "I feel like I'm coming out from under an anesthetic after an operation." Then joy filled my heart as we all said "Hallelujah, thank You Jesus." The more we praised God, the more joy we had; and the more joy we had, the more we praised God.

It was 7 p.m. and I had been delivered!

I went back to my hotel. This whole thing is unbelievable, I thought. How do I know it wasn't just a bad dream? Or maybe an acid flashback? I looked down at the bruises all over my body; I took inventory of my aches and pains. "This wasn't imagination," I said aloud. "It was real."

Was this the end of it, at last? I figured it had to be, but I wanted to make sure. I called Father McGrath, and he invited me back to the House Of Prayer. He and I both wanted to talk about my battles with demons. "But I can't stay more than one night," I said. "I'm flying home to California right away, then on to Hawaii so I can be with Heather."

So I checked out of the Barbizon and returned to the House Of Prayer. "I really thought it was done that first night," said Father McGrath. "But as soon as I heard you were still having battles, I realized it wasn't. My problem was that I didn't have any support from Sister Pauline or Vince because they were skeptical. We weren't working as a team. We were divided."

"Skeptical?" I said. "Why were they skeptical?"

"They didn't believe the deliverance was real," he explained. "They said they didn't feel right about trying to pray for you, at least not a prayer of exorcism, because they simply didn't believe in it."

"I guess that makes sense," I replied. "I was right in the middle of it all, and I still find it hard to believe. It almost seems that Satan wants to blind us to the fact that he even exists."

"I think you're right, child. Everything in our society opposes the whole idea of the supernatural."

We sat up late discussing what I'd been through. The next day Father McGrath took me to the airport; he was also meeting the Linn Brothers, who had written *Healing Of Memories*. They were going to be staying with him for a while, and he was anxious for me to speak with them. "Are you sure you can't postpone your trip for a few days?" he asked. But I assured him I needed to get back to Heather as soon as I could.

I came downstairs the next morning to go to the airport. I dressed in a designer jumpsuit, big jeweled belt, felt cowboy hat, and high top boots. Father McGrath took one look at my outfit and groaned, "Must you wear that?"

"What do you mean?" I said, but I knew very well what he was talking about. I had gone with him to the Charismatic Convention in Atlantic City, and he had said my clothes were so outlandish that he wanted me to walk behind him in case he ran into any of his Jesuit friends.

"Well," he said resignedly, "I've already warned everyone that you dress – shall we say – differently? I guess the Lord is working on my pride, so let's go." His pride? What if I started dressing like one of the conservative ladies that came to the Catholic prayer meetings? I laughed aloud at the thought, and when he asked me what was so funny, I said it was nothing.

We arrived at the airport and met the Linn Brothers, and then had time for a visit as I waited for my plane. They were eager to hear about my life. I shared what had happened when I took the L.S.D. and got pulled into the tunnel. I'd never told anyone before and was surprised when they said I should get a book entitled *Life After Life* because many people who have been brought back after dying have had the same experience.

The three priests prayed over me before I boarded the plane. It was as if I had three fathers sending me off on my first journey away from home, making sure I'd be well taken care of. "I've called ahead," said Father McGrath, "and one of my friends will be waiting for you at the airport in Oakland. He'll take you to the Holy Redeemer Center. You'll be well cared for there."

The Lord gave me beautiful scriptures on the flight, promises that soon Heather and I would have a home and I would be married. One scripture mentioned remembering my widowhood no more.

I arrived at the Holy Redeemer Center in Oakland. Like the House Of Prayer, it was a Charismatic Community and several people lived there. Father Weber met me at the door. Tall and good-looking, he carried himself with the confidence of a born leader. But he also was very kind, like Father McGrath.

I called Garrett and told him I'd given my life to Jesus. He became violently angry, screaming terrible obscenities about the Catholic church. Suddenly the call ended. I tried calling back but couldn't get through. He must have hung up on me, I told myself.

Barbara called later. "I was at the house when you called," she said. "I wondered what was going on. He got madder and madder. From what I heard I could tell he was talking to you, but I couldn't imagine you'd gotten involved with the Catholic Church. Suddenly he jerked the phone right out of the wall. He was way out of control, and I was so scared I had to get out of there."

"So that's what happened," I mused. "I thought he'd hung up on me."

"Oh, no," she said. "I've never seen him so wild. He tore the phone right out of the wall..." This wouldn't be a big deal today, but it was then. People couldn't connect and disconnect their own phones in those days. Garrett's phone would be out of order until he got the phone company to send repairmen to reinstall his phone.

I told her my story and invited her to the healing Mass they had every Friday night. The sermon was about Mary Magdalene and the Lord's forgiveness. She was really touched during the service and told me she was going to start searching for God and going to Mass.

One night I had a nightmare about demons. I told myself it was only a dream. The next night I had another. But again I woke up, and it was only a dream. I went through the day normally. But that night in chapel, the unthinkable happened: I lost control of my words as I was praying and cursed Jesus. At that point I was afraid to pray any more.

I told Father Weber what had just happened, and he called Father Mc-Grath immediately. While he was on the phone, I could feel myself spinning out of control again. I tried to look at a picture of Jesus but His head split in two and I couldn't see Him clearly. My jaw became clenched and those awful faces started.

Father Weber came out of his office and handed me a phone number. "Father McGrath has two friends who have a lot of experience with demons," he said, handing me a scrap of paper. "Call Joe and Mary Ferguson. I can vouch for them; they are devout Christians and lead one of our prayer groups. They'll be able to give you the help you need. And now if you'll excuse me, I need to get back to some things in my office."

I called the Fergusons. "We can meet you at 7:00 p.m.," said Mary. "We'll be glad to pray for you." I told Father Weber, and he said he wanted to be with us.

It wasn't a long wait but it felt long to me. I was getting sicker by the minute.

Joe and Mary came in with a crowd. "We brought our whole prayer group," Mary said with an engaging smile. "There's strength in numbers, isn't there?" I wondered. Father Weber walked in, said hello to everybody, and stood by a wall where he could watch everything.

They started praying and the demons began to stir. Father Weber watched without a word, but suddenly someone called him to his office for a phone call, and he walked out. Meanwhile, there must have been twenty-five or thirty people hovering over me, and I felt like a freak in the circus. Had they come to watch the show? Their prayers grew more intense and the manifestations got stronger. I got really angry and told them to stop.

A priest heard the commotion and came in. "Excuse me," he said to catch our attention, "but what's all this?"

Everyone simmered down and Joe answered. "We're here to cast demons out of this young woman," he replied. "It's all cleared through Father Weber. He called us on the phone and asked if we'd come and pray; he said he had to be away. So we've brought our whole prayer group – we felt it would be good training for them."

"Well, I've just talked with Father Weber," he said, looking around. "He wanted to be here when the demons are cast out, but he just got an emergency phone call, and now he has to go out for the rest of the night. So he told me to ask everyone to leave. He doesn't want the demons cast out until he can be there to keep an eye on things."

I couldn't believe it. First I had felt like a freak in a sideshow because twenty or thirty people had showed up instead of the two I was expecting; then they had managed to get the demons stirred up; now everybody had to go home until Father Weber could be here. Did he want to watch the show too? Everybody left. Mary's eyes were filled with tears and she looked me in the eye and mouthed the words, "I'm sorry." I could tell she really meant it.

The prayer group left and now I was alone with the priest. Another stepped in. I tried to tell them what was going on. "Can't you pray for me?" I asked.

"We can pray," they said sternly, "but you really just need to relax. You've got yourself worked up, and frankly some of what you're saying sounds quite fanciful. The best thing to do is to wait for Father Weber."

My heart sank. I had already learned that disunity doesn't work when it's time to cast out demons. These priests were skeptics like Vince and Pauline. What would Father Weber be able to do?

I had never felt so discouraged. Whenever I had thought the demons were gone, they had always come back. Would it ever end? Would the demons ever come out once and for all, or were they just going to leave me for a few hours or days at a time so everyone would stop praying, and then they'd come back and take over again? If this was my future, I may as well kill myself right now. But no; I couldn't do that; I had to go on for Heather.

I called Joe and Mary and they encouraged me. "We're really upset about what happened," Joe said. "As soon as we came in with the prayer group, we realized they had no business being there. We're so sorry..."

"But be certain of this, JoAnn," Mary said in a strong and confident voice. "Jesus will set you free. We've been sent home and we can't pray with you right now, but we'll be praying here at home. And I'll say it again: Jesus will set you free."

I hoped she was right, but I was the one who was here alone, harassed by demons in a house full of priests who thought it best not to pray. Nevertheless I felt a flicker of hope; Mary's warmth and love really helped. If nothing else, I knew somebody understood, and somebody cared.

I went back to my room and prayed. I asked God to teach us all; surely there were lessons to be learned in all this. I asked for strength; I wanted to give up but knew I couldn't. I told Him the evil spirits were laughing at the attempts made in His name. Every effort to cast them out seemed to have been in vain.

Shadows of darkness were swirling about my head. It was so hard to see because everything was spinning around the room.

"I need You, Jesus. I trust You, Jesus, because You know what is inside me. If there is any deceit in me, please cast it out. I'm asking you for help, even though it's getting hard for me."

I got up and looked in the mirror and saw the devil in my eyes. They weren't my eyes.

Afraid of my own thoughts, I was in a living hell.

"Jesus, what am I? What am I to my daughter but a letter arriving every day? Am I a filthy wretch filled with evil spirits? What have I done, Jesus? Please help me, Lord. You are able to do all things. Can You cast them out while I'm fast asleep? You can do it in my dreams. Praise You, Jesus. Hallelujah. Glory to You, Father."

I wrote down this prayer in my diary, but while I was writing it another set of voices inside me was jeering and mocking. I wrote down what they were saying too, but have deleted their profanity:

"This is a bunch of garbage. There are no such things as evil spirits. You are a jerk. If there was a Jesus, would he let you go through this hell? Huh? NO, YOU FOOL. You are alone and captured by your own sick mind. Ha Ha Ha Ha Ha Ha Ha. Pooh on all this, forget it. Go get drunk or smoke a joint. That'll do you a lot of good. The rest of this is trash, utter trash. Religion is trash. It has no place in the world. Satan is not anything but a word. You silly fool, you are possessed with insanity and it is your fate. You can't be helped because we have blocked the gate. Kill yourself before it's too late."

"No, I won't." I spoke the words aloud. "I love Jesus and He will win a victory for me and He will set me free. I love Jesus. Lord Jesus, save me. I've gotten to the point where I'm afraid of my own thoughts. HELP ME PLEASE, JESUS."

It was getting late and I went to bed; somehow I fell asleep. I dreamed there were spirits hiding inside of me. They were in a circular enclosure, and outside the circle stood a young man.

The biggest spirit was grey, plump, and hairy; he had sharp teeth stained with blood. At first he was trying to frighten the young man, but then he put up a room divider and tried to sleep in the dimly lit room.

I could see the young man looking down at the spirits who were foolishly trying to hide from him. They were sneaking around behind the room divider, looking for a place to hide, but the young man was much bigger and his piercing eyes saw everything that was going on. He was so tall his head brushed the ceiling and so large that he could have spread out his hands and touched any wall in the room. He watched intently wherever the spirits went.

A child could have removed the silly room dividers they had put up. It was comical. The spirits looked foolish trying to hide because there wasn't anywhere for them to go. They could not get away from the young man.

I woke up startled and sat up in bed as the ugly gray demon with pointed bloody teeth came tearing out of my mouth with an unearthly scream. It disappeared with a puff of smoke.

I was not afraid because I knew Jesus was the young man in my dream. "Praise you Jesus," I said aloud. "I know that I am now delivered. I just know in my heart it is over." I fell gently back to sleep, safe in the arms of my Jesus with no fear at all.

The next morning I woke up. I couldn't believe how good I felt. Drugs had made me feel like this sometimes, but I hadn't been using drugs lately. I called Mary to tell her what had happened.

"Mary, do you know what happened last night?" I asked excitedly. "The demon came out of me and..."

"...It disappeared in a puff of smoke," she said, finishing my sentence.

"How did you know?" I said in amazement.

"We got together and prayed for you, and saw it in the Spirit."

We both praised God together. "I was so disappointed when they asked us to leave," she said. "But when we got home and started praying for you, I realized that God is sovereign. He Himself was setting up the whole thing."

"What do you mean?" I asked.

"He arranged for your final deliverance to happen with nobody else around. If we had been there to pray for you, you would have felt the need to call us if you ever had another problem. And it's not that we wouldn't be glad to pray for you, but God is a jealous God. He wanted it to be just between you and Him."

This made sense. "I get it," I said. "He didn't want me to think it was people who were setting me free; He wanted me to know He was the one doing it. A lot of people prayed for me, but it's true – if they had been the ones to cast the demons out, I would have been dependent on them. The Lord wanted me to know He's my best friend, and I can depend on Him alone wherever I am."

"That's it," she said. "And the Bible says, 'Whom the Son sets free is free indeed.' He did it, not anybody else. You're free, JoAnn."

We got off the phone and I called the airline to get my flight to Maui. I was on my way back to my precious little Heather at last, and she was getting a brand new Mommy.

Thirty

A NEW BEGINNING

More than thirty years have passed since the day I returned to Maui and stood with pounding heart, waiting for my daughter to get out of school. I can still see her face when I called out, "Heather," and she turned to me.

"Mommy, Mommy, is it really you? Is it REALLY you?" she cried as she ran towards me. I scooped her up into my arms and the separation fell away. We snuggled and I buried my nose in her hair.

I took her hand and we walked to the Schaeffers' house. Heather flung the door open and excitedly announced, "My mommy is home! My own mommy!"

The other children spilled into the house, and they all glanced at me as they heard Heather's announcement. Then they swarmed back outside to play and I followed them, unable to take my eyes off Heather. Sometimes I laughed and sometimes I cried, but again and again she looked up at me and waved or smiled.

Karen came to the door and invited, "Let's have a cup of tea." We sat on a sofa overlooking the Pacific. "Paul and I have been reading your letters and you've been on quite a spiritual journey."

"Yes," I nodded thoughtfully. There was so much to say, but where could I begin? I simply waited.

"I've told your case worker that you are ready to take Heather back to California. He's already started making the preparations, and he's anxious to talk to you." Karen smiled. "I'm so happy for you, JoAnn. You were such a broken woman, we didn't know if you would ever be able to take care of Heather again."

"Neither did I, and I was terrified." I looked Karen in the eye, and suddenly my eyes filled with tears. I said, "How can I ever thank you and Paul?"

"Knowing we have helped you and Heather is all the thanks we need."

I stayed at the Schaeffers' until it was time for Heather to go to bed.

"Mommy, are you going to go away again?" she asked sadly. She looked so fragile as she snuggled under the covers.

"No, little goose, Mommy is not leaving you." I kissed her forehead. "I have some things to do and then we're both going back to California soon."

"This many days?" she asked, holding up all ten fingers and wiggling them around.

"Maybe, but I will be with you every day until we get on the airplane," I assured her.

"Okay Mommy." She lay down, squeezing me tightly. "Then will you will be with me always?"

"Yes sweetheart, Mommy will never leave you again."

The next day I called Mr. Sinclair, my caseworker. He wanted me to come in right away, and we conferred for a few hours.

"You really are a different young lady," Mr. Sinclair said with a warm smile. He had seen me when I was taking lithium, and I wasn't surprised that he could see that I'd changed. "This doesn't happen very often, JoAnn. Karen and Paul have read me parts of your letters. You have had an amazing transformation. I've made arrangements for you to meet with Dr. Farris from the Department of Mental Health in my office tomorrow. I don't see any reason why we can't release Heather to you after these formalities are cleared up."

Within a week Heather and I were headed for Oakland, California. Joe and Mary Ferguson had offered their home for us to live in until we could get settled.

I was deeply changed, but still fragile. Sister Rose Alice had described it perfectly: there were holes in my personality where the demons used to be, and it would take a while for the holes to be filled up with something new.

In the next year, I met and married a man named Bob. He owned a few houses in Santa Cruz and was an expert builder. He could remodel anything, and my house gave him plenty to work on. We lived there as he methodically made it into a beautiful home.

Bob provided the stability Heather and I desperately needed. He was a wonderful father for Heather. And recognizing I was fragile, he carefully shielded me from pressure. "Don't do anything you don't feel like doing," he often said. Many wives secretly dream that their husband might give them a day like that. Bob gave me all the time I needed.

What did I feel like doing? I had time to start being a wife and mother. Heather loved animals and we got her a pony. Often when I went to the feed store I'd see the chicks, and they were so cute I always brought a couple home. Then came the rabbits and kittens and puppies. A visit to the pound always meant another animal would come home with us. One day I saw a beautiful full-grown rabbit in a cage. "Matilda" became a part of our family.

She would run to Heather and me as soon as we went out the front door. We loved feeding her carrots. Matilda will always be my favorite pet. She seemed to know she had been rescued. I knew how she felt.

Bob, Heather, and I attended Mass each Sunday. Then I met a neighbor and she invited me to a Bible study. I went, and it was a few ladies who met in a cheery living room, filled with antiques and heated with a wood fire. Everyone made me feel welcome, and I resolved to come back next week. I did, and I made sure I arrived early enough to sit by the fireplace. I savored the popping sound of the burning logs and the fragrance of the fire, mingled with the smell of a fresh-baked apple pie. A moment later, the others came in and sat down.

"Tell us how you came to Christ," the leader asked, her eyes sparkling with anticipation.

I shared a bit about how I lost my husband and then I told them about the drug overdose and the being of light at the end of the tunnel.

The excitement drained out of the leader's face. Warily she glanced around at the other ladies, and I wondered why they all looked so startled. Then she stood up and spoke resolutely. "JoAnn, there's nothing in scripture about a being of light, except that Satan will disguise himself as an angel of light, to deceive people." A few of the ladies nodded silently. "I'm afraid that's what's happened to you." A murmur of agreement rippled through the room.

I hadn't expected this, and it was confusing. They'd seemed so friendly a few moments ago, and now they were as stony as Mt. Rushmore. I knew the group leader had grown up in church, studying the Bible all her life, and I didn't know much about what the Bible taught. I tried to digest what she had said, and yet something still didn't quite add up. "But if it was Satan," I stammered timidly, "Why did he lead me to Jesus?"

"Well, it wasn't the being of light that led you to Jesus," she insisted.

"You are deceived, and I don't want to hear any more about this. I think you'd better find another Bible study," she added as she looked at the door. Clearly, she wanted me to leave.

I felt devastated as I drove home, and kept wiping the tears away so I could see to drive. I felt confused. How could this woman who knew so much say such a thing? Didn't all Christians believe the same thing?

A few weeks later I was walking down the road and met a neighbor my age. Cindy and I fell into conversation. "You know," she confided, "Santa Cruz is the murder capital of America. There are several witches' covens in the area, and sometimes they do human sacrifices." A few minutes later she told me she had just found Jesus.

We had a lot in common and she was easy to talk to. We started spending a few hours together each day while Heather was at school and Bob was working on the house. One day she asked if I'd like to visit her church.

Bob seemed reluctant, but he shrugged and said, "I'll take you." I called Cindy and arranged to pick her up.

When we got to the church, we found the musicians doing a sound check with drums, keyboards, and a lot of guitars. "I always sit in the front so I can hear the music better," Cindy announced cheerfully. "Go ahead," I said to Cindy with a nod as Bob wordlessly chose an aisle seat near the back and Heather and I sat with him.

The pastor was an egg-shaped man in a suit with a bright shirt and a garish tie. He was prematurely bald and surprisingly energetic for such a heavy man. He greeted people loudly from the platform, flashing a smile that reminded me of the pictures I'd seen of a whale's teeth and the small gaps that allowed them to feed on plankton. Then he opened the meeting with a prayer. When he said "Amen," the music began and he started dancing, twirling around like a spinning top. In years of acid trips, I had never imagined anything like this.

Bob moved quickly. He gave me a hollow look and disappeared through the door. Heather stayed with me and nestled in my arm, looking up at me with her eyes large, round, and startled. I gave her a squeeze and smiled reassuringly. I suspected she had never seen anything like this at the Schaeffers' Episcopalian church. I had heard guitars in the Charismatic Catholic Masses and in the Aglow meetings, but never as loud as this. I had seen people lifting their hands before, but not spinning like tops. I was so uncomfortable I wished I could melt into the floor and escape. And yet I couldn't leave until Cindy was ready to go home.

I endured whatever they were doing. The more the pastor shouted and twirled, the louder the music got; the louder the music, the more he shouted and twirled. In spite of everything, the noise simmered down once in a while, but never for long: it seemed to be a signal for someone to start shouting somewhere else in the church.

Each second was agony. Time skidded into slow motion when the pastor preached. Heather leaned into my arms and tried to sleep, but as soon as she'd nod off he'd jump up and shout "Glory! Glory!" or variations. At last it ended and I grabbed Heather and hurried out. We found Bob smoking a cigarette in the car, and waiting for us serenely.

Minutes later, Cindy caught up with us. "What did you think?" she asked enthusiastically as she hopped in the back seat.

"Hmm," I said thoughtfully, buying time until I thought of something to say. "Never seen anything like it."

"I know," she said contentedly. "There's nothing else like this for miles around. Most of the churches around here are dead."

What a strange thing to say, I thought. How can a church be dead?

By now, Bob had backed out of the parking space and started driving home. Cindy continued to chatter about her church, using a lot of lingo I didn't understand. She was so talkative nobody else in the car had to say anything. It a relief not to have to talk, and it was even more of a relief when we dropped her off at her home.

The next day, she called me, "JoAnn, I told my pastor about what you went through in the Catholic Church, and he said there was no such thing as demon possession, and he doesn't want me to talk to you anymore. He's going to call you." Click went the phone, and it rang a few moments later.

"Is this JoAnn?" the man asked.

"Yes."

"This is Cindy's pastor, "I don't want you to ever speak to her again. You are very confused, and she told me you attend a Catholic church. The Pope is the antichrist, and you are deceived. Don't ever come to our church again." Click went the phone for the second time.

"Antichrist??" What in the world was he talking about? And where was Christian love? This man was abrupt and cruel. What was going on with the Christians I'd met in Santa Cruz?

I was glad to go back to our Catholic church on Sunday, where people were kind and I felt safe.

After a few more episodes like this, I learned not to share my testimony. It always caused conflict, and I found theological debates tiresome. The few people I did confide in who seemed to know the Bible were puzzled or even angered at the spiritual journey that had begun with my drug overdose. They reluctantly agreed that I had found the right Jesus, but it bothered them that I had found Him the wrong way. I was like the kid in Algebra class who looks at the problem and immediately knows the answer, but didn't go through all the right steps to come up with it.

"I don't know why those things happened to me," I would apologize. What could I say? Did they expect me to alter my story to fit their religious beliefs? Why couldn't I simply tell what happened, without an argument?

"It makes no sense; why would He put you through all of that?" said many.

If my conversion was controversial, so was my exorcism. "Catholics always call it exorcism, but the Bible calls it deliverance," one person insisted. "Besides, whenever Jesus cast out demons, He did it with a word. There wasn't any folderol."

I've met many other people who have had demons cast out, and few had a battle like mine. Usually, one short prayer session was enough. But we all had this in common: we needed to renounce our ties to the occult, and we needed to forgive those who had injured us in any way.

After reading the New Testament a few times, I did notice that sometimes Jesus cast out demons simply "with a word". But there were other stories where the demons "tore" their victims on the way out. People would ask why I'd had such a struggle. I still don't know, though one thing is clear: it was a struggle while people were trying to get me set free, but then it happened in a moment when Jesus appeared in a dream. At that point, He really did cast them out with a word. The important thing is the victory, not the battle that led to it.

Bob finished remodeling our house in Santa Cruz. We found magazines that listed properties for sale all over the country, and started daydreaming about farms and Victorian houses. Prices were unbelievably low.

We flew to New Jersey and rented a car. We toured several states, and fell in love with the beauty of New England. Every small town had its unique charm: maybe a park with a gazebo, maybe a pond, maybe a river with a covered bridge. Scene after scene was as charming as a movie set.

We found a three-story Victorian mansion in Maine, 30,000 square feet, with a two-story carriage house. It had an acre of land, a large rolling lawn, and even an ocean view for less than it would cost to buy a small house in the Santa Cruz Mountains. Our new home was big enough for us to live in a few rooms while working on others.

We settled into our routine, with Bob working on the house and Heather attending school. I enjoyed being a wife and mother. Bob continued to shield me from pressure, and I could tell I was becoming myself again. I spent my days cooking and cleaning, and listening to the Bible on tape. We found a new hobby: shopping for antiques. As often as not, they were for sale in someone's rickety old barn or storybook home. The sign that listed their business hours might simply say, "By Chance". Those were our favorite places. It was like a treasure hunt, and we never knew what we'd find. We filled our home with antiques.

I tucked one special box into a closet: my diaries. They were a hodgepodge of spiral-bound notebooks, photographs, and snippets I'd scrawled on napkins or scrap paper. I decided I should go through it and get it all in order.

The job was huge, but I felt I needed to do it for Heather. When she grew up, she was bound to wonder why I had left her with various baby-sitters and with the Schaeffers for so long. Would she feel rejected? If I could get my story together, she would be able to read it when she was old enough. And then she would see how broken I had been, and that I had always loved her and yearned to give her a normal life. I hadn't always been there for her, but I had always loved her.

As I pulled the scraps together and assembled the story, I never dreamed anyone else would read it. The years of work were a labor of love for Heather.

I set up the typewriter on a table in a large bay window. It seemed to be a place designed for writing, like my little desk in Hawaii. Day by

day, I spent hours transcribing my journals. Then I would take the original handwritten pages and burn them in the woodstove. Many of the
pages were things I had written by automatic writing. For some reason
now, it gave me the creeps.

Meanwhile, I had found the only church nearby. It was Pentecostal,
but milder than Cindy's church in Santa Cruz.

I enjoyed it and Bob liked the preaching, but they did two things that
made us both uncomfortable. Once in a while the pastor called for everyone to join hands with others and pray. Or he would have us turn
to the person sitting next to us and repeat something he had given us to
say. Sometimes I wondered if the pastor thought we were all parrots,
but I decided to stay with the church. Bob didn't. As he grew increas-
ingly reluctant to attend, I was saddened that these church traditions had
become a barrier between him and the preaching he enjoyed.

Heather loved the Sunday school, and I started going to some of the
prayer meetings and Bible studies. But this time I kept my testimony to
myself, and I got along with everybody.

We made it through two winters in Maine. Our first Christmas there
was the best Christmas of my life. I made Heather a large rag doll and
fitted her in one of my dresses. Heather is probably one of the few children who had to be woken up on Christmas morning. I invited her to
a tea party. She ran down the stairs to see Bertha, the doll I had made,
sitting at a table with gifts. It snowed Christmas Eve, and it was our first
white Christmas. After opening the gifts we all went outside and made a
snowman. Back in the warm house, with a fire in each of the fireplaces
and the smell of turkey cooking, I made a large breakfast.

But later in the winter when it really got cold, even a fire in every fireplace wasn't enough. If the temperature outdoors dipped below zero, I
had to wear gloves and a winter hat to keep warm. It took thirty cords
of wood to get us through the winter.

We looked forward to summer, until it came. It took hours every day
to clean the 30,000 square foot house. All summer, Bob mowed the
lawn every week. In the fall, he raked our lawn and burned the leaves.
And he spent months preparing another thirty cords of wood for the next
winter. With all this work, the air was thick with bugs that bit. The bugs
helped us look forward to winter.

We had another white Christmas, but it wasn't as enchanting as the one the year before. The fun was wearing off of the ritual of clearing the walks and hiring a plow to clear the driveway. Then on our second New Year's day in Maine, I watched the Rose Bowl parade on TV, and saw everyone in shorts. I started feeling homesick, so I called my mom and asked her what she was doing. "Oh, everybody's outdoors right now. We're having a barbecue."

Shorts! Barbecue! That was California, but here in Maine I couldn't have gotten the house warm enough even to wear shorts indoors. What was I doing here? I got off the phone and wailed, "Take me home!"

Surely the house would sell quickly. Bob had restored it – it is now listed in the historic house registry. It took months to sell. The buyers were from out-of-state and may not have realized what they were getting into: the winters, the bugs in the summer, the hours of cleaning and maintenance. But they turned it into a bed-and-breakfast and didn't seem to mind the full-time job of keeping the place up.

We sold most of our furniture at an auction and filled a U-Haul truck with the rest. Then we drove back to California and got settled in a house on California's central coast, near my family. Bob got a job, Heather got into a school, and I got back into my routine of being a wife and mother. Just as a hobby, again I found a table by a window and played with art and writing.

I had begun drawing an alphabet during my crazy years, all in black and white. But now I started a new one, this time in color. I noticed that my art had changed somehow. I hadn't tried to change it – it had just happened when my life had changed. You can see the contrast on the cover of this book: "Mind Lost" is in the old alphabet; "Mind Found" is in the new, a series I call "The Alphabuddies."

I hadn't gotten anywhere with my book about Strawberry Jan – she's the "S" on the cover – so I tried to revise it. It became another book, *The Secret Trap*. This time I knew I was the one who was writing, but I couldn't come up with an ending for the story. Eventually I attended a Catholic retreat in Santa Barbara, and finished the story on my knees, asking God for help and inspiration.

I returned home and told a few friends at church what had happened. One of the ladies said she'd signed up for a writers' convention at Biola University. "You'd be welcome to come with me," she said. "They have several workshops for children's writers."

So I went with her, taking *The Secret Trap* and a short version of my testimony. I had written it so I could hand it to anyone who asked how I had come to Christ – it was amazing how many people asked me this question – but now I could give them a photocopied piece of paper and change the subject or walk away before the arguments started.

I was attending the workshops for children's writers and showed my work to a few people, and I met one of the editors at Biola, a woman named Mary. As we chatted she asked, "How did you come to Christ?" I told her it was a long story and I'd written it all in my diary, but I'd written a short summary. She seemed to want it, so I handed her a copy.

She found me at breakfast the next morning. "This is an amazing story," she said. "Didn't you tell me you have a longer version – a diary?"

"I do at home," I replied, "but it's really long."

"But it's already written?" she exclaimed. "I want to make sure – did I get that part right?"

"Yes it's all typed up," I replied.

"I hope you don't mind," she added, "but I've given your testimony to the senior editor of Thomas Nelson. He wants to speak with you today."

"To me?" I couldn't take it in. "What for?"

I found out a few hours later when Bill and I met. He came right to the point. "Mary gave me your testimony," he said. "I read it, and saw right away that this is a story that has to be told. And the amazing thing is that she tells me it's already written down – is that right? She tells me you kept a diary."

"I did," I replied. "It was all handwritten, but I took time to type the whole thing."

"Amazing! You actually kept a diary during all of these events," he said. "Can you get it to me? I want to show it to our whole editorial staff."

The convention ended and we all went home, but not before Bill could remind me to send him my diary. So I had the copies made and shipped them. Phone calls went back and forth for the next few months.

Bill and Mary started converting the diary into a narrative so it would be presentable to the other editors, and soon I had a professionally written version of the first few chapters. Then Mary drafted a summary of the whole story. We agreed on a title: *Diary Of An Exorcism*. "The editors I've showed it to agree that this book really has possibilities," said Bill. "They all said it would make a great movie." I wasn't surprised; Nate had said the same thing.

"But there's one more thing we need," Bill said. "Can you get verification of these events, especially the exorcism?" He told me what to do, and I spent the next several weeks getting letters from everyone involved. The only one who would not write a letter was Father McGrath because the exorcism had not been done with permission by the Pope. I learned it takes a long time and a lot of red tape to perform an official exorcism.

A few months and many phone calls later, Bill called and said, "Our project went to committee. The editors have all read your journal and we've had a meeting. They decided not to publish the book. They voted, and it was close – four to three – but they said it's far too controversial. The being of light? The exorcism? Far too controversial." He sighed with disappointment.

I was more bewildered than disappointed. How had my diary gotten into the hands of the committee at this publishing house? It had seemed to be a miracle, and I had taken it as a sign that the book would get into print. Instead, the project was dead.

Or maybe not. Bill spoke again, and now he sounded determined. "I'm not giving up. I'm going to find a way to get the book published. This story needs to be told."

We got off the phone and I got on with my life, but Bill kept his promise – he really didn't give up. He would call to tell me he was taking the journal to another publisher, and his dispassionate optimism would stir up my hopes.

One Monday morning I got a call from an editor at a large Christian publishing house, "JoAnn, this is Jenny. I am the senior acquisitions editor and Bill sent me your testimony. I get about 3,000 submissions a year and read only a few. I spent the weekend with your story. I couldn't put it down. I had to find out how you were going to get out of everything and how the story ended. It's an amazing story but we would never publish it. It's far too controversial."

There was that word again – "controversial". I got off the phone and took my disappointment to God. With a fragile laugh I prayed, "Well Lord, the way You do things seems to be too controversial for the church world these days. I guess nothing has changed in 2,000 years."

From time to time, Bill and I would touch base and he always encouraged me to keep trying to get it published and to let him know when it was. I lost touch with him after a few years.

I put the journal on a closet shelf, wondering if my story would ever get into print. But I reminded myself that the most important thing was to let Heather see it when she was ready.

An opportunity came up for Bob to build spec houses. We chose a lot and I started drawing. I had never done anything like this before and neither had Bob, but about a year later I got to open the front door and wander through the finished house. It was like walking through a painting, a euphoric moment when what had been just an idea had now become a reality.

We sold the first house, and then built one after another. Each was a unique design, and Bob was a great contractor. I made the designs and he built the houses. I became known as "the framers' nightmare" as my creativity went into finding a way to capture the best views on each piece of property we selected. Our last spec house was on a lot overlooking the Pacific, and I figured out how to have the living room, dining room, breakfast nook, kitchen, family room, master bathroom and master bedroom all capture the ocean view. The house had high ceilings and a marble octagonal entryway, which surrounded a courtyard. Eventually I got to design my dream house, which Bob built on a hilltop in Nipomo.

Bob had given me the gift of being able to stay home and raise our daughter. Whenever she came in the door one of her first words was always, "Mom," and I was there.

Years were passing, and Heather was growing up. I have too many cherished memories to list here, but a few stand out: her Arabian horse, Shadow; proms; her first job as a cashier at McDonalds; surprising her with a car on her sixteenth birthday. Then, all too soon, Heather left home and went off to college. I cried for days and Bob brought me a flower bouquet in a chicken soup bowl. Time rushed by so quickly.

A few years later, another sorrow entered into my life. Bob decided to divorce me after twenty years of marriage. I got all the counseling I could, but probably the best advice I received was to get involved in the outpourings of the Holy Spirit in Toronto, Pensacola, YWAM,

Smithton, Morningstar, and elsewhere. It was like what had happened with my deliverance: God used people to help me, but much of what I needed happened as His presence touched me.

Then I met Stan. A long string of coincidences brought us together – the kind of coincidences that make it clear that God's hand is directing the situation. We got married late in 1999.

I knew he was a preacher, but I never heard him in the pulpit until we'd been married for a few months. He was a traveling minister. I had secretly wondered if he would go around and preach canned messages. I dreaded the thought; it would be a bore to have to travel with him.

One Monday our pastor called and asked Stan to preach; the pastor was going to be out of town. I'd heard pastors saying it took a week to prepare a message for Sunday, so I kept waiting for Stan to start studying.

But he never did. By Saturday night, I was worried. "Honey, when are you going to prepare your message?"

"Oh I never prepare a message," he said nonchalantly. "I read a few chapters of the Bible and pray every day. But that's to prepare my heart. I never prepare a message."

"Never? What do you mean?"

"The Lord will give me the message when I stand up to preach."

So we went to church, and I wondered what was going to happen. He spoke, and I was astonished at how good a preacher he was. "Why didn't you tell me?" I exclaimed as we drove home after church. "You're really an amazing preacher."

He shrugged. "What was there to tell?"

"Well, I've heard some of the best in the world, and you're as good a preacher as any of them!"

He shrugged again. "I don't know if I'm a good preacher or not," he said. "All I know is I have a great message. If I can get even a little of it out, my preaching will be good."

We've turned out to be a perfect match. We're so much alike that our old friends marvel. One met me and laughingly said to Stan, "I never would have imagined there'd be a woman somewhere who's just like you."

He had other gifts, and they came into view one by one. I found out he's a gifted musician and a prophet, but there was still one more discovery I was to make: Stan has always wanted to be a writer. "I never

had time for it," he said. "I was busy as a pastor, or traveling in ministry. Maybe I'd write a short article now and then, or Bible study notes
for the small groups in our church. But I never had time to do any real
writing."

I'd showed him the short summary of my testimony before we got
married, and I'd wondered if it would scare him off. It didn't. "Either
Jesus is big enough to give you a new life or He isn't," he replied. "If
He isn't, I'm in the wrong business."

But even then, it took me a few years to show him my journal. "Do
you think you could turn it into a book?" I asked.

He was reluctant. "It's quite a story, but it would be a huge project.
And then, even if I tried to write it, I'm not sure my writing is good
enough to do justice to the story." We had this same conversation many
times in the next few years. Eventually the Lord told him to write my
book and he got to work. Soon he found encouragement.

"It's like my preaching," he said. "I don't think I'm such a great
writer, but you've given me a great story. Who else could come up with
a story of a grieving widow whose life was a ghost story one day and
something that belonged in a tabloid the next? Who else could write a
conversion story that would tie theologians in knots? In one respect,
reading your journal has been like reading the Bible: if you don't know
the person who wrote it, it seems to contradict itself." Stan keeps insisting that this is one of the things he loves about me: that I'm conservative one minute and outrageous the next, that I'm strong one moment
and vulnerable the next, that life is never boring if I'm around. I can say
the same about him.

So in the past few years, Stan has spent many hours trying to bring
my story alive. "Describe how you felt when…" he would ask about a
scene in my diary, and I would have to try to remember. Or he'd name
a character in my journal and say, "What did he look like? If he spoke
to me right now, what would he sound like?" More than once we reen-
acted a scene from my journal so he could picture how everyone looked
and moved. "It isn't your story," he kept insisting. "First God made
you unusual, then He wrote a story with your life. I want to bring out
the story He's written."

"It may stir up a lot of controversy," I warned him. "It's upset a lot of
Christians."

"That won't hurt anything!" he said mildly. "We'll stick to telling the truth, and we'll let truth speak for itself." With that, he has worked tire-lessly to make the story as accurate as he could.

Heather is now married to a wonderful man, and they have two beau-tiful children. She's become Vice-President of strategic planning in a major corporation. She's worked hard to get where she is, and I'm very proud of her.

So I present this story to Heather, so she will know that however bro-ken I was, at every moment I loved her dearly. And I present it to the rest of the world because I've met a lot of broken people, and I want you to know that however broken you are, at every moment, God has loved you dearly – and will continue to.

There's a lot in this story that I'm not proud of, but this scripture sums up how I feel about it –

"What benefit did you reap at that time from the things you are now ashamed of: Those things result in death! But now that you have been set free from sin and have become slaves to God, the benefit you reap leads to holiness and the result is eternal life. For the wages of sin is death, but the gift of God is eternal life in Christ Jesus our lord." [Ro-mans 6:21-23, NKJV]

Thanksgiving Day, 2010, 11:11 p.m.

Today, Stan and I finished the book. We paced ourselves for the last few weeks, so we could finish by Thanksgiving. "Then we'll really be thankful, because the book is finished!" we agreed. But it's been quite a year.

In February 2010 Stan almost died from brain cancer. Brain surgery followed, and the biopsy revealed that it was the most aggressive form of cancer there is. But in the next few months, Stan went through radia-tion and chemo. Unable to travel, he kept working on the book. God was good to us; Stan had almost no side effects from his treatments, and the doctors marveled at how well he had bounced back after his surgery.

At the beginning of this month, Stan finished his last draft and I was reading it, reliving the pain I had gone through when I lost Bob. Suddenly the phone rang, and the oncologist told me Stan's latest MRI showed that the cancer had returned.

We have traveled the world together and seen many miraculous healings. Now Stan needs one himself. The first prognosis was that he had two to three months to live. Further tests and treatments have upped his life expectancy.

How much more time do Stan and I have together? The doctors have made it clear that we can only guess. All we know is that our lives are in the hands of the Lord and He will be the one who decides. We take one day at a time, and each day is a gift.

I have learned much, being married to this incredible man. He is so close to God, perhaps he's learned all there is to know in this world. It is an honor and privilege to be married to him.

The letters he's received from those he's ministered to over the years are a testament to what one man can do who follows after the Lord with all his heart.

So I will close with thanksgiving to God, knowing that we all face eternity. Whatever the future holds, I thank God for the last eleven years with Stan. They have been the happiest and most rewarding years of my life. And my comfort is that Stan and I will be together in eternity with our Lord and Savior, Jesus Christ.

November 25, 2010,
Thanksgiving Day, 11:11 p.m.

Acknowledgements

Just write a book, and you'll soon realize that the author is indebted to many others who made the process possible:

Stan's mother, Charlotte Hale Pindar, whose career as a writer has challenged and inspired Stan for decades.

Joseph Councilman, whose valuable help in many technical aspects made the book possible.

The professionals in the early 90's who encouraged me to not give up: Mary Reid, William D. Watkins, Jarrell McCracken, Charles 'Kip' Jordon and Dan Olson.

John Paul DeJoria, who rescued me from one mishap after another.

My sweet mother, Georgette Russo.

My sister and brother-in-law, Marie and Ron Kerr, who also put up with me during the difficult years.

Barbara Moore, who was always there for me.

Winston Brooks Parsons, who did so much for Heather and me.

My friend Mickey – "Cowboy" – who read the diary and said that if anything, I had understated the real story.

The wonderful Briggs family.

The Burgers, truly a godsend.

Scott, my wonderful attorney.

Bob Oldemeyer , who was there for Heather and me and who gave me the time to type my handwritten diary – before anyone could imagine I would need it for this book.

Pamelah Porter, who helped us in many ways and made a retreat available so Stan could turn the last half of my diary into a story.

Rose Spagnola, who gave so much of her time, which allowed us to work on this project.

Julie Meyer, who encouraged us to get the book done.

Terrance Sheppard, mentor, cheerleader, and a great friend.

Lynnie Walker, who inspired me by writing faithfully.

Many of you I can't mention by name because we changed your name in the story, to preserve your privacy.   Thank you all for standing by me when my life was falling apart.

Dr. Kissel, Dr. Stella, and Dr. Spillane along with other medical people who kept Stan alive when he had a brain tumor, and who made it possible for him to finish this book.   There is life after cancer.

The many people all over the world who have prayed for Stan after his surgery for brain cancer, and to the God of grace who has answered those prayers.

Contact Stan and JoAnn Smith

MindLostMindFound.com